THE HABIT OF

HAPPINESS

AND THE ANATOMY OF INSPIRATION

Michelle Bradshaw Kanti

BALBOA.
PRESS

A DIVISION OF HAY HOUSE

Balboa Press books may be ordered through booksellers or by contacting:

Balboa Press
A Division of Hay House
1663 Liberty Drive
Bloomington, IN 47403
www.balboapress.com
1 (877) 407-4847

Print information available on the last page.

Library of Congress Control Number: 2016907918

ISBN: 978-1-5043-5716-6 (sc)
ISBN: 978-1-5043-5717-3 (hc)
ISBN: 978-1-5043-5718-0 (e)

Balboa Press rev. date: 10/04/2017

Table of Contents

Part 2
The Anatomy of Inspiration
(and the seven paths of happiness)

Preface

*"Happiness is the chief good, the end
towards which all other things aim."*
<u>*Aristotle*</u>

Happiness, everyone wants it, yet not everyone succeeds in finding it. We may want to have more of it, yet not know how to get it. What if simply cultivating the habit of happiness helped you get there? Would you be willing to do what it takes to have more happiness in your life? Achieving this experience may not be what you think.

This book, all the bookios (audio and video tools), and toolkits are inspired by my twenty-plus years of working with clients and is my response to their earnest requests for a simple step-by-step guide capable of helping them overcomes the challenges they faced. This book is my response to their ever-present, unexpressed, deeper question of what they could do to be happier. Together we discovered how to reclaim their inspiration, regain their influence over their health and actually increase their experience of happiness. It occurred to me that others could also benefit from the acquisition of these skills and the passion and purpose for writing this book was born. I have duplicated as closely as possible, the journey that I share with my clients, to skillfully navigate life's inevitable problems so that they become the portals to greater opportunities for a more fulfilled life.

You are holding in your hands an essential guide capable of increasing your inspiration for and your experience of well being, enhancing your health and happiness by establishing the habit of happiness. Happiness is the skill that you can learn here. Habits are the consistent thoughts and feelings that we feed with our time, energy and attention that create neural pathways in the brain and lead to our habitual behaviors and choices; as such these patterns are within our influence and can be changed. The most interesting and surprising discovery while working with my clients is how similar and predictable our negative patterns and habits actually are. This predictability reveals the weakness of the ego's protective mechanisms and allows us to benefit from this predictability, understanding them makes it possible to develop the skills to transform them. The Habit of Happiness is about acquiring and practicing the skills that can lead to the habits of positivity, faith, and wisdom that then result in inspired creation, healthy habits and greater happiness.

In response to my clients' requests for practical help in dealing with fear, grief, loss, depression, anxiety and most of life's difficulties I created the Lifeguides Transformation Program. This program uniquely combines the most potent transformative tools available and breaks them down into a simple to follow formula including a three-step approach to master the mind and master the emotions. This program contains the spiritual technology (the techniques capable of reconnecting you to your essential nature, your purity, your spirit) capable of establishing happiness as your new habit. You will be supported in gathering the skills that can help you naturally manage your moods and overcome your fears. You will learn how to overcome negative habits and shown how to create new healthy habits.

I am excited to share this journey with you and hopefully inspire you to take the action steps necessary to create the profound and permanent changes that you want that can lead you to a happier life. My goal with this book is to empower you to the point where you can extract the technology from these pages and apply it to your everyday challenges in an efficient way so that you can free yourself to your potential. I am committed to providing you with the same experience of transformation that my clients have enjoyed that goes far beyond the simple sharing of information and actually inspires you to take the action steps capable of creating your life by design. The happiness in your life depends on your choices and upon the quality of your thoughts and your emotional vibration. If you are looking for an all-natural holistic system of health, well-being, and happiness, then this is the place for you.

Inspiration is the divine motivation that arises from the spirit to take innovative and creative action. When our mind, body, and spirit are balanced we gain access to our essential nature that is bright, positive, peaceful and powerful. The chakra system is the internal structure (the anatomy, that I invite you to be in right and powerful relationship with) through which you can gain access to your inspiration (your innate motivation towards creation). This choice empowers you to realize your creative potential so you can create your life and even yourself by design. The anatomy of inspiration shares how to reclaim and awaken that spark of divine motivation to take innovative and creative action. By reading the stories, my client's shared illuminates how you can stimulate this vital energy for yourself.

Some people seem to be born lucky and be happier than others; they appear to be born with a temperament that is positive and inspired, which gives them a more fulfilled experience of life. Happiness, inspiration, and positivity naturally bring many benefits including an ability to discover the opportunities that sit in the center of our challenges, turning difficulties into gifts. This quality, amongst other advantages, does lead to a happier experience of life, and the good news is that if these qualities are not naturally present, they can be learned and integrated as the habit of happiness. Armed with greater self-awareness, a commitment to the choice to be happy, and some potent tools you too can acquire the skills of happiness and actually increase the set point of happiness in your life. You are invited to be the author and artist of your life, your reality, and even your biology.

The Roadmap to happiness

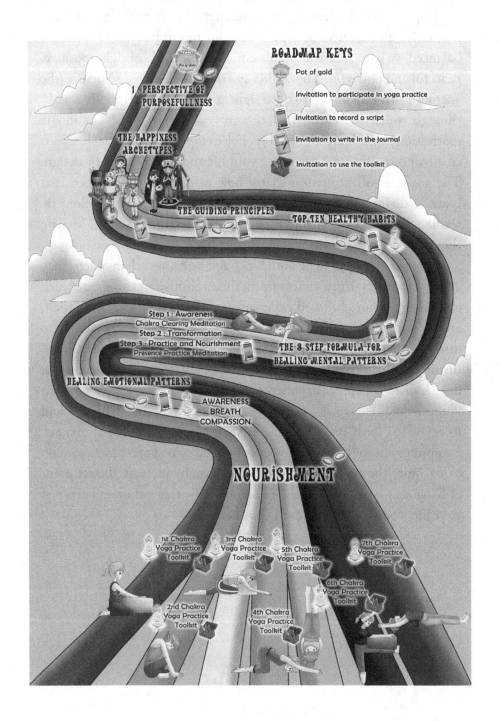

The Roadmap to happiness

I created this illustration so that you could see at a glance where we are going on this journey together. This image will clarify the steps you can take to raise your happiness set point. There are pieces of gold sprinkled throughout this path, and they represent the benefits that you can gain by accepting the invitations that are presented to you as you progress on your journey through this book. There will be icons that represent invitations for you to journal, to participate in exercises, to create and to listen to meditations, and to do some yoga practices.

The Perspective of Purposefulness

The first destination and opportunity to begin to establish the habit of happiness is, by mastering your perceptions. We start by learning how to shift your perception of the challenges in your life so that you can see the gifts that sit in the middle of your difficulties by adopting the perspective of purposefulness. This shift will strengthen you with the skill of understanding how to discover and utilize all the challenging ingredients that arise in your outer reality that triggers predictable and negative patterns in your inner reality. By recognizing and transforming those patterns, you can change those negative perceptions and attitudes into positive ones. This transformation will be reflected in both your inner and outer life.

The Happiness Archetypes

The next destination on our journey to greater happiness is to identify and understand your happiness archetype. This insight will empower you by understanding your specific negative mental and emotional patterns and vulnerabilities that rise up when you are challenged, stressed and tired. This wisdom empowers you with the choice to shift from your lower unhappy, negative thoughts and feelings and invites you to choose new happy, positive ones.

The Guiding Principles

Now we are ready to move on to the guiding principles; here you will see my template for keeping my compass true north so that positive forward movement along the path is always possible. You are invited to use my principles or create your own list of inner values, beliefs, and agreements that are your standards that can strengthen and guide you when things get obstructed, confused and foggy on your path.

The top ten Healthy Habits

The next destination on the map is to establish the top ten healthy habits that you can choose to adopt as you learn how to develop positive, healthy habits and let go of negative ones. You are invited to use the skills shared in this book to support you. Also, if you feel like you would benefit from more guidance, you can work with the meditations shared on my website and in my toolkits and my programs.

Healing mental patterns

Then you can learn the three step formula to healing your mental patterns which arms you with the skill of mastering your mind. You will be given specific scripts capable of rebalancing your vulnerabilities so that they can become your strengths. You are invited to include the physical body by using the affirmations as mantras in your yoga practices, this accelerates and amplifies your learning and transformation opportunity and accelerates your progress.

Healing emotional patterns

The three steps to healing your emotions are 1.) Awareness 2.) Breath 3.) Compassion. There are two primary tools that we use to support emotional healing which are meditations and yoga practices. You will be given scripts that you can record to make your own meditations that guide you through the three steps and share the secrets of how to transform negative patterns into positive ones. The yoga practices are designed with these opportunities in mind and are particularly potent practices that target the predictable negative patterns. If you do not practice yoga, you can work with recording the scripts so that you can reach and positively affect your subconscious mind and your emotional and energetic system.

Nutrition and Nourishment

Finally, you are invited to a greater awareness of the role that nutrition plays not only on your physical health but also your emotional and spiritual health. When you take care of your physical health, the potency of all the tools is amplified. A valuable tool for me to establish great eating habits and improve my diet has been Juice Plus; this is also available for you to use.

The Seven pathways

There are seven pathways to happiness that are related to the seven chakras. Everyone has a primary archetype that is prominent on their journey. However, everyone's journey includes an experience with all the archetypes. Each pathway will not only guide you on your journey but will also give you deeper insight and understanding of the people in your life that challenge you. This insight will benefit you by understanding how to support yourself and the people in your life. You will also benefit by awakening the spark of inspiration to manifest your life by design.

Introduction

A Perspective of Purposefulness

This book can teach you how to make stress your friend, which enables you to utilize your challenges as opportunities that can actually make you happier, healthier and stronger. The journey of life is enhanced when we engage with our difficulties in a way that grows us and helps us to ultimately understand that each challenge contains the exact right ingredients for us to find the strength we need. This set up allows us to gain the skills necessary to reach our highest potential. I created the Roadmap to Happiness to illustrate this journey from your unhappy lower self to your higher happier self to further illuminate how to arrive at an experience of greater happiness. New research has demonstrated that those who learn the skill to positively navigate stress actually live longer than those who have low stress. The same principle applies to all of life's difficulties and the best way to manage life is to learn the skill of positively interpreting challenges as opportunities. Then we can use the ingredients present to motivate us to grow and strengthen in the exact way that the problems invite us to, as we can benefit from the lessons that are laid out in our lives for us to step up into. The skill of holding a perspective of purposefulness can increase your lifespan and improve your level of happiness.

My private sessions always begin by strengthening the inner reality starting with an invitation to develop the muscle of positive perception by choosing this perspective of purposefulness, (which is a re-evaluation of the difficulties in your history and your present reality through the lens of faith.) Faith is rooted in an assumption that you live in a benevolent universe that is constantly conspiring to support you to realize your highest potential and that everything that happens can help you in realizing that potential. You are supported and invited to also participate in that same re-evaluation so that you can fortify yourself by choosing if you want to decide that you are participating with a friendly universe. Next is the invitation and support to thoroughly know yourself, your strengths and weakness, your values and your agreements. This knowledge brings these agreements up to the level of conscious awareness so that you can actively participate in choosing them. I have provided a template for how to do this in the guiding principles chapter. I have also created a quiz to help you identify your personal happiness archetype that will give you insight and information about your patterns and your strengths and your weaknesses. This information will reveal the exact edge of growth that you can best focus on to give you maximum progress on your path.

We will show you how to recognize the predictable story that may be ruling your internal dialogue, giving you the opportunity to be aware enough to free yourself from an internal story that could attempt to negate your intrinsic goodness. You will also gain a deeper understanding of the anatomy of inspiration, why it's important, how it relates to you, and how to reclaim any lost inspiration. By consciously choosing the thoughts that contribute to your sense of well-being and by nourishing your subconscious mind with these ideas, enable you to transform the physiology of your brain and skillfully support yourself in being happier and healthier.

Social scientists have arrived at the happiness formula which is $H = s + c + v$

This means happiness is the sum total of S which is the brain set point (40%) meaning the conditioning we were exposed to in childhood, C (10%) which is our life conditions, our job, our environment etc. and V (50%) which is our voluntary action and our lifestyle choices. Many of us understand and participate in our happiness by taking part in our healthy lifestyle choices, yet we may struggle with consistently implementing these choices. We may have an awareness of our influence over these things and know that it is our responsibility if we want to be happy to make healthy lifestyle choices. We may not have considered the impact we can have with the deeper levels of our being. Knowing that we really can have and assert our influence on the quality of our thoughts and the emotional states that we occupy, allows us to make sure that we make choices that are positive and productive. You will be guided into understanding how to create deep, meaningful connections with the deeper levels of your being, in the subtle energy body, in your emotions, and in your thinking states. These connections bring about a more in-depth understanding of how to manage your moods and your thinking so that you can make the choices that support a happier experience of life.

The program available here has such depth that it not only empowers you with the skills and tools to actually implement your healthy lifestyle choices but also with resetting the set point. These tools allow you to get to the root of your misperceptions, which is capable of freeing you of the continued creation that arises from your conditioning. Yes, that means that I am suggesting you can change your conditioning and you are not limited by your past or even by the choices you made yesterday. Nor are you limited by your subconscious mind and the information here shows you how. By consciously choosing the thoughts that contribute to your sense of well-being, you can transform your thoughts, your feelings and the physiology of your brain so that you can skillfully support yourself in being happier and healthier.

My intention is to provide you with the experience of transformation by sharing all the information and giving you access to the tools that you need that can bring you to the very best version of yourself. You are invited to experience the technology capable of awakening and empowering you to be all of who you are, liberating you to know how it feels to be deeply happy. I have been in the transformation business for the last twenty years, and from my observations, I am certain that people can change into the very best version of themselves. The necessary ingredients for this to occur are the personal choice for the possibility of self-improvement, combined with effective technology. The spiritual technology in this book holds the opportunity for you to be more positive, fully creative, authentic, and happier while living your true heart's desire.

I will provide the tools, information, skills, and practices capable of creating profound and lasting change in your life. You are invited to cultivate the habit of happiness and make the choice to acquire the skills that establish the habits that support you in finding your highest potential. We become what we habitually do. Habits are important, as they lead to behaviors that can increase your sense of well being, bringing you to a state of deep happiness. An opportunity inside *The Habit of Happiness* resides in establishing the knowledge that you have the skills and the tools that allow you to influence the outcome of your future positively, which on its own invites a greater experience of well being and happiness in your life

When you participate in the practical alchemy of turning your vulnerabilities into your strengths, you will meet your highest self in a way that allows you to understand how to get there and live there consistently. This book contains all the information you need to cultivate the habit of happiness and actually be more optimistic, and the offering does not stop there. I have a series of audio and video tools, practices, and processes that bring this experience of transformation alive for you. These tools elevate the status of this book to the level of a bookio (a book with supportive audio and video tools that provide the experience of transformation, and they are all available via my website.)

Whether we are aware of it or not, we are continuously putting orders in with the universe for our tomorrow's reality. The feeling and thought states that we occupy today are creating the vibrations that will determine our tomorrow's reality. Choosing to reside in positive thoughts and emotions today is the best investment you can make to create your best possible tomorrow. Learn how to be skilled in creating the vibes today that will make all your tomorrows reflect the things that you want: health, wealth, and happiness.

I will show you how to break free of fear, negative habits, and the habit of negativity. You will be supported in cultivating the healthy habits of choosing positive thoughts and feelings, providing the inner nourishment necessary for you to reside in the positive internal environment of your own creation. These healthy habits will place you in the driver seat of your life, as the master of your thoughts, the master of your emotions, and the creator of your future. This is simple physics, not wishful thinking or some idealized Pollyanna version of reality, where deep emotional experiences are denied or dishonored. We need to experience the full spectrum of emotions to be happy, healthy human beings. You benefit greatly from understanding how to navigate through negative emotions so that you can meet and digest and honor your emotional reality as it is and then transmute it to its opposite positive possibility. Practicing with this edge that fully abides with your true inner reality, yet resists indulgence in painful and difficult thoughts and feelings is a worthwhile life changing skill to acquire. All this supports you in developing the habit of happiness.

I will be revealing how to choose which thoughts and emotions you want to occupy so that you know how to gain to clarity, wisdom, and happiness and know how to stay there. You will be given more insight into your personal vulnerabilities and shown how to best support yourself to become clearer and stronger internally so that you can create externally more of what you want. As a Lifeguide, I will support you in your awakening and expansion into the truth of who you really are—a powerful spiritual being—allowing you to be the creator of the life that you choose to live. Through some simple alchemy, you will be empowered to become your own guide your own magician (the magical creator of the life that you want). The information provided in this book is designed to support you in becoming your own guru, therapist and life coach. The greatest goal we have in life is happiness. Most of everything we do is with the intention of being happy, our work pursuits and our relationship pursuits are all motivated by the goal of being happy. As a society, we have embraced the use of pharmaceutical drugs that support us in coping with our pain. Here, you will find some useful practical options that can help you find peace, clarity and balance the natural way, through some practices and processes that support you in naturally managing your moods providing an all natural, holistic approach to wellness.

The happiness habit and the anatomy of inspiration

Happiness is defined as "a state of well-being characterized by emotions ranging from contentment to intense joy, emotions experienced when in a state of well being." Attitude matters, thoughts are creative, and our character, health, and general well being are the direct result of our habitual thoughts and emotions. Knowing how to choose our thoughts and our emotions directly affect the levels of happiness we can experience. One of the ways we disconnect from our happiness opportunities is by placing them sometime in the future, connected to a future destination: a new job, house, income, or partner. As long as it is there, it isn't here. We can choose right now, today, to cultivate the happiness habit that allows us to fully have the goodness that we have been waiting for and is sitting right in front of us, now. Allowing happiness to become our habit empowers us to be the creator of our destiny, rather than hoping that one day, some event may grant us our wish for a happy life.

The anatomy of inspiration is intimately connected to your energetic system, your nadis, meridians and chakras. A chakra is a vortex of energy that aligns with the spine that can be considered to be like a transportation zone between the physical and spiritual body.

As you rebalance this system, you naturally reclaim your lost inspiration and find the essential energy necessary to create your happy life. Chakras provide subtle energy to the functions of the body's organs, mind, and emotions. When we choose to consciously activate the anatomy of inspiration (explained more fully in part 2) within the chakras, we progress on our path of spiritual evolution and growth. This energetic inner structure has an anatomy that is known, predictable, and available to all of us anytime we decide to turn towards it to embrace and strengthen it. Our energetic system that consists of nadis, meridians, and chakras, which is the physical system that relates to our subtle energy body, which relates to our spirit. As we participate in our spiritual growth and correct our misperception and reclaim our trapped energy from our past traumas and the related energy centers we can work productively with this structure and we can increase our happiness and feel our divine motivation. Most of the energy used in the functioning of our body, mind, and intellect comes via the subtle energy system, which can be perceived by sixth sense and the ancient yogis mapped this system out for us many centuries ago. All spiritual growth naturally leads to the awakening of the chakras

Each chakra is related to an area of experience in your life and to predictable mental and emotional patterns that can be either positive when unobstructed or negative when wounded by un-integrated past trauma. We can go out of balance and lose our inspiration when our chakras are fed with negativity, and we can reclaim our balance and our inspiration as we choose to feed new positive patterns of thinking and emotion. As we transform the patterns within the chakras to their highest positive possibility, we can also reclaim a specific motivating aspect of our inspiration. By bringing the chakras back to balance, we can reclaim our connection with our essence (whom we are in our purity and our truth.) We can make conscious choices that support our connection to our essential nature that strengthens the depth of both our happiness and our inspiration.

The reclamation of our inspiration is specifically and directly related to the experience in which it was lost. If our inspiration is floundering as a consequence of an experience of first chakra wounding, we experience thoughts and feelings of instability and insecurity or feeling unsafe. It is within meeting that same energy vibration with our awareness, our breath, and our compassion that we can reclaim that aspect of our inspiration. (I will be explaining this concept in greater detail as we progress through the book.) We all know someone who has lost their enthusiasm and their motivation as a consequence of heartbreak, and we know intuitively that the resolution of that loss of mojo resides in healing the heart that broke. We may ourselves, or we may know someone who has gone through an experience of loss and inside that experience, motivation, and interest was lost along with our energy to create. It is the experience of meeting and transforming the emotions and the perceptions we created as a consequence of this experience that we can reclaim our inspiration and our happiness. I use heartbreak as an example here because we can all usually connect to some empathy for the person having this experience yet may not so easily find it for someone who has suffered financial devastation or suffered a loss of self-respect or pride, but the experience of loss and the healing of that loss remains the same.

I will provide a guide for you in these subtle yet essential aspects of the self to support you in reinforcing and understanding these aspects of who you are. You can strengthen and balance your system, reclaim your inspiration and address disturbances on this subtle level of your being before they have to reach the physical and manifest as physical disturbance in the form of illness.

I haven't met a client yet who doesn't want to understand how to manage their reactivity better and be in charge of their anger or some other lower emotional state so that they don't react when they are tempted to. Nor anyone who is not interested in understanding how to naturally strengthen their immune system so that they don't catch every virus that they bump up against. Or know how to love and feel good about themselves in the face of someone else's criticism and negativity. Imagine how good it would feel to clearly find out when someone is projecting onto you so that you don't suffer at the hands of someone else's negativity and not internalize someone else's problem. Understanding and strengthening your relationship to your energetic system supports you in achieving all of these things and rebalancing this system fuels your rockets to their maximum capacity and frees you to be naturally re-inspired.

There are many various experiences, feelings, and thoughts that can cause us to lose our inspiration and understanding the terrain in which it was lost, can also provide the map and the guidance for understanding how it can be reclaimed. Understanding this energetic system holds many benefits, empowering you with the knowledge of how to effectively work with your emotions so that you can skillfully manage your moods and replenish your energetic wellspring when you are depleted and exhausted. You can learn how to skillfully navigate any emotional challenge so that you can understand how to come back to your essence and be calm and peaceful in the face of any emotional difficulty.

Our journey together through the chakra system is about reclaiming this lost energy, understanding how to reestablish it and clarifying what to do to keep it ignited. Many experiences in our lives can support our experience of inspiration and the most potent way we can be in the right relationship with our health, our inspiration, and our happiness is to know it as and claim it as an inside job. This wisdom allows us to assert our influence as much as possible in our relationship to this precious experience. Transferring the experience of inspiration into our inner universe in relation to our emotional and thinking states allows us to create it at will. As each of the chakras holds an aspect of our inspiration and as we heal and balance and align the chakras we free and activate that spark of energy that ignites our inspiration. In the first chakra we can experience inspiration when feeling grounded and safe, and in the second when we are feeling connected to and nourished in relationship, we can again feel inspired in relation to creativity by reconnecting with ourselves. When in the third we can feel powerful and potent or when we feel accepted and loved in the fourth. The fifth chakra ignites inspiration for us to feel free to express our truth and the balanced sixth chakra supports our inspiration with clarity and certainty. The balanced seventh chakra frees us to trust deeply which supports our inspiration. All these outer experiences can also be generated in our inner world with specific tools and practices. Inspiration is also a natural consequence of rebalancing and aligning the chakras without a specific focus on it, but with our focus, it amplifies the possibilities.

As we establish a deeper, cleaner, more profound connection with this system, we can support ourselves, and each other, to realize our highest potential for happiness. By learning how to connect to the body's energy centers, you can learn how to open your inner channel of light, pleasure, and happiness. By illuminating and removing all obstructions of thought and emotion associated with each of the chakras which is directly related to the difficulties in your everyday thinking and feelings (which translate into the difficulties in your life), you can increase your experiences of daily happiness. These obstacles can dilute or numb your own sensations with your connection to your vitality, aliveness, light, inspiration and your happiness quotient.

Each of our chakras has a happiness archetype and a specific internal dialogue that transforms into a series of affirmations with a specific emotional vibration that is healing and transformative. By shifting our perception and our mindset a little in the optimistic direction, we vote for the experience of happiness that we seek and desire so deeply. We can train our minds, and our emotions to create, cultivate, and nurture positive thoughts and feelings that reflect the experiences that we desire, rather than ruminating over everything that went wrong, could go wrong, and most likely reflects what we do not want. Happiness can become a simple-to-understand habit that is perhaps not necessarily easy to practice, but a practice it certainly is. We are habitual beings, and we can use this often-challenging fact in our favor by consciously choosing the habits of positive thought and emotion to feed with our time, energy, and attention.

Well-being can be described as a state of inner harmony, balance, and coherence. We can create this inner state by attending to the health of our energetic system. (Our inner energetic system—nadis, meridians, and chakras—connects with our outer energetic system, our subtle energy body that contains our aura, our thoughts, and our emotions.) Transforming insecurity into stability is the opportunity of the first chakra; from fear to wisdom in the second; from anxiety to peace in the third. By embracing unconditional love in the forth; evolving from control to surrender in the fifth, and in the sixth transmuting confusion into clarity and isolation to connection in the seventh. Understanding how to work with our vulnerabilities so that they transform into our strengths and establishing this practical alchemy allows us to occupy our energetic harmony so that we can have a full experience of our well being.

Awakened, the chakras allow you to realize your full happiness potential, achieving an experience of life truly worth having. By using positive memory and imagination to create the emotional frequency that you want to occupy, you can create the biochemistry of your choosing. These skills liberate you to know yourself as the creator of your behavior, physical reality, and life. All this will be explained in a simple step- by- step guide in the section containing the individual chakras.

Science is useful in showing us the effect of our hormones, but it is within our own spiritual awakening that we discover how to choose our emotions, so that we are then free to choose our behaviors, transforming happiness into a skill that can be learned. All a feeling needs is to be felt thoroughly so that it can be digested and integrated. By honoring our true emotional state, with presence, breath, and compassion we actually free our inspiration and transmute a negative emotion into its opposite positive possibility, which can compress time and reduce how long we are required to occupy our negative emotions. This honoring means we are not vulnerable to becoming stuck and unwittingly indulging in our own negativity and pain. (This will be explained more fully in the emotional healing chapter.) This speeding up of time means that we are not indulging or unwittingly languishing in negative emotional states rather we can skillfully transform them. This transformation allows us to navigate more efficiently through our difficulties with grace and skill so that we can be free to experience the fully integrated and digested reality of each negative emotional state, effectively raising our vibration to its highest positive possibility. We are then free to consciously and consistently practice occupying states of pleasure, harmony, and happiness that support our coherence. This practice is how we can demonstrate our emotional mastery and finally come to know the truth of our own creative potential.

Understanding how to cultivate new healthy habits that expand your happiness potential is casting a vote for increasing your general well being. Researchers have discovered that the happiest people are the ones who balance quality relationships with other pleasurable experiences, meaning, or purpose in the things that they do. These values can translate into habits and attitudes of accepting the challenge of meeting your own needs and the desires of others while adapting to difficulties so that you can find the gifts that reside within them. Underneath the external things we associate with happiness is a deep emotional need, which when satisfied, results in a feeling of deep happiness. When you expect to have this need met and have happiness, you increase the likelihood of this happening. Knowing that this is within your influence gives you the ability to exercise your power of choice and consciously participate in creating your inner emotional state. By choosing to focus on what you like, admire, and appreciate about yourself, others, and your experiences mean you are voting for greater opportunities to experience higher levels of happiness in your life. These values can translate into attitudes and beliefs that can be included in your guiding principles (explained to you in that section). Thoughts create words, words create habits, and habits create behaviors, which creates character. If you seek to embrace healthy, happy characteristics, then the place to start is inside by creating the words that can construct the thoughts that can lead to the habits that create the behaviors that create the character.

Please remember that thoughts are alive and creative; they create neural pathways in the brain, and thoughts that fire together wire together. In the healthy habits section of the audio portion of this bookio are guided meditations to help you create some of the characteristics identified with happy people. I recommend you get the toolkits if you know that you are unlikely to actively participate in the exercises provided in this book. Please be honest with yourself about this so that you can ensure you can have positive forward movement to ignite your inspiration and increase your happiness to support you to take action sooner rather than later.

In the section on how to create positive thoughts, you have all the information you need to create your own happiness meditation with your own words. Working one-on-one with me to create your own unique guided meditations is also an option. What is important is that you take a step that leads to a change because for things to be different you need to do things differently.

Science has revealed that those with intrinsic happiness values are more adaptable, flexible, resilient, creative, and social: traits associated with the happiest people. Those with intrinsic happiness values take full responsibility for finding happiness, place the expectation for finding it on themselves, and have confidence in their success. You can choose to establish these intrinsic values by establishing the habit of happiness at any moment, and they will lead you to a greater experience of well being, allowing you to feel more joy and satisfaction.

My intention is to support you at whatever level you need in understanding how to make these choices by cultivating those traits by establishing those habits. While some may be lucky enough to be born with this intrinsic value system and have an innate understanding of how to be positive and optimistic, we can all choose to adopt and cultivate the habits that result in greater happiness and well-being. We can strengthen our choice for these values with the simple support tools outlined here, if you are self motivated you can use this book as a self help guide if you are not I designed the toolkits for you to take with you through this journey of change.

> *"The long span of the bridge of your life is supported by countless cables called habits, attitudes, and desires. What you do in life depends upon what you are and what you want. What you get from life depends upon how much you want it—how much you are willing to work and plan and cooperate and use your resources. The long span of the bridge of your life is supported by countless cables that you are spinning now, and that is why today is such an important day. Make the cables strong!"-L. G. Elliott*

My story

I have always been driven to understand why we are the way we are, exploring what distinguishes my way of being from yours, from other members of my family, and from that of my friends. This fascination with what makes us who we are led me to study (and later discard) psychology and hypnotherapy. Then I trained in breath work, yoga and meditation, which were motivated by my interest in discovering the most potent transformative techniques available. This education led me to understand how to work with and later create the spiritual technology capable of creating profound and permanent change in relationship to our habits, our fears, our internal stories, and our moods. I am excited to be able to touch more of you positively in a way that can increase the happiness in your life. Fueled by the incredible results, I have witnessed in my client's lives I have created this book and additional tools for you too to improve your lives in the same ways so that you can realize your potential.

I am eternally grateful to my clients for their deeper and deeper questioning, pushing me further into an exploration for answers. I am grateful that they challenged the limitations of conventional psychologically oriented answers, igniting a necessity to explore deeper into the root cause of issues that consistently presented themselves. These experiences enabled me to recognize patterns and to understand more fully the role of the unconscious and the chakra system in our evolution towards wholeness, health, and happiness. I am grateful for the times of clear inspiration and information that I have no earthly right to know. This education of using my intuition on a consistent and accountable basis has been the greatest gift of all and has enabled me to bring forth my gifts to the world and to you. Research has demonstrated that the biggest factor to creating happiness is finding your innate gifts and sharing them with the world in a way that adds value to you and others. I hope that offering my gifts can contribute value to both you and me and increase both of our happiness: a real win/win, my favorite kind of creation.

The consistent requests that my clients pursued about wanting to know how to love themselves more, how to be more positive, and how to overcome their fear pushed me further down the path of creating the tools that responded to these requests. I went on a quest to discover the most potent tools of transformation and brought them together into my practice. Through trial and error, I discovered what worked, what was effective, and what had the most positive results. I combined the most effective techniques using sound, breath work, affirmations, visualization, yoga, positive memory, and compassion meditation and created the tools that make up the Lifeguides Transformation Program. The expansion of my professional path was paralleled by my personal journey of expansion through the experience of loss.

Loss, the catalyst that invited
me into my authenticity

"Being young, wild and free, it didn't dawn on me that in order
to go into deep ecstatic places, I would have to be willing to
transform absolutely everything that got in my way. That included
every form of inertia: the physical inertia of tight and stressed
muscles; the emotional baggage of depressed, repressed feelings;
the mental baggage of dogmas, attitudes, and philosophies.
In other words, I'd have to let it all go – everything."
Gabrielle Roth

December 2004 was a really packed and significant month for me I
had recently broken up with my boyfriend of four years, and he had
gone back to his family home across the country. Our beloved 17-year-
old family dog had just died, and my mom was in town visiting from
England when we got that dreaded phone call that changed everything
that call that nothing can really prepare anyone for. We all know that
death is inevitable yet we continue to be surprised by it when it lands
at our door. Like life has betrayed some secret promise of immortality.
My brother called to break the news that my father who was 67 had
suffered a massive heart attack and died. I will never forget the death
screams that escaped from mothers heart at that moment and the shock,
grief, and confusion that this loss threw us all into for the months that
followed. Shortly after that my brother moved back to England, and I
got notification that my landlord was moving back into his property.

My slate was completely cleaned and I was starting over. Looking back, now I can see that I was not breathing and nor was I able to feel and experience all this loss fully. I went into coping mode and navigated through the next few months in a haze underneath a weight of grief that I was, at that point unable to touch. As the weeks passed, I was slowly able to get back to my practices and then fully integrate this experience. Thank god for those practices and the knowledge that I had gathered on my path I truly believe that it saved my life. I know how it feels to lose everything and not know how to carry on and move forward.

Transformation through loss has been a consistent and intimate part of my journey. I wish I had had a coach, a roadmap, a series of tools, or a toolkit to help me navigate through the fear and the confusion. I wish I had had a Lifeguide to help me to overcome the demons that attempted to seduce me into maintaining the status quo and ultimately to stagnate each time I went through the experience of loss, transformation, and ultimately reinvention. Instead, I had to figure it out the hard way. I alone had to find the faith and the determination to reach inside myself to contact my courage. I had to wade through all the internal noise and chatter to find the small still voices that could lead me into positive forward movement. Ultimately, I found my own mastery in navigating this territory, drawing the map for this landscape to share and support you inside this ordeal.

Now this process of loss, transformation and reinvention holds more curiosity and anticipation than dread, as I look back at each reinvention that has brought me home to this life, to this self, to this work, to this place I call home. With the roadmap I created along the way, my attitude has changed. This process of death, rebirth, and reinvention required my being radically honest about who I am, what I value, what truly matters to me until my authenticity had no choice but to speak up for itself and lead the way. Now when things start to fall apart, I can more quickly feel enthusiasm rather than resistance rise in me, as I can finally trust that this ending is the new beginning of who I am now.

I learned that reinvention is possible, necessary, and even inevitable for me walking this path of transformation into authenticity. It should not be surprising to me that as a transformation coach my path is perhaps more intensely transformative than most. As things naturally transform in my life, I know that feeling challenged is a sign that something sacred is occurring and that I benefit from practicing presence, by holding a perspective of purposefulness, by leaning into the guiding principles, by breathing deeply, extending compassion, choosing positive thoughts, and raising my emotional vibration. All these skills are explained later and can be learned here, and I invite you to practice the habit of happiness and watch your life transform for the better.

I listened. I paid close attention to that small still inner voice and its persistent messages; the intuitive messages that rose up from the language of the body. The hunches, the insights, the gut instincts that dutifully did their job of delivering messages of passion, excitement, and joy when I chose the right path, and the loud screaming voices of agitation, anxiety, and discomfort that rose up as I strayed from the path that aligned with my spirit.

My professional journey has taught me how to separate the voices of fear from true inner guidance and I wish to share this skill with you so that you can do the same. I gave myself greater permission to expand and rise to the calling of my purpose and live both my personal and my professional life exactly the way that I wanted to. In harmony and alignment with my gifts, my calling, and my purpose, the universe co-operated by opening the right circumstances for me to be able to do so. These choices allowed me to establish myself firmly in the foundation of a happy life.

As I look back at the many decisions that brought me to this place of fulfillment and happiness, I see that I was making those decisions mainly on the basis of both the subtle and the obvious signals that spoke both softly and loudly to me in the form of physical sensations. Some of them were comfortable, and some of them were not. By following the feelings of passion, joy, and excitement, I discovered my mission, my path, and my purpose. I realize that to do this, practicing presence is necessary; a simple yet courageous willingness to experience everything fully that arises as it is, in an attitude of grateful acceptance. I sought out all the best information and tools available to support me in establishing this healthy habit and translated that into a practice in the form of a guided meditation that I could use personally and easily share with my clients and students. This simple yet profound practice is the foundation to all my practices that awakens our light. The willingness to be curious and interested in what is happening within allows the space for us to be powerful in making the choices that lead us home to ourselves. This practice has been such a foundational, essential and profound tool of support that I have decided to make it my service, my free offering to the world and to you. (You can download it from my website all the information for how you can do this is available at the back of the book in the tools section.) Even if you do nothing else this simple and elegant practice will invite a profound shift in your levels of happiness by supporting you in being more awake and more conscious of who you are.

The pursuit of happiness includes the necessity of the acceptance of the reality that life contains suffering which can actually have many great benefits of strengthening character. I want to be clear that the tools and practices shared here are all about honoring and being with your pain exactly as it is, to feel it thoroughly, and to integrate it. (You integrate your pain by using the breath; this will be fully explained in the emotional healing section.) Before we even consider the possible gift of transformation, we benefit from having skillfully abided with our pain; this helps us to purify our emotional field, and this skill is shared in the Presence Practice. This personal path of faith, growth, expansion, and trust, aligned with my professional understanding, coaching, and teaching. This path combined with the issues that lived on my uncomfortable edges of growth, (and are the same emotions, thoughts, feelings) that supported the magical manifestation of the evolution of both my personal and professional life.

I know how uncomfortable it can feel to be pushed against your own raw edges of growth, and I am aware that my own kindness and understanding directed towards that pain helped me. I know that a smooth sea never made a skillful sailor, and it is with this understanding that I know better than to expect a smooth ride. Seeing the beauty in the inevitable difficulty that is predictable for us all to sharpen our skills motivated me to create my tools of support to be saturated with the energy of compassion.

By meeting all the inner emotional visitors at the door—the good, the bad and the ugly—with a heartfelt welcome allows this mechanism of growth to be ignited to co-create in a cooperative relationship with the universe, the creation of your life by design. Fate is what happens to you in the absence of your choice; destiny is what you create in collaboration with all arising conditions. Holding a perspective of purposefulness, trusting that everything that happens is valuable, whether it appears to be seemingly good or bad, knowing it has a positive possibility contained within it, is essential to arrive fully in the synchronistic flow.

We all know what it feels like when situations just seem to be unfolding easily and effortlessly, just the way we want, indicating that we have arrived in a positive flow. It is important to understand the things that we can do and the internal choices that we can make to increase the chances of this happening. I have discovered that the more I let go of attempts to control and direct external situations in a specific direction and the more I allow life to happen from a strong foundation of positive internal navigation, the more I am able to let go of external control the more magical my life is. Following this synchronistic flow, especially when fear and logic screamed that this may be risky, was the path that invited me to me, to live a full, vibrant, passionate life, and allowed me to create the roadmap so that I can invite you to do the same. Having faith and trusting this guidance aligned me with my higher self and placed me in the flow. Sharing the tools and practices that support this possibility is my version of teaching a man to fish.

My invitation to you is to live fully in this moment, to turn the volume up to your own inner guidance, listening to the invitations of your higher self that knows what is right for you. By aligning with and listening to your inner stirrings, you connect with your true self that has gifts to share, and you are charged with the responsibility of connecting to and expressing them. These stirrings come in the form of inner sensations, voices, insights, and hunches. Purifying these signals to ensure that they are free of negativity is an essential step in connecting with your intuition. The world needs you, so you are invited to know the stories you hold about yourself, to examine them and rewrite them if necessary to support you in creating your life, as you want it so that your gifts spring forth and are contributed. Adversity is the portal to your own potential, difficulty is inevitable and an indication that you are in a sacred time where you are being invited to connect with your inner strengths in a way that empowers you. It is safe to assume that your challenges will be worthy of your skill set. When you identify and ultimately transform your negativity, you are supported in arriving at the place where you can demonstrate through your choices, your behaviors and your actions that you have finally released your inner demons as you express the confidence externally in and ownership of your new positive pattern and the habit of happiness.

I learned over and over again that everything that can be lost will be lost. I know what it feels like to lose everything: everything that you have, everything that you love, everything that you worked so hard to build, and everything that you depend upon. I know that feeling of fear that automatically arises upon facing the unknown, that taste of dread, as you sit at the top of the collapsed mountain you just climbed and at the foot of the next mountain to climb, as that rebuilding begins and that seemingly insurmountable task of reinvention beckons.

I understand how it feels to resist change, by any means possible, to tolerate the intolerable rather than risk the emotional experience of loss, yet again. I have caught myself negotiating for a safe passage, only to discover that there really isn't one. I have considered the possibility that it would not be so bad to live a small safe life that contained no risk of loss until I saw that perhaps learning how to navigate this experience I had resisted maybe a worthwhile investment. Now I embrace fully the experience of loss with the curious anticipation of the new delights to come, and I invite you to confront your challenges with the same possibility.

With each rebirth, I arrived closer to my own center, to myself, to my essence. I discovered that the more I let go, the freer I became, and that loss actually lightened my load. Each time, it showed me that I could endure loss without being emotionally overwhelmed, that I really was strong, and that in each rebirth, I created a life I liked better. This transformed my fear of loss into a willingness to embrace change with a renewed sense of awe and excitement, to discover the real me that emerged at the other side of the ordeal. I saw that my best investment was one that could not be lost. Then everything that I cultivated I cultivated within myself, in a place in me that could never be lost, that could never be taken from me.

I wanted to create a framework to support others in making the best possible investment in themselves that could not be taken by, but only be enriched through the experience of loss. This framework is something that you could acquire that actually makes you richer each time you experience loss, as you strengthen your capacity to surrender and let go of what you no longer need and melt into the highest possible experience for you. When we let go of the external things that need to be surrendered we grow internally in our strength, our clarity and our own intrinsic values. So, I discovered loss is simply a redirection onto a path that brings you home to you, to the cultivation of what cannot be lost. I learned that periods of loss are great portals of growth and accumulation that, if approached open heartedly, can catapult you into next level of your life, and that much of the suffering can be averted when we approach them that way.

Now when my inner voices scream at me to hold on and never let go, I recognize them as fear and insecurity, and as such, they contain no truth and no wisdom. I have learned to let go of them and let go of whatever is leaving averting the suffering of clinging to what is shedding and leaving no matter what I have learned how to transform that inner dialogue into wisdom and positive voices that affirm my new beginnings and positive opportunities that await me.

I have created a quiz to help you identify what your blind spots are and where your areas of vulnerability may be. These apparent vulnerabilities, challenges, or difficulties are, in fact, the portals that you can walk through to find your greatest assets, the best parts of yourself. By expanding into this mindset, you allow for the possibility of your own personal growth by residing in the correct relationship with your shadows, so that they can finally be illuminated with truth, acceptance, and pride. This allows an integration of all aspects of yourself to become possible, allowing you to have the experience of wholeness and full acceptance of who you actually are.

My Pathway Home

I graduated from the University of San Francisco (USF) with a degree in Psychology. I had transferred my credits from the American University in Paris where I had been a student ten years earlier. In transferring, I discovered that my Psychology credits had transferred easily enough but that lots of the requisite courses for graduation had not. This set of circumstances required me to take classes, such as Theology, Ethics, and Religion, courses I would not have necessarily chosen myself. To my amazement, I found that these subjects were both stimulating and inspiring. This opened up my spiritual path, introducing me to the information I had not been exposed to before because of my atheist upbringing. I found that I had an incredible connection to and thirst for these subjects, and because I was spiritually uncontaminated and blank, I could embrace the purity of these spiritual teachings. I had found my niche. I had come home to the knowledge that led me to truth... I felt like I was returning home to myself... I was a spiritual being.

After leaving USF, I searched for a graduate school to continue my studies in Psychology and Spirituality only to be disappointed by the limited options. I really wanted to go to a spiritual university because it felt like truth lived there... But I could not find one. As I pushed my search further in the direction of alternative options to this traditional path of education, I discovered Hypnotherapy training. This stirred something in me and instantly resonated as an appropriate path to follow... It felt like it was the closest thing to truth that I had found thus far.

We focused on short-term, solution-oriented processes that helped people change their habits. My education on this path was a profound and mystical experience. Spending extended periods of time in non-ordinary, heightened-states of consciousness ignited memories of latent gifts and reconnected me with innate abilities long forgotten. While training in the hypnotherapy school, I started learning the Tarot. I was magnetically drawn to them. The cards spoke to me in a very clear and direct way. I found I was able to read instantly and this became a vehicle to express my natural intuitive gifts in a way that supported others on their spiritual journey. These two paths of Hypnotherapy and intuitive readings merged and became my educational path of teaching, training, and learning. I followed this path for almost a decade.

The intuitive work taught me more about the journey of my own personal empowerment and transformation. I gathered a deep understanding of the internal mechanism of transformation and transmutation. I discovered that our awakening is achieved through our mental and emotional maturity into a state of mastery, of our thoughts and our emotions in each moment, so that we can know we have choices and are the creators of our reality. We can gain knowledge of how to have mastery of our internal reality, our thoughts, and our emotions so that we can reconnect with our spirit. I discovered that the liberation from fear and the feeling of being emotionally overwhelmed is the key to this path to awakening, freedom, and peace. This allows us to exert our influence on our external reality, empowering us to manifest and create the reality of our choosing. (If you are interested in learning more about how to manifest I highly recommend the manifesting chapter and all the associated tools to integrate this mechanism and maximize all the benefits. You will find a deeper explanation in the manifesting chapter.)

As a Hypnotherapist, I learned that most people's issues stemmed from trauma, creating both mental and emotional injury. The mental injury stems from misperceptions and illusions that arise from the language and perceptions contained in the trauma that become the commands that determine misbehavior. These perceptions gather into a fear-based consciousness that if left alone, would create a reality that we do not want. Fear has two meanings: either we can "Forget Everything And Run" or "Face Everything And Rise." You are supported in expanding your capacity to face the difficulties and the challenges of life so that you can confront and transform these difficulties and rise.

> *"Happiness does not depend on what you have or who you are. It solely relies on what you think."* Buddha

I became more interested in different bandwidths of consciousness and what was possible, as we inhabited various states? I found that the state of heightened awareness produced as a consequence of the Presence Practice I created was the most beneficial state to support the experience of raised awareness (both inside and outside of the practice). This state is necessary to catch the first moment of a discursive thought or feeling as it arises and to transforms it in the moment. This skill is crucial if you want to transform your mind and your life. The practice of noticing the very first moment a negative thought arises gives you the opportunity to starve that thought of time, attention, and energy so that it expires into the ether. My guided transformation practices are most similar to mindfulness practices and support you in arriving at the state of consciousness that the Buddhists call relaxed wakefulness. I recognized that as we invite and confront the traumas in our history, it must be done with the full power of our consciousness and alertness. Wakefulness is necessary to be powerful in the territory of the mind. Being fully in the present time facilitates your evolution down the path of spiritual growth.

> *In mindfulness one is not only restful and happy but also alert and awake. Meditation is not evasion; it is a serene encounter with reality."* Thich Nhat Hanh

I have now navigated away from Hypnotherapy towards the guided meditations I created as the primary tool to support the transformation of consciousness. This is because they support the level of awareness necessary to choose your thoughts in each moment as they arise. The Presence Practice is available in all the yoga practices and the guided meditations for each chakra. The purpose of this practice is to strengthen you when confronted with stress and difficulty in life, with more awareness and reinforcement of the tools to make positive, healthy choices. We all know, and we hear all the time that we should love ourselves, and I have no doubt that we all want to do that, but this can be an elusive behavior to acquire… How do we actually love ourselves? How do we cultivate the habit of kindness and friendliness towards ourselves? How do we practice the art of self-love?

> *"Everything we do is infused with the energy with which we do it. If we're frantic, life will be frantic. If we're peaceful, life will be peaceful. And so our goal in any situation becomes inner peace."* Marianne Williamson

The answer is making self-love an actual practice. We begin to know what loving the self actually is by cultivating the vibrational frequency of love in the body and bathing the cells in that positive frequency. This is one of my primary motivations to develop the Presence Practice. In this practice, I guide you through the experience of loving yourself and show you how to elevate the idea of loving yourself into an act, a practice. This is explained in fuller detail later, and you actually have the script so that you can record and listen to it on a daily basis. I also want to ensure that all my processes directly access the aspect of consciousness that is aware that it is aware. I want to evoke your full awareness and presence in the cultivation of new healthy habits intentionally so that you can maintain a relationship with this part of yourself and lean into it when invited to fall asleep and regress into old unhealthy habits and patterns when life gets stressful and challenged.

At these times, it's easy to reenact behaviors that may be old and familiar but have their roots in automatic thinking patterns not consciously chosen or preferred ways of being. By practicing residing in these states of consciousness while stressed and by being invited into intentional discomfort in the yoga practice, our brains develop new circuits that encourage us to stay fully present. Being aware that we have choices about the thoughts that we choose and the feelings that we occupy, even when we are uncomfortable, which is when we most need it. This creates a new template for us to function from. By practicing this on the yoga mat, we expand into ownership of this template and then become able to transfer the learning into life. It is not an accident or laziness that causes me to work with the Presence Practice at the beginning of all my guided transformation practice…. It is guided by an intention to access this particular state.

The emotional injury we suffered in our past may have resulted in an experience of emotional overwhelm, which was not an enjoyable experience. As a consequence, every emotional decision becomes a protection against emotional overwhelm leading to the choice to shut down emotionally or to avoid feelings to the point of disassociating with the body. I was spending the majority of my time with my clients processing negative self-perceptions that came as a consequence of wounding experiences in childhood and even further in the past. This pushed me into a deeper study and further exploration of the mechanism of acquiring a healthy relationship with my own emotions. I was drawn to workshops, classes, and courses that shared the tools and the technologies of dealing effectively with our emotions to the point of Mastery.

As I combined this information with the experience I was gathering through working with clients; it appeared that another pathway of forgotten information was opening up for me. I could clearly see how to apply and expand on these tools and to see how all my experiences were supporting me in creating my own process of internal transformation and change work, leading to the creation of the Lifeguides Transformation Program.

My work naturally matured and evolved with me, and I was attracting more clients who were interested in transformation. They were at a point in their lives where they were ready to see change. No matter how they found me, they had already put this mechanism of change into motion and they simply needed further guidance and support, with more knowledge, tools, and information about how to go through this process. I was happy to be able to provide that.

Gradually, I realized that this is who I am. I am a Transformer. I am here to be a Lifeguide… to support and empower people on their path of transformation, of reconnection to truth, the truth of who they are in their spiritual nature by mastering thoughts and emotions; inviting others to connect with, stand in, and manifest the lives they truly want and deserve. What do you yearn for? What are your deepest heart's desires? What does your authentic self long for? I invite you to sit with these questions and arrive at your intentions, your aspirations, and your goals for yourself. Together, we can remove the obstacles preventing you from manifesting your desires and liberate you to create your life by design.

Establishing the habit of happiness through the anatomy of inspiration is a skill worthy of your time, energy and attention. Each chakra has a series of affirmations that are antidotes to the predictable negative self-talk that arises when life challenges us in a particular area that relates to a particular chakra. Nourishing the mind with the food, the opposite positive ideas to the negative inner dialogue give us the support necessary to have a greater range of choices to draw from in our consciousness when we are challenged.

Most issues arise as a consequence of self-forgetting, disconnecting from the truth of who you are. Remembering and reconciling with our true self is the path to health, wealth, and happiness. I feel that the way that I best serve my clients lies in my ability to see them in their divinity, to see them in their already perfect state. I can meet you where you are now, inside your difficulty, and hold the space and invite you towards the vision of who you are in your spiritual truth and of who you want to become until you can easily find that for yourself.

The purpose of my work is to remind you of the truth of who you are, to reconnect you with your essence, your happy higher self, and your divine nature. I am here to support you in understanding what your obstacles are and in introducing you to and removing the ones currently preventing you from truly knowing your own divinity.

Once you understand the obstacles that you are dealing with, you are supported in removing them, in transforming them, and in coming back to the home of yourself. Most spirituality approaches this task and invites us to remember ourselves as we truly are. I feel that the time has come to support people in this task in a way that speaks to more than just the mind.

We have reached a critical mass in consciousness that demands more than books to support our transition. We require processes, journeys, and practices that include the transformation of our bodies, our emotions, and our minds, leading us back to the home of our spirit. This book is a gateway to all my tools and services and allows you to have the experience of transformation. Videos and audio tools are readily available to you, turning this book into a bookio (My word for a book with audio and video connected to it).

The Lifeguides Transformation Program

INTRODUCTION

Many of us have reached a point in our lives where we have discovered something we would like to change about ourselves. It may be the inability to forgive or perhaps a negative habit or pattern of behavior that we desperately want to break. You may discover in identifying your happiness archetypes, the patterns that you want to work on but you haven't yet fully understood or been shown how to do that. Some of us may be aware that we are capable of more, that our lives could be richer, fuller, more creative, and satisfying. There may be a vague sense that we are on the wrong path and not fully realizing our potential. We may have acquired success in one area of our life and be at a complete loss as to how to create it in another. We may be filled with deep and important questions about ourselves, but not know where to go to find the answers. We may just simply know that something needs to change but not know what or how to change it.

Lifeguides provides the tools, the steps, the how-to, as you are guided and supported and shown how to make the changes that you desire. Our processes actually take you by the hand and guide you through the internal mechanism of change and energetic transformation. This is the alchemical process of turning your lead into gold. Lifeguides processes provide the spiritual technology capable of creating the habit of happiness and igniting your inspiration. This gives you the opportunity to leave the past in the past and reclaim your energy for your present moment. This in itself is empowering and inspiring.

The well-known secret is that we create our own reality based on what we believe. We know the power of positive thinking and the importance of keeping our mind focused on positive thoughts, ideas, and beliefs. Our consciousness, however, only creates 10% of our reality; 90% of our reality is created from our lower mind, which is filled with wounds, fear, illusions, and misperceptions. All of our fears, doubts, and anxieties reside with our lower self in the area of our subconscious, along with every single wounding experience that has not yet been integrated. It is essential that we shake hands and make friends with our lower self and our subconscious so that we can use it as a supportive tool that helps us create what we want, not what we're afraid of. The not so well known secret is that we create from where our energy is most highly charged. As long as our fears or wounding experiences remain in the realm of the unknown, they have the power to create exactly what we don't want.

> *"Until you make the unconscious conscious, it will direct your life, and you will call it fate."* Carl Jung

So the reason it is necessary to shake hands with and embrace the subconscious and become familiar with those fears is that they have the potential to create your reality and decide the quality of your life and the content of your future experiences. If you do not become powerful over it, it will become powerful over you and decide what is going to happen in your life for you. It can determine your happiness set point if you allow it. Most of the challenges that we face in our health, in our levels of happiness, and in our wealth are created as a consequence of trauma and stress. Most of these consequences are within our influence and can be changed. These experiences can create internal obstacles that stand in the way of our realizing the full potency of our power and our potential. The Lifeguides Transformation Program offers you the opportunity to meet, to integrate, and clear these internal blockages. It gives you the opportunity to attain your full strength and power and the ability to realize your full potential.

Lifeguides is a transformation program that shows you how to recognize and change limiting mental and emotional patterns, into power, love, and creativity in a simple three-step formula. We focus mainly on two levels of healing: the mental level of healing and clearing and the emotional level of healing and clearing. It is true that everything that has happened in your biography lives in your biology. Your body actually has access to all your experiences and the consequences of them. It is necessary to go on a journey back down your timeline to uncover and resolve any emotionally stressful and traumatic events. We will not be looking through a straightforward psychological lens of who did what, when, or why. Really, this has little or no transformative, healing value. We focus on what that event did with our emotions by trapping our vital life force and freezing it in that time in our history, connected to the related area of our body. We benefit from knowing and liberating ourselves from whatever perceptions our mind created as a consequence of those events, we focus on healing and transforming that blocked emotion and false perception. Perception is critical; it determines the lens that we look at life through and that lens is colored by the interpretations we place on our experiences. Fully illuminating our perceptions with awareness empowers us with choices.

> *"Your destiny is too great, your assignment too important,*
> *your time too valuable. Do not let fear intimidate you."*
> Joel Osteen

Whenever we are exposed to trauma, a couple of things happen automatically. First, we stop breathing fully. The reason we stop breathing fully is that we don't want to feel fully, and limiting the flow of breath is the most effective way of doing this. The reason we don't want to feel fully is that we don't want to be emotionally overwhelmed, we tend to do whatever is necessary to avoid that experience. We believe that if we don't feel fully, we can survive, so not breathing fully is a brilliant tool of survival. The consequences of that decision are one, it creates emotionally frozen places within our chakra system that act like energetic obstructions and vampires (I call these karmic lumps, as I see them, as an energetic accumulation of backed up unresolved, un-met, and un integrated emotional energy). Two, it teaches us a pattern of response to emotion that is about not fully feeling our emotions. These choices are negative and disruptive and they keep us limited and trapped in our lower self. Connecting to and living in healthy relationship with your energetic system supports you in connecting with your higher self. This is the goal of the Lifeguides Transformation Program.

> *One of the highest truths of healing is all*
> *feelings fully felt and integrated transform into*
> *love, joy, happiness, power, and energy*

We will provide the exercises and processes that will guide you into fully feeling and integrating your feelings. These processes expose the difference between effectively and ineffectively feeling our feelings so that we can support you in digesting the emotional and energetic blockages that come from trauma in the past. This book invites you to participate in exercises capable of increasing your happiness by reclaiming trapped emotional energy reconnecting you to your inspiration and clearing your mind.

At the same time that you stopped breathing fully, your mind did what your mind does: attempt to make sense out of the experience, so it creates a perception. As a child, you have an egocentric perspective, (you see yourself as the center of the universe) therefore, your perception is likely to be egocentric, self-blaming and negative. The internal dialogue probably sounded something like "it's all my fault " or "I'm stupid" or "I must be bad or not lovable, " and because of the emotional stress at that time that perception went straight into the subconscious. This thought literally became ingrained in the brain as a physiological trench of frozen thoughts that were believed to be true. These trenches contained a life force that was originally intended for positive creativity but diverted into a negative charge that can negatively create the very thing that we do not want. The higher aspect of yourself knows and remembers with clarity your intentions, but the lower part of yourself contains all the obstacles and all the reasons not to manifest what you want. If we were to take your brain from your skull and slice it, you'd see a series of dendrites that look like roots to a tree. When exposed to stress, repetition, or trauma, the perceptions we create cause these dendrites to clump together and form these trenches, a physical manifestation of our misperceptions that scar the landscape of our brains.

We literally have trenches in our brain that are encoded with negative beliefs and ideas about ourselves that have been ingrained at the time of trauma, then got reinforced, fed, and established each time that illusion received time and attention as those perceptions were accepted as true. Those negative ideas and beliefs about you are misperceptions that are not real and not true. They come with a traumatic event and are perceived through an egocentric lens. They come through a child's perception, which can be about doubt, self-blame, guilt, and self-deprecation, disconnected from the brilliance of our true essential nature. These perceptions then, are frozen and powered with energy through intensity from the original trauma. They are fed with focus and attention each time they are re-stimulated and then they can create your experiences and your reality.

This is worth repeating for us to wake up and be empowered enough to be able finally to choose differently. We really are powerful and capable of liberating our past through understanding that at any point, we can choose to stop feeding the fears and the negativity and shift our focus onto feeding its opposite positive possibility.

The Lifeguides Transformation Program applies a simple three-step formula that enables you to transform these patterns into positive and genuine beliefs about yourself. We will show you how to become aware of your negative beliefs and self-perceptions. Not forgetting that these beliefs may be buried in your subconscious mind, making no sense to the conscious mind. Then we clearly show you how to transform those thoughts and liberate you from these trenches in your brain. We will also show you how to create new trenches that are encoded with thoughts that are in alignment with your truth so that you can be supported in using your mind as a tool to create the reality that you choose. These new trenches can lead you to make the positive choices that are aligned with your desires. The truth is always in alignment with your divine nature and in opposition to all illusions, misperceptions, and fears that feed insecurity, powerlessness, and negative inner talk.

We will also take you on a journey of emotional healing and clearing that centers around your chakra system. A chakra is an energy center aligned with your spinal column. There are seven of these centers, and each one correlates to your thoughts and feelings on a different area of your life. Every thought and emotion you've ever had filters through this system. Sometimes the chakras become blocked, and this can lead to disruption and disease in your body and in your life. The emotional healing and clearing processes offered to you through this program help unblock your chakras giving you the opportunity to claim and maintain optimum emotional and energetic functioning and health.

We all go through certain archetypal (every man) experiences and challenges. These experiences are predictable and designed to reveal who we really are. They create the perfect circumstances and conditions that present challenges, which contain the opportunities for us to reach within ourselves to make choices to bring forth our virtues of strength, integrity, honesty, and compassion or our vices of fear, anger, selfishness, greed, etc. How we respond to these challenges, the choices that we demonstrate through our actions determine whether we progress further along our path of growth and evolution or not. If when faced with challenges, we choose to respond with kindness, patience, understanding, forgiveness, and integrity, we open the doors to evolution, growth, and empowerment.

> *"Everything that happens to you in your life is your teacher. The trick is to sit at the feet of your own life and let yourself be taught by it." Unknown*

If we respond with attempts to control or threaten or punish another playing a god-like role, we will remain stuck. It is not necessary to know all the intimate details of every individual's particular circumstances and challenges to ignite the mechanism of healing and balancing because they are mainly archetypal. This means that the resolutions are also archetypal, general, and predictable. Each of these processes is beneficial to everyone, independently of where the trauma and imbalances reside and independently of the specific storyline of what happened. The five affirmations I created for each of the chakras (The Anatomy of Inspiration) are characteristic of what that chakra needs to rebalance and heal independently of an individual's specific experience. If you want help with a personal solution (that can be revealed in your self-discovery process), I can support you privately through email. You will find all this information at the back of the book.

My Yoga Path

I am someone who defers to my guidance, to the small still voices of insight and Intuition, that constantly communicates with me in both subtle and obvious ways. I am on the path of the sixth chakra and have learned that the highest source of guidance comes from within, and when I attend to and respond to those voices, I arrive at a deeper place of truth and peace, both in myself and in my life. This is one of the reasons why I am inviting you to connect with your higher self to become your own guru so that you have unobstructed access to your own wisdom and truth.

I have had brilliant and important teachers along the way, and I am grateful to all those who have contributed to my path of knowledge and education. I studied the Sivananda style of yoga and was fortunate enough to be taught by swamis. I had transmitted the yoga principles in the most spiritually pure way. I later apprenticed myself to one of the leading yin yoga teachers in the country, and I bow down in gratitude for the brilliance they laid down for me to move forward with and discover my own path of yoga that allowed me to bring forth and express what was intrinsically within me. Nowhere have I felt the resonance of past life knowledge burst forward into my current experience of life, more powerfully than on my path of yoga.

Very early on my yoga journey (I took my first yoga class at sixteen), I felt an intuitive recognition and understanding of the purpose of this practice. I felt my reconnection with my essence inside each of the asanas, and the more I practiced, the deeper I felt myself arrive into the home of my body. I practiced yoga throughout the years, more for the joy of coming home to myself than anything else and I never intended to become a teacher. I missed the obvious connection between it and the rest of work for many, many years.

Finally, I felt it 'd be good to elevate my practice to the next level and started my search for a suitable teacher-training course. Now, I realize that I was drawn by my internal radar of karmic recognition and found the right ashram for me in the Bahamas.

On a conscious level, I was attracted by the idea of doing yoga on a beautiful beach in Paradise but when I arrived, I found an entirely different reality. It must have been the hardest thing I have ever done, as I found myself in a constant state of anxiety about not knowing, about not running my own schedule, about not being in control. Little did I know that I was confronting my ego and the edges of my spiritual growth and that this battle with my ego had begun.

The whole experience was highly structured, requiring me to surrender completely; the very last thing I wanted to do and enjoyed the least but needed the most. I found myself having no time even to play on the beach in Paradise. I would not recommend this experience to everyone, nor was it the experience I was looking for. But it was exactly the experience I needed to allow me to reconnect with the essential part of myself through all the obstructions that arose to be purified.

I encourage you to be alert to the experiences in life that challenge you and feel difficult, as this is usually a sign that you are walking on sacred ground. I encourage you to pay close attention to everything that is present, as it is all purposeful and can be used to open a portal to your next edge of growth. Trust that the circumstances are perfect and that they contain the exact ingredients capable of elevating you to the next level. Usually, you are invited to meet your automaticity, your ego, and your lower self in a way that can be very illuminating and transformative.

"Yoga is the martial art of the soul, and the opponent is the strongest you've ever faced.. your ego." Unknown

However, what I found there was far more essential for me. Information about Vedanta philosophy struck so many chords of recognition in me that it was like a symphony playing in my head. Everything that I had learned about working with people was confirmed in those scripts, giving me such a strong feeling of inner peace and a sense of belonging to some lost ancient tribe, a family. Towards the end of the training, I recognized that the practice was, in fact, a descending chakra practice. I started to connect the dots until the intuitive impression of how this practice could merge with my other work became apparent.

Shortly after completing my training, a longstanding client invited me to attend her yin yoga class. Here I saw how the universe was guiding me back to myself, to my body and of how this practice could combine with my work and expand my offering. I am grateful for her information on alignment, which refined my teaching skills and brought me deeper into understanding the subtle energy body. As my practice and my classes grew, I found that yoga and the chakras were inseparable for me and I couldn't help but utilize the practice of yoga as a vehicle to share all my work. I then developed ascending and descending chakra practices in both the active and passive styles of yoga so that I had a physical practice that I could offer everyone at every level.

Whatever your level of practice and whatever level the mental, emotional, spiritual or physical issues you are dealing with, know that there is always something you can do and help is available to you. I have practices that caton address and rebalance whatever the issue is that you are dealing with. If you want a custom made personalized practice for your specific combination of challenges, I can offer you a service that will specifically and personally address all your current issues in a way that supports you as you navigate through your edge of growth into your highest possibility. Simply email me outlining your concerns and your happiness archetype, and I will design a personalized practice for you.

It is not necessary to practice yoga already to do these practices, and if you really do not want to do the yoga, the other tools will be sufficient to support your transformation. It is important to use the tools as instructed to fulfill my intention of transformation but if you want to set your own intentions and participate in the yoga practices or the meditations in other ways, it is possible to do that also.

Last year was a year of detoxification and purification for me. I received strong guidance from my intuition that I needed to release and let go of everything that was no longer serving me or in alignment with my mission of fulfilling my purpose of sharing my work with the world. I felt that I had been clearing and detoxifying on the mental level, but weeding out the disturbances on a consciousness level revealed a need to apply that same wisdom to my energy and physical body through a diet and exercise regime. I felt that I already had a healthy diet, and I knew about making healthy choices. I was careful to have plenty of fresh fruits and vegetables. I tried to keep my sugar and dairy intake down and have three nutritionally balanced meals and snacks a day to support my blood sugar stabilization. I guess that I probably fell in the higher percentile of the healthy population. In the guiding principles section you are invited to evaluate and connect with your deepest values and arrive at your agreements with yourself, others and life and then create your own guiding principles that you can rely on to be your compass that keeps you on the evolutionary track on this journey through life.

I now realize that I was not nearly as healthy as I thought and was in need of real information, support, and help. That I found in the form of a raw food chef. She came to my home and helped me clear out my cupboards and clean up my food act. I learned that my body needed a variety of fresh, unprocessed foods to be healthy, which meant eating more raw organic foods to allow my body to detoxify and balance. I discovered that to be in peak condition, our bodies benefit from natural foods whose colors mirror the charkas.

I always knew it was a good choice to ingest as much fruit and vegetables as possible. I recently discovered a great product something I had been searching for many years, since I started in the weight management business, twenty-three years ago, when I started working for a well-known weight loss company. Juice Plus is an excellent product and a great way to compliment our deficient Western diet that lacks real nutrition. If this interests you, please go online and check out the Juice Plus page on my website. You can contact me or go to my website to get this excellent product. I encourage you to do your own research and decide what works most seamlessly with your lifestyle and to take serious steps today to detoxify, reduce inflammation, and stabilize your blood sugar. I am passionate about supporting you in making great choices for your health on every level. I have created a whole life detox toolkit to support you in that choice. This is a ten-month journey through each of the chakras, a month in each beginning with the Transform 30 detox using juice plus, then a month Awakening Intuition, a month Awakening the Inner light, then Manifesting. Starting with nutrition and the food is essential, as good physical health is a great foundation for the more subtle body detox to follow.

Fresh locally grown produce is the highest nutritional choice possible. Research suggests that digested food is changed into color light impulses, creating a level of vibrational energy in our blood that the individual cells can absorb. To activate or balance a chakra, eat foods in its own color, and to calm over-activity, eat food in its opposite color. It is important to maintain balance and variety in the diet and to choose one that is sustainable and that works for your lifestyle. Juice Plus is simply the best nutrition product that I have found thus far and is the one that I personally use. It is the next best thing to fresh fruit and vegetables; it is affordable and easy to use which adds up to being actually doable and therefore effective.

The year before I started my new lifestyle, I made the new healthy habits chakra rebalancing meditations one through seven, which propelled me into an unexpected and profound transformational journey that directly mirrored the chakra that I happened to be working on creating a guided meditation for. This unconsciously took me about a month to create the meditation for each chakra and to progress through the seven steps of transformation, a journey everyone would benefit from taking. This lead to the creation of the whole life detox toolkit: a deeply purifying journey that guides you through a self-discovery process to reveal where your energy is blocked, stagnant, or toxic. Then you are guided to transforming your obstacles into gateways that transport you into the highest expression of your authentic self. I highly recommend doing that course alongside this one, as a purification journey, which ensures the fluid movement of energy through the chakra system. Working with nutrition and exercise supports the progress you can attain alongside the massive life improvements that accompany the mastery of the mind and the emotions. Good nutrition is at the foundation of any real transformation, as it allows the smooth transition towards your highest expression of yourself.

Here, I have laid out how to remove the obstacles that prevent us from connecting with and living fully in our essential nature. These obstacles may take the form of energetic blockages rooted in emotional trauma, or they may be wounds in consciousness that take the form of illusions, misperceptions, or fears on the mental level. My intention with the Lifeguides Transformation Program is to remove any illusion, misperception, or fear that stands in the way of your connection to the truth of your innate perfection. This perfection is not just in some of us, it is in all of us. Just as Michelangelo chipped away the excess marble to reveal the already perfect David that existed underneath, my intention is to chip away at illusions and fears created by misperceptions that came as a consequence of trauma. These perceptions may still be commanding our behaviors and choices, even if we know better and know they are no longer serving us. Everyone has all they need to change into the person they want to be within them. By freeing up from our habitual patterns, choices and behaviors we become liberated enough to establish new healthy habits.

Nothing I could write here would create transformation or awakening in your life. The best I could hope for is to inspire you to participate in the processes and practices that I have provided to guide you into your own personal transformational journey. You actually have to participate in your journey. You can benefit from working with the audio and video programs made available to you with links, mp3s, and personal access to me that elevate this communication beyond the sharing of information to the level of life changing transformation practices.

The Lifeguides Program is obviously not the only path available to you to transform, awaken, or become enlightened. But it is a direct and accelerated path. True awakening happens once we have worked in these awakened states of consciousness and integrated all aspects of whom we are, and we have remembered our true spiritual nature.

I feel that we are living in very exciting times and that we are supported in transforming our fear and our wounds into love, joy, energy, and happiness. We have arrived as a group consciousness at a point where we need tools that take us beyond simple intellectual understanding and assist us in arriving deeply into the home of our bodies. Here we can take up residence with ease and with comfort and do our spiritual growth work together, with love, support, and assistance. I realize that not everyone can dedicate years to their spiritual path and may not be in a regular practice of meditation and yoga. This program has something to offer for everyone, whoever you are, and whatever your practice and wherever you are starting from, I will meet you there. Some say that we are monks without monasteries and we have the opportunity to truly realize our spiritual reality inside our ordinary lives.

The Art and Science of Happiness

As it turns out, scientific research has uncovered interesting facts about happiness that aligns beautifully with my transformation program. We can cultivate certain characteristics, choices, habits, and skills that will contribute to our experience of happiness and well-being. According to the research, it is of primary importance to discover what your natural talents and gifts are and understand how to share them with the world in a way that contributes value to you and offers value and service to others. This experience provides meaning and great satisfaction that contributes to your happiness quotient. According to science, this is the number one factor that creates a happy life.

I am grateful to come from a family that encouraged me to pursue only what I am interested in. In school, I was encouraged only to take the courses that I liked and enjoyed and that brought a sense of satisfaction, held my interest, and inspired my natural curiosity. I was supported in walking the road less traveled if it was what I really wanted to do, and this allowed me to pursue the work I really wanted to do and be passionate about it. This choice supported my early and direct connection to my purpose, which allowed me to create and provide the roadmap for you to come home to yourself and do the same. (independently of all your circumstances and path you may have walked thus far). I have helped many clients align with and pursue their passion, discover their gifts and fulfill their purpose.

Having the information contained within the Lifeguides Transformation Program enables you to work with whatever circumstances may be present, trusting that they are workable and able to be utilized in a way that supports your journey home to your purpose and the awakening of your own natural gifts. This program will allow you to discover how you can find your natural talents and share them with the world in a way that contributes value to you and all those you share your gifts with.

Science supports the idea that having permission to be human, to make mistakes and still be embraced and accepted by those that we love allows us to be more ourselves, and experiencing this acceptance contributes to our sense of happiness and well-being. Giving us, and others permission to feel the full spectrum of our emotions from the lower negative vibrations of anger, fear, and anxiety actually supports our ability to have and experience the higher, more positive emotional states of peace, joy, and excitement. Fully experiencing all our emotions is natural and necessary to ensure a positive, healthy, and happy experience of life. This practice also helps us expand in our patience and acceptance of others that we love which improves the quality of our relationships. The guiding principles section in this book supports you in establishing this experience in your life.

The truth is that it is not wise to attempt to suppress a natural emotional phenomena with medication or any other means because when we try to suppress, we actually intensify that emotion and it becomes the lens that we see and experience life through. Allowing ourselves to have the full spectrum of our emotional reality gives us the capacity to learn how to navigate our own emotional intensity in a mature, conscious way that creates the template for us to exercise a wider range of choices regarding which of our emotional states we choose to inhabit.

When we learn and cultivate the skill of choosing positive thoughts and emotions and choosing happiness, we support ourselves by increasing our levels of wellness. Happiness is the main principle that leads to living an extraordinary life and increasing our wellness. Research has demonstrated that those who know that they influence their thoughts. and assert that influence by choosing their thoughts are happier. In his book, "Learned Optimism," Martin Seligman explains that optimists explain adverse events in specific temporary and impersonal ways and that conversely, pessimists explain them as pervasive, personal, and permanent and vice versa for positive events. Learning the habit of seeing challenges as specific to a certain situation, which is temporary, and thus able to be changed and not related to personal deficiency, means you are more likely to be positively energized and change the problem situation to your advantage. If you perceive the challenge as a pervasive life problem, as permanent, and unchanging, and even as a personal failure, you are more likely to feel depressed and resign yourself to failure. Through the course of this book, you will understand how to include the thinking that supports your happiness and cultivates it in your physiology liberating you from ingrained negative habits that may have been ruling your freedom of choice

The good news, of course, is that all this is within your influence. You can elevate your mood, transform your thinking patterns, and train your mind to expand into a perspective of purposefulness and find the opportunity at the root of your challenges so that you can support yourself in escaping the trap of self-loathing and self-blame. It is important to stay present enough to yourself not to fall into the trap of a negative spiral of thinking. Optimism and gratitude are a few of the little treasures of happiness that increase our sense of well-being and increase our happiness quotient. Continuing with negative self-protective patterns is like entering into a contract with darkness and expresses a lack of faith in the light. When we choose to trust the power of positivity and the light, we are making a significant statement of trust, love, and surrender. We can make many choices to detoxify our minds, our emotions, our habits, and simplifying our lives and going on a positivity diet helps. The bottom line is happiness pays, and that positive emotions lead to more creativity, more productivity, more loyalty, and more inspiration.

Love is more important than money when it comes to the happiness scale. Once our basic financial needs are met, money makes little difference to our levels of happiness; love makes a major difference. Relationships and love are important factors. When they are oriented towards growth and deepening connection, we are supporting ourselves in creating increased levels of happiness. Little things make a big difference and the moments we spend in positive, growth oriented relationships with the ones we love are the second most important factors in making us happier. Having gratitude and appreciation for the good things in our lives and the people that we love enhances our health, creativity, and satisfaction in life. I encourage you to look at Happiness 101 on you tube to see this research.

Research also supports the truth that exercise makes us happier. Understanding the mind/body connection allows us to gain the benefits of moving physically, as exercising is akin to taking an anti-depressant. I have come to relate to yoga as so much more than just exercise; it is medicine that heals the mind the emotions, as well as the physical body, and it opens a portal to our spirit that nourishes us on every level. The yoga in the Lifeguides programs amplifies these offerings by including the spiritual technology capable creating the profound and permanent changes you choose for yourself.

> *"In a way exercise can be thought of a psychiatrist's dream treatment. It works on anxiety, panic disorder and on stress in general, which has a lot to do with depression, and it generates the release of neurotransmitters- norepinephrine, serotonin and dopamine- that are very similar to our most important psychiatric medicines. Having a bout of exercise is like having a little bit of Prozac and a little bit of Ritalin right where it is supposed to go."* John Ratner

We can also improve our cognitive functioning by choosing to exercise. Studies have shown that meditators increase the activity on the left side of the brain, which results in a more positive outlook and a happier person. Deep breathing reduces the negative emotional states and increases the positive. I have created the Happiness yoga practice that amplifies these benefits by bringing all these skills together in one practice. Overall health is improved as we transform our negative mental and emotional patterns into their opposite positive possibility, suffering is reduced by skillfully navigating through it.

"In addition, when old repressed emotions, negative thought forms, and blockages- all lower vibrational energy patterns that can result in physical disease- are entrained and integrated into higher healthier frequencies, overall health is enhanced." Judith Kravitz

Real change only comes when you incorporate these changes in your life, that is why I created my Lifeguides Transformation Program. By providing you with the tools of audio and video practices, which include deep breathing and exercise (if you want it) you are supported in incorporating these positive changes, so that transformation becomes an experience, not just an idea. The real art of happiness resides in this practical application in your own life. It is when we commit to changing our daily routines and our habits that we actually see our lives transform, this is the most critical step you can take. The transformation toolkits I have assembled bring all these benefits together in a simple, understandable, easy-to-follow program that supports you to change your habits, to transform your life, and increase your happiness.

When we understand how to free ourselves of our own self-inflicted internal torture, by using our life challenges as opportunities for growth, we can release ourselves from the repeated wheel of karma and move closer to freedom. By reaching deeper into ourselves and finding our virtues of courage, integrity, compassion, and strength especially when stressed, allows us to advance along the spiritual path. This power translates into self-esteem and courage, which provides the energy necessary to mature, expand and evolve. Each task or challenge that life presents us that we successfully navigate leads to our maturation and our empowerment. By knowing whom we truly are, by knowing and experiencing our virtues and our ability to handle life and the challenges that it presents, we become ourselves. These experiences liberate us from fear and illusion, making us more alive and more able to realize our true potential. The maturation of our self-esteem and the establishment of our empowerment are essential for us to realize our true potential and have an optimum experience of life. Gifting us with a perspective of purposefulness allowing us to confront life and everything that it presents with full presence and capacity, forever shifting us away from the illusions of powerlessness and purposelessness.

The Lifeguides programs and toolkits provide the framework and foundation necessary to confront and successfully navigate through life's challenges. This program also enables our transformation of consciousness, which is required to support our evolution from fear-based beings into love-based beings. As we gather a purposefulness perspective, seeing that life continually presents us with the perfect conditions and experiences to support our growth and awakening we can see how the seeds of our own karma are constantly co-creating a reality that holds the promise of our liberation.

As we are, in fact, co-creating and inviting, moment to moment, the exact opportunities that we are ready to embrace, to wake us up. We will consistently be presented with challenges, struggles and difficulties that have contained within them the very solutions necessary for us to expand into the healing, transformation, and transmutation of all of our wounds into their opposite positive possibility. This practice, I feel, is the greatest spiritual practice, to actually use life and the experiences that we constantly co-create as purposeful and as a container for our spiritual growth. It is beneficial to recognize all of the challenges and struggles that we bump up against as ways to reveal all our habitual patterns of negativity, struggle, and stagnation. When we take the time to practice patience with ourselves, so that we can fully illuminate our inner dialogue with awareness, to the point that we know what our inner voices of fear are saying to us, we open up the space for our enlightenment.

In times of stress those voices burst forth with an enhanced force making it virtually impossible to ignore them, yet still, we try, we tend to ignore those voices as a distraction when in fact we benefit greatly from turning towards them with tenderness, presence, and clarity. The tools contained within these pages help to illuminate your blind spots with awareness so that you are better able to meet life and it's challenges in a purposeful way. Our minds are brilliant creators, and our karma will work endlessly to bring forth our wounds in the form of our experiences. When we meet those injuries with expanded awareness armed with transformative tools we create the opportunity for us to be free spiritual beings. Each day we can wake up and choose to see life as a gift and to be fully present in that day. We cannot always control the outcome, but we can control our reactions.

Each day we can bring all we have to that day, choosing to live it fully, seeing it as a great gift. Each day we can train our mind not to obsess on regret, nor to worry about tomorrow, but to be in this present moment. Each day, we can be grateful for what has happened that day. And we can choose not to judge our lives from moment to moment (am I happy, successful, unhappy, a failure, good, bad) but simply to live our life.

We are living in exciting times where science and spirituality are merging into the same awareness of what the true nature of reality and ourselves actually is, and I feel this affords the opportunity for our true renaissance to happen. We really have not known who we are and what we are capable of. If we knew, we would be truly free beings, manifesting instantly. We are beings with pure essence without limitation, and every physical force is merely a manifestation of the invisible forces. Every human being is a miniature Universe, and each person contains all the greater possibilities of, the greater Universe. We are holographic by nature; the pure conscious mind within us and in outer space are all one being. We are all part of this infinite holographic Universe. Our bodysuit of skin, cells, and bones and organs and cells can be very convincing, but it is a disguise, an illusion that veils our infinite potential: the human being and the universe are one being. We are invited at this time to know ourselves, to know our souls, to discover whom we are and what we have to give.

The roles we choose to play within our personal relationships are essential to our personal and spiritual growth. The actions, the language, and the choice of those around us mirror what we have become within to us. Romantic relationships are the most highly charged containers of spiritual growth, as that lens of reflection seems to be highly polished. It is a reflected reality. In others, we see the reflections of that which we are in the moment or of that which we judge in the moment. When there are consistent patterns of reflection, it is mirroring who you are being in the moment exposing where we can grow and who we can become.

I feel excited by the fact that we are now ready to embrace the real renaissance of our karmic healing, the reality of whom we truly are, free of the karmic wheel of wound, illusion, negativity, and automaticity. By transforming our fear-based consciousness and our lower negative emotions, we can avail ourselves of the possibility of awakening and enlightenment. When we understand how to free ourselves of our own self-inflicted internal torture, by using our life challenges as opportunities for growth and the skillful means described here, we will release ourselves from the wheel of karmic repetition and finally be free. This freedom allows us to be truly loving beings free of the eternal suffering that fear will entrap us in.

The yogis define karma, not as a record of wrongs that we have practiced or inflicted upon others, but as seeds of misperception and illusion that we hold about ourselves, about others, and about the nature of reality that we have not yet resolved. These ideas have a strong creative ability and will have their say in our reality. By exposing their existence as we recognize and transform them, we progress along our path towards freedom.

Archetypes

I have created a quiz to support you in recognizing the specific mental and emotional pattern, that are currently influencing your experience of life, this will empower you to ensure that the influence becomes the positive one that you choose. When you establish a clear and strong relationship with your happiness archetypes, they become capable of reclaiming any lost inspiration and becoming the architect of your future happiness. Making friends with and shaking hands with your happiness archetypes will support you, in establishing a strong connection with your inner energetic system, which contains the map that can navigate you into your highest happiest self. Abiding with, and navigating through the same emotional vibrations and perceptions that arose inside past traumatic experiences can reclaim inspiration that may have been lost inside the experience of trauma. When they are touched and fully felt, until they are healed, rebalanced and reintegrated into your system, you have the opportunity to arrive into your highest, happiest self, aligning your subconscious mind with your conscious intention. This integration and alignment enable you to understand how to manage your moods better and how to free yourself from fear and negative thinking which allows you to reclaim your own creative potential so that you can live your life by design. I would like to introduce you to your Anatomy of Inspiration.

<u>*What is your happiness archetype* and</u> <u>*what color is your path to happiness?*</u>

1.) When at my best, the strongest feeling I feel is

   1.) Secure

   2.) Connected

   3.) Powerful

   4.) Love

   5.) Expressive

   6.) Clear

   7.) Trusting

2) When I am feeling good in my relationship with my partner, the strongest feeling I feel is

   1.) Safe

   2.) Whole

   3.) Worthy

   4.) Loved

   5.) Free

   6.) Certain

   7.) Faith

3.) At times of difficulty, my tendency is

    1.)   Gather support from friends

    2.)   Withdraw

    3.)   Feel paralyzed

    4.)   Seek revenge

    5.)   Get control

    6.)   Feel confused and Indecisive

    7.)   Feel like there is a conspiracy or set up

4.) In conflict, I tend to

    1.)   Feel insecure and unstable. / Be angry and frustrated

    2.)   Feel isolated and alone. / Feel afraid

    3.)   Feel powerless and anxious

    4.)   Feel resentment, jealousy, or hatred

    5.)   Feel out of control and/or suffocated

    6.)   Feel overwhelmed and want to drink

    7.)   Feel like others are plotting against me

5.) My greatest physical vulnerability is

    1.)   Liver, legs, hips, feet

    2.)   Kidney, reproductive organs, low back pain

    3.)   Digestion, stomach, mid back pain

    4.)   Cardio vascular system, heart disease, lung problems

    5.)   Thyroid, eating problems, mouth/dental problems

    6.)   Headaches, vision problems

    7.)   Dizziness, stroke

6.)   When stressed, the strongest emotion I feel is

    1.)   Anger

    2.)   Fear

    3.)   Powerlessness

    4.)   Jealousy, ingratitude

    5.)   Out of control

    6.)   Confusion

    7.)   Betrayed

7.)   My biggest fear is

    1.)   Death

    2.)   Abandonment

    3.)   Disapproval

    4.)   Being un-loveable

    5.)   Suffocation

6.) Being lost

7.) Isolation

8.) My stinking thinking sounds like

    1.) I am not safe

    2.) I feel alone

    3.) I'm not good enough

    4.) I'm not lovable

    5.) I can't express myself

    6.) I don't know

    7.) I don't trust life, others, myself

9.) When I overcome obstacles, the strongest feeling I feel is

    1.) Safe

    2.) Connected

    3.) Peaceful/ triumphant

    4.) Courageous

    5.) Free

    6.) Clear

    7.) Faith

10.) I would most like to feel

1.) Stable

2.) Creative

3.) Powerful

4.) Loving

5.) Free

6.) Clear

7.) Trusting

Answers

The Seven Happiness Archetypes

If you have more than two categories with an equal number of points, then look at your answer for number 5 and go with that number. Otherwise, you can contact me, and I will help you.

Mostly 1.) The Chief walks the red-grounded path of safety

Mostly 2.) The Adventurer walks the orange pleasure path

Mostly 3.) The Nurturer walks the yellow path of deep self-love

Mostly 4.) The Lover walks the green path of unconditional love

Mostly 5.) The Artist walks the pale blue path of freedom

Mostly 6.) The Guru walks the deep blue path of clarity

Mostly 7.) The Master walks the violet path of enlightenment

What follows is an introduction to the seven happiness archetypes, and I will go into greater detail and depth of the success stories that I share in the last section of the book. We all embody each of these archetypes to a varying degree in either its positive or negative states. It is useful to know the strengths and vulnerabilities of each of these archetypes so that you can know how to bring yourself back to balance when something stresses or challenges you in your circumstances and one of these aspects of yourself and your life. The negative aspect of each of the archetypes contains the information necessary to know and overcome to bring you back to your path of happiness, to embody the anatomy of inspiration to arrive at the positive archetype.

We each have a primary archetype that contains our current lifetime vulnerability. This vulnerability exposes our current spiritual edges of growth and our main archetype, which is a consistent edge that will show up to a larger or lesser degree on our path to enlightenment depending on how conscious, awake, and evolved we are. This vulnerability contains within it, our highest potential for happiness, balance, and health, and by courageously confronting what is required we are shown how to travel from our weakness to our strength. The negative patterns reflect where our thoughts and feelings go when we feel stressed and crazy (surprisingly crazy isn't random or chaotic, it is very structured and predictable.) This structure makes the journey back to our sanity predictable. The tools and the method of transforming your lower self to your higher self is described in the Lifeguides Transformation program and the three steps to healing the mind and the emotion.

1

Charlie The Chief

The Chief walks the red-grounded path of safety

When balanced, the chief is grounded, stable and solid connected to the earth, his history, and his ancestors, in a way that provides a strong sense of stability, security, and safety for himself and all those around him. He is reliable and predictable in his interest in family, structure, and support. He is strong in his foundation, which emanates calmness, courage, and compassion. He likes simplicity and nature, which strengthens him and positive support, group connections, family, and a sense of continuity feed him.

When imbalanced, he can feel irritated, unstable, insecure, and unpredictable. Stress causes him to feel unsafe, which releases adrenaline throughout his system, causing him to reside in fight/flight mode, weakening him on every level. His emotional vulnerability is anger, and the mental weakness is an inner dialogue that ruminates around the wounded belief that he is not safe. These thoughts and feelings can lead him into some challenging behaviors like road rage, criticism, complaining, and negativity. Tending to focus on what is wrong and not working within him and others that perpetuate the creation of challenge and difficulty in his life, fueling the whole cycle of anger.

As you balance your thoughts and emotions, you support the habit of happiness that creates new positive behaviors of enthusiasm, kindness, active listening, forgiveness, tolerance, and the expectation that others are capable and trustworthy. This allows you to hold the vision for positive possibility and gives you and others the space to rise to your highest possible behavior choices. This brings more peace, equanimity, and harmony into your life. As you expand into feeling safe, secure, and supported, you behave in ways that reflect these feelings, allowing yourself to be more vulnerable, alive, and present. Being grounded and solid about whom you are and where you belong translates into acting in ways that make you dependable and trustworthy, becoming a known entity both to yourself and others.

By walking the grounded path of safety, the Chief gathers strength by being in nature, being connected to the negative ions that rise through the earth and grounds him. Gardening or walking barefoot and putting his hands in the earth invite balance and strength for him and bring him back to himself. He learns to fortify his emotional vulnerability of anger by strengthening his liver meridian. Pushing more chi through his system allows him to digest his anger by meeting it with awareness breath and compassion. Transmuting his angry adrenalized state into his harmonized happiness state of compassion and courage which liberates him into understanding the truth that he is safe and supported to be in his body and in his life with full presence and open-hearted compassion.

Applying the three steps to master his mind supports his sense of well-being and safety. Recognizing that his mental fitness is supported by his choice to practice and nourish his mind with positive, optimistic thinking eradicating his illusions and predictable default negative inner dialogue. This, along with applying the three steps to master his emotions, provides the tools and practices that he needs to liberate from his old limited conditioning and his habitual patterns so that he can be connected to his essence, his natural state, and his happiness. This releases his trapped energy and ignites his inspiration through the experience of being safe and stable and secure.

Here we are invited to connect with nature and our tribe. For us to be balanced here, we are invited to live in harmony with nature inspiring a feeling of being connected to the earth, our family, our community, and our societal considerations. You benefit and increase your happiness quotient by being part of a community of people, a community of life, in a way that matters to both you and them. Meaningful relationships can be found everywhere, not just in the romantic arena, and by actively contributing to your community, you will find deeper your inspiration and deeper meaning and greater satisfaction.

When stressed and challenged, be vigilant of being more reactive and feeling agitated, irritated, or angry. Pay extra attention to your inner dialogue, being extra sensitive to inner dialogue that may speak loudly or softly and seduce you into the idea that you are not safe, supported, or secure. This inner conversation originated in a traumatic experience early in your history that you perceived yourself as being unsafe, expanding into the illusion that you are not safe. At those times, you are being presented with an opportunity for transformation, and it is important to take advantage of that opportunity by being present and awake to your emotions and your consciousness so that you can exercise your power of choice and practice your tools. You are consistently choosing to navigate your thinking and your emotions back to their true harmonized inspired and happy state.

We all like to feel safe and supported; it carries a high value for you, perhaps the highest. When stressed, you tend to become ungrounded and can easily feel lost like you don't fit in and like you need a high degree of stability, consistency, and security to feel at peace, relaxed and at home. The home and everything that it stands for is important, and you may be willing to sacrifice lots of fun adventures in deference to having a strong anchor that allows you to feel safe. Your gifts reside in establishing an internal sense of stability so that you no longer seek it externally.

You are walking the red path of aligning with safety. This transformative journey clears all wounds related to your sense of safety, security, stability, and belonging, liberating you from the wounds of the past. Supporting you in feeling grounded, safe, and connected. This path is physically related to symptoms of low back pain, immune disorders, sciatic problems, and depression. By working with the tools available in the first chakra toolkit you have everything that you need to create a new inner reality that is firmly rooted in an inner and outer reflection of the truth of your safety. This experience can provide a source of inspiration for you that motivates you to create the life of your dreams.

2

Aden The Adventurer

The Adventurer walks the orange pleasure path

When balanced and harmonized the Adventurer is playful, free, wise, connected, and creative. Interested in deep, meaningful relating with the self and others, the Adventurer travels his path seeking and finding pleasure, purpose, and meaning. He sees connection everywhere and lives in an abundant reality without limitations.

You are highly creative and can easily find joy through your creativity and your connections. The more willing you are to risk emotionally and show your vulnerable under belly, the greater your rewards through deep intimacy and lasting connections will be. When imbalanced, it is easy for you to feel isolated, alone, outcast, or disconnected. This isolation can exist on many levels even in relation with the self from your own creative flow, leaving you feeling overwhelmed challenged and afraid. Fear rules the imbalanced Adventurer, causing you to feel paralyzed, isolated, or trapped, disconnecting you from flowing with abundance and catapulting you into an experience of scarcity, lack, and deprivation.

You become susceptible to addictions when out of balance, so it is important to be present and connected to difficult emotions of isolation and perceived aloneness so that you are not seduced to escape the emotional pain through distractions, ranging from substances to television, all forms of escaping the overwhelming pain of disconnection. You may substitute life-threatening risk taking activities, such as extreme sports or gambling of any nature, rather than risking losing the self to emotional vulnerability. Fear is the demon of the adventurer, although sometimes you would never know, as you can appear to be highly courageous, willing to risk life and limb for a temporary adrenalized thrill, this is the mask that obscures the terror of risking the exposure of the authentic self in case it is rejected.

These thoughts and feelings can lead you into some challenging behaviors like disconnection with the ones that you love when you are hurt or stressed or challenged. You may find yourself constructing walls of self-protection that can feel insurmountable for yourself and the ones you love. The fear of intimacy or emotional pain may cause you to make poor choices about your partner, such as distancing, rejecting, and ultimately, abandoning them. These destructive behavior choices trap you in a low vibration pattern of reach and withdraw, doing a two-step in intimacy that is painful and limited, leaving the most precious and vulnerable parts of yourself lonely, unknown, and untouched. You may indulge in a whole variety of additions to hide out and avoid the possible pain that sweetness, surrender, and vulnerability brings because the fear of getting hurt is too strong. As you balance your thoughts and emotions, you support the habit of happiness that creates new positive behaviors of optimism, balance, courage, and curiosity towards intimacy.

You may experience greater abundance in your life as you bring balance into this chakra. This allows your creativity to flow, providing a greater sense of fulfillment and satisfaction. Holding the vision of positive possibility of connection and goodness happening gives you and others the space to rise to your highest possible behavior choices. This brings more balance, peace, equanimity, and harmony into your life. As you expand into more connected, creative, and wise choices, you behave in ways that reflect these feelings; this allows you to be more vulnerable, alive, and present. Being connected to your higher power and the highest power of the universe ignites your wisdom, which feeds and benefits your choices and behaviors.

For us to feel fully happy and satisfied, we benefit from having deep, strong, and meaningful relationships. Once we mature and know ourselves well enough to understand our values, we can then connect with others with a shared value system, which is a necessary ingredient for a happy life. This chakra is also the center for our creativity, another necessary ingredient for a balanced and happy life. A happy, creative life includes both expression and input. Happiness and joy are activated in the second chakra, which produces a sense of well-being and happiness that uplifts everything that we do.

Happiness and pleasure are not the same things. A continuous stream of pleasure experiences does not necessarily result in increased happiness, which is actually an internal state of consciousness that arises out of a deep sense of meaning and satisfaction. In fact, small things consistently done, create the major impact. When it comes to deep happiness, connection is highly important to you, and in fact, it may carry the highest value for you. It may also be the place where you are most challenged. You are probably highly creative and may find joy, peace, and happiness in expressing your creative abilities. Money could be an area that challenges you, and when stressed, you may tend to feel completely alone in the world. Your gifts reside in fully participating in open-hearted, vulnerable intimacy. You can reclaim lost inspiration inside the experience of intimacy and connection. Your path is about clearing the wounds surrounding abandonment fears, betrayals, addictions, and experiences of scarcity. You benefit by rebalancing sexual and creative energy, supporting you in connecting with abundance and creative expression, this rebalances all desires, appetites, and addictive patterns. This is physically related to arthritis, potency, and desire problems, fibroids, and menopause issues.

The Adventurer learns to fortify his emotional vulnerability of fear by strengthening his kidney meridian. Pushing more chi through his system allows him to digest his fear by meeting it with awareness, breath, and compassion. Using positive memory or imagination to connect to times when intimacy, closeness, and connection were strong and supported, and present strengthens you. He works with positive affirmations to nourish the inner dialogue of the lower mind with positive food leading to positive possibility. He transmutes his fearful adrenalized state into his harmonized happiness state of wisdom and clarity, liberating him into understanding the truth that he is always connected to his own higher power and the highest power in the universe.

Applying the three steps to master his mind supports his sense of well-being and connection. He recognizes that his mental fitness is supported by his choice to practice and nourish his mind with positive, optimistic thinking eradicating his illusions and default negative inner dialogue. This, along with applying the three steps to master his emotions, provide the tools and practices that he needs to liberate from his old limited conditioning and his habitual patterns so that he can be connected to his essence, his natural state, and his happiness. He benefits from being vigilant when stressed and challenged not to be reactive and feel isolated, alone, and disconnected.

Pay extra attention to your inner dialogue, being extra sensitive to inner dialogue that may speak loudly or softly and seduce you into the idea that you are alone, outcast, or somehow unwanted. This inner conversation originated in a traumatic experience early in your history where you perceived yourself as being alone, and perhaps feeling emotionally overwhelmed and afraid inside this experience, expanding into the illusion that you actually are all alone at those times. You can recognize that you are being presented with an opportunity for transformation, and it is important to take advantage of that opportunity by being present and awake to your emotions and your consciousness so that you can exercise your power of choice and practice your tools.

Consistently choose to navigate your thinking and your emotions back to their true harmonized happy state. Working with the tools and practices for rebalancing the second chakra will support you in transforming these vulnerabilities into your strengths.

3

Nancy The Nurturer

The Nurturer walks the yellow path of deep self-love

When balanced, the nurturer is giving and kind and generous towards the self and others. She knows how to extend kindness and compassion to support all those she touches. She is empowered when in the right relationship with her personal power, knowing how to assert for her needs to be met, never forcing or pushing too hard, nor being weak on her boundaries, appearing whishy washy. She is in the right relationship with her confidence striking the perfect balance so that her self-assurance is a great asset magnetizing everything and everyone that supports her manifestations.

She knows about self-love and practices excellent self-care. There is a deep sense of inner-peace, calmness, and inner equanimity. The Nurturer contains a bright inner-light that shines out and touches everyone with its positive glow of caring, kindness and deep compassion. There is a knowing of her true value and a deep sense of worthiness that shines through.

At your best, you are confident, kind, caring, and powerful. You could be considered to be an unstoppable force to be reckoned with. You have a deep connection to your value that communicates this truth to others, and you can easily command respect and easily be the most powerful force in any room.

When stressed or challenged, it is hard for you to remember the truth of your own value. You are vulnerable to limiting yourself, as you question your capacity, ability, and worthiness and all the goodness that you are very capable of creating. Your gifts reside in knowing your value to the degree that you feel worthy of having all the goodness you are capable of creating for yourself. You may struggle with power issues in relationships and find yourself inside power struggles.

An imbalanced third chakra can lead you into over exertion of power and seduce you into being vindictive, mean, cold, calculated, and manipulative, which of course, leads to nothing but problems, sleepless nights and an even deeper commitment to your self-loathing, as you give yourself more cause to hate yourself. It is important not to give yourself any more reasons to dislike yourself, as this is the vulnerability of this chakra. This vulnerability makes you want to strike back harder when someone hurts you. Freedom and healing reside in resisting that temptation that would lead you into finally healing this painful wound. Or conversely, it can lead into feeling like a victim and powerless which also can stimulate the same desire for revenge or manipulation. This reflects an imbalance in relationship with power and a loss of inspiration inside this imbalance and liberation to reclaim inspiration as you rebalance this chakra.

I know that it is tough to convince an ego that wants revenge that turning the other cheek really is your salvation but practicing this tough lesson actually liberates your spirit to finally forgiving those who have hurt you. This choice supports the growth of your spirit into the joy of knowing your intrinsic value and worth without any exertion of effort on your part to seek revenge, control, gain the upper hand, have authority, or a pseudo puffed up sense of your power.

These thoughts and feelings can lead you into challenging behaviors like finding yourself wrong and beating yourself up leading you to sabotage your own happiness and trap your inspiration leaving you depleted, repressed and unmotivated, deciding that you are unworthy and unloved. Others may perceive that you waste time feeling sorry for yourself, losing yourself inside a self-indulgent pity party. You may find yourself both voluntarily and involuntarily involved in power struggles all around your life, in your work relationships, and in your love relationships. You may be very sensitive to others' negative judgments of you, while at the same time, indulging in your own judgments of them and of yourself. Your skin may be thin in relation to feeling wrong and be intolerant of the slightest hint or suggestion that you have done something incorrectly. Your anxiety may cause you to worry and ruminate unnecessarily about everything, spending lots of time and energy involved in being concerned about things, that most likely, will never happen. Phobias of all kinds could surface if you get too far out of balance.

Expanding into your natural state of confidence and magnetism causes you to become the life and soul of any party. You will be easily able to exert your positive influence positively, knowing your own worth supports you in acting with dignity and strength, power and balance, allowing you to be completely yourself. At your best, you can create a win/win in all situations so that everyone feels loved and cared for. This brings more balance, peace, equanimity, and harmony into your life. As you expand into allowing yourself to be more confident, alive and present, you find your positive power and exert that positive, balanced influence that brings abundant, nurturing energy, love, and happiness to everyone around you. Being connected to your own self-love and balanced personal power allows you to invite others to find that place within them.

The art of self-love is of utmost importance to self-esteem, and developing a healthy sense of your own intrinsic value is extremely important to your happiness. The third chakra is the center where you can develop a healthy sense of your own value, both with yourself and others. This is the center where we are invited to discern the difference between healthy and unhealthy ego function. Being in alignment with our truth and our intrinsic values is necessary for us to create balance in this chakra. Connecting with and operating from your own guiding principles liberates you to your highest happiest self. Walking our talk supports us in finding our power, which is another fundamental element to arriving at health here in the third chakra center.

The vulnerability of this chakra is to believe in your own powerlessness, the opportunity, and the strength resides in understanding that you are all powerful in the creation of your life and your happiness. In relationship to happiness, it is important to realize that you can create your life your way and that your choices contribute to your experience of happiness.

The Nurturer learns to fortify her emotional vulnerability of anxiety by strengthening her stomach meridian. Pushing more chi through her system allows her to digests her anxiety by meeting it with awareness breath and compassion. She uses positive memory or imagination, connecting to times when feelings of positive confidence and positive pride were present inside, with experiences of feeling good about herself when she knew she was worthy of goodness. Working with positive affirmations to nourish the inner dialogue of the lower mind with positive food leading to the positive possibility, transmutes her anxious, adrenalized state into her harmonized happiness state of peace and equanimity. Liberating her into understanding the truth that she is always perfectly loved and lovable just as she is and knowing she is deserving and worthy of love both from herself and others. This helps her to remember that she is powerful and confident and capable of creating a great life for herself.

She applies the three steps to master her mind which supports her sense of well-being and connection. She can recognize that her mental fitness is supported by her choice to practice and nourish her mind with positive, optimistic thinking which eradicates her illusions and default negative inner dialogue. This, along with applying the three steps to master her emotions, provides the tools and practices she needs to liberate from her old limited conditioning and her habitual patterns so that she can be connected to her essence, her natural state, and her happiness.

Be vigilant when stressed and challenged to be more reactive to feeling unworthy and anxious. Pay extra attention to your inner dialogue, being extra sensitive to inner dialogue that may speak loudly or softly and seduce you into the idea that you are unworthy, less than, and somehow undeserving. This inner conversation originated in a traumatic experience early in your history where you perceived yourself as unworthy and perhaps feeling emotionally overwhelmed, and you maybe are afraid of repeating this experience expanding into the illusion that you actually are undeserving of love.

At those times you are presented with an opportunity for transformation, it is important to take advantage of that opportunity by being present and awake to your emotions and your consciousness so that you can exercise your power of choice and practice your tools. Consistently choose to navigate your thinking and your emotions back to their true harmonized happy state. You are invited to clear all wounds related to your sense of self-esteem and personal power, enabling you to be fully empowered so that you can realize your full potential. This supports you in cultivating a strong sense of confidence. This path is physically related to stomach disorders, ulcers, liver dysfunction bulimia, and hepatitis. Working with the tools and practices for rebalancing the third chakra will support you in transforming these vulnerabilities into your strengths. Any inspiration that may have been trapped, suppressed or lost inside the experience of feeling unworthy or losing personal power is available to be reclaimed here by revisiting that experience and bringing awareness, breath, and compassion to it.

4

Lilly The Lover

The Lover walks the green path of unconditional love

When balanced, you are the most loving, joyful, giving heart-centered person around. Your love is palpable and a vibration that attracts everyone around you to their own loving hearts. You are capable of great joy, generosity, and kindness. You have a willingness to be vulnerable, as you have an innate understanding of the gifts of that choice. You understand about intimacy and naturally practice the three spiritual laws of intimacy. You can be connected to your emotions in a way that allows you to be truthful about what you are feeling in each moment. You can remove the walls of self-protection that you built around the heart that prevent you from experiencing the pain of rejection and at the same time, prevent you from fully giving and receiving love, which is, in fact, the opportunity of the fourth chakra. You are also able to confess all your fears and worries and doubts that may be plaguing you and those you are closest to.

Your greatest strength is the gift of unconditional love yet when stressed; you may find that you have a lot of grief, sadness, or jealousy. You are invited to free yourself of all automatic self-protective mechanisms of avoiding love, vulnerability, and open-hearted connection so that you can fully open your heart and share the abundant well spring of joy, happiness, and care that you have at your fingertips. Your gifts reside beneath the armoring of self-protective walls around the heart, and in choosing to dismantle those walls, you will expand into a well spring of unconditional love. The Lover learns to fortify her emotional vulnerability of heartbreak and grief by strengthening her heart meridian. Pushing more chi through her system allows her to digests her grief and sadness by meeting it with awareness breath and compassion. The Lover uses positive memory or imagination when connecting to times when feelings of love, compassion and kindness, and open-heartedness were present. If there truly is no memory to recall from then, simply imagine what it would be like to have love in your life.

Working with positive affirmations to nourish the inner-dialogue of the lower mind with positive food leading to positive possibility transmutes her grief, sadness, and heartbreak into her harmonized happiness state of unconditional love. This liberates her into understanding the truth that she is completely free to open her heart fully so that she can fully give and receive love. Then she is free to be generous and loving even when those around are not free or able to love.

She recognizes that her mental fitness is supported by applying the three steps to master her mind and by her choice to practice and nourish her mind with positive, optimistic thinking, eradicating her illusions and default negative inner dialogue. This mental mastery along with applying the three steps to master her emotions provides the tools and practices that she needs to liberate herself from her old limited conditioning and her habitual patterns. She can be connected to her essence, her natural state of fully giving and receiving love and live in open-hearted connection to her happiness.

When stressed and challenged these thoughts and feelings can lead you into challenging behaviors like being cold-hearted, distant, uncaring, and even jealous and vindictive. When you are hurt or stressed or challenged, you need to watch out for these demons when your Lover goes out of balance with the ones that you love. You may find yourself constructing walls of self-protection that can feel insurmountable for yourself and the ones you love.

The fear of intimacy or emotional pain may cause you to make poor choices in relation to your partner, such as rejecting them and finding fault. If you don't have a partner, you may remain single and always find a fatal flaw with each new relationship possibility you are presented with, navigating you back to the heartbreak in your history that you are attempting to heal. These destructive behavior choices trap you in a low vibrational pattern of reach and withdrawal, doing a two-step in intimacy that is painful and limited, leaving the most precious and vulnerable parts of yourself lonely, unknown, and untouched. Similar to the trauma of the Adventurer, the Lover wants deep love and intimacy more than anyone, yet holds every possibility at arm's length in deference to the sense of pseudo safety that arises from self - protected aloneness. Open-hearted kindness and connection is the way forward for the Lover, yet as simple as it sounds, when wounded and stressed by difficult circumstances, opening the heart may feel impossible. When you do make a choice to open your heart and extend love with kindness and compassion, you discover a never - ending supply of love available for you to give and receive. This contributes to an endless supply of energy, vitality, and health that is available to you, allowing you to be accepting of what is. As you balance your thoughts and emotions, you support the habit of happiness that creates new positive behaviors of optimism, balance, courage, and openness towards love and intimacy. Any lost or trapped inspiration can be reclaimed inside the choice to fully open your heart so that you can fully give and receive love.

Cleaning out your heart center allows you to start fresh. If you want to be happy, reboot, take inventory, and clean the slate and create your updated version of your guiding principles. Carrying baggage and repeating your wounded inner dialogue and old stories, again and again, is self-destructive. Punishing others for your bad days and unhappy childhood is cruel – although many find it useful as a control mechanism. If you want a happy life with someone, or just yourself, you will benefit from cleaning out your heart center and falling madly in love with your life, or at least, falling in love with something about your life.

> *"Happiness is about cleaning out your heart and nurturing the graces that matter: hope, love, and forgiveness. Let the past go. And don't be shy about telling others you love them or that you are sorry for something. You may not have a second chance." Unknown.*

You may experience greater abundance in your life as you bring balance into this chakra. This allows your creativity to flow, providing a greater sense of fulfillment and satisfaction. This holds the vision for positive possibility and gives you and others the space to rise to your highest possible behavior choices. This brings more balance, peace, equanimity, and harmony into your life. As you expand into open-hearted giving and receiving of love, you behave in ways that reflect these feelings, which allows you to be more vulnerable, alive, and present.

Be vigilant when stressed and challenged; to be less reactive to feeling jealous or vindictive and disconnected from the heart. Pay extra attention to your inner dialogue, and be extra sensitive to inner dialogue that may speak loudly or softly and seduce you into the idea that you are unlovable. This inner conversation originated in a traumatic experience early in your history, where you perceived yourself as being unloved and somehow un-loveable. This may have lead to feeling emotionally overwhelmed and afraid, expanding into the illusion that you actually are un-loveable.

At those times, you are being presented with an opportunity for transformation, and it is important to take advantage of that opportunity by being present and awake to your emotions and your consciousness so that you can exercise your power of choice and practice your tools.

Consistently choose to navigate your thinking and your emotions back to their true harmonized happy state. You are invited to clear all wounds related to your sense of grief, heartbreak, and sadness, enabling you to be fully open-hearted and unconditionally loving so that you can realize your full potential. This supports you in cultivating a strong sense of compassion and kindness and unconditional love, allowing you to release all protections and defenses around the heart, which actually isolate and separate you. Rebalancing this chakra supports your open-hearted compassion in relationship with yourself and others. This path is also physically related to all heart issues, asthma, allergies, and lung and breast cancer. Working with the tools and practices for rebalancing the fourth chakra will support you in transforming these vulnerabilities into your strengths.

5

Ari The Artist

The Artist walks the pale blue path of freedom

In his best, balanced state, the Artist is expressive, creative, authentic, surrendered, and free. He has overcome control issues and can communicate all his wants and needs and boundaries effectively. The Artist speaks effortlessly and easily in a way that attracts and magnetizes everything that he wants and needs. His hormones are balanced and harmonized, and he takes full responsibility for the life he consciously creates. Surrender is the path to harmony for you. Mastering the art of letting go and finding your voice are the keys to your liberation. Freely speaking your truth inside an energy of compassion allows you come back to your center and reclaim lost inspiration.

When stressed, you may run into control issues, and power struggles both with your higher and lower self and with those you are in close relationship with. You are vulnerable to repressing your emotional truth to maintain the peace and continue being liked or approved of. This vulnerability can lead to a loss of authenticity and a challenge with knowing who you truly are and what is right for you. It is part of your journey to shed the many roles you have adopted to survive and know the difference between what is you and what is not you, what is the true self and what is false self and not you, not your natural state. This distinction may start out as something obvious and lead to more subtleties as you journey along your path. Practicing the wisdom contained within the serenity prayer is essential for you to find balance and harmony. Your gift of purity and truth reside in the act of practicing the art of surrender. Releasing and letting go of your self-protective mechanism of self-suppression and skilled adaptation around being who others need you to be, are essential for you to find your true self. Surrender here is not at all about giving in or giving up on the self, rather it is about melting into the highest.

These negative thoughts and feelings can lead you to some challenging behaviors like being inauthentic and repressed and unable to express your emotional truth, which can cause you to carry resentment about sacrificing your needs because they were not expressed and they remain unknown. This adaptation can look like you becoming a chameleon and being the person others want you to be, which can cause you to lose who you really are. Your creative expression could become compromised as you unconsciously energetically push back on your own expression. You benefit from observing when your artist becomes repressed and out of balance. At these times, you can take a step back into your witness and really be observant of your own reactive patterns when you are hurt or stressed or challenged.

You may find yourself constructing walls of self-protection that can feel insurmountable, but they are not. It serves you to illuminate your wounds fully and know with certainty what they are constructed of. Identifying your fears and inner dialogue in relation to expression, creativity, and power struggles allow you to transmute the repressed emotional energy into powerful, potent, creative energy. Learning to make important choices when you need to make them and having the courage to be spontaneous are essential lessons on your life path.

Be careful not to let others make important choices for you that you have to live with. Learning to speak up for yourself is an important lesson on your path. Remember that you are an adult and overcome the seductions of the inner child that may attempt to silence you, as if they are successful, they will never lead to happiness. Happiness requires that adults act like adults, and an expansion into being entirely responsible for yourself is necessary on this life path. Ego struggles transmute through the fifth chakra and knowing how to navigate this territory successfully is essential for you.

Speaking your truth in a balanced, powerful and effective way is important, and practice makes perfect. As you balance your thoughts and emotions, you support the habit of happiness that creates new positive behaviors of expression, communication, and truth. You may experience greater creative expression in your life as you bring balance into this chakra. This expression allows your creativity to flow providing a greater sense of fulfillment and satisfaction, bringing more balance and harmony into your life. The Artist learns to support his emotional vulnerability of force, control, and over assertion or repression on the physical level by strengthening his thyroid. Pushing more chi through his system allows him to digests his excessive tendency to force or push too forcefully by meeting it with awareness, breath, and compassion. Or if there is a repressive pattern the opposite imbalanced tendency of suppression of truth or expression is supported by meeting it with awareness, breath, and compassion. Using positive memory or imagination that connect to times when feelings of flow; surrendering and being authentic, where strong and available, rebalances this chakra. Working with positive affirmations to nourish the inner-dialogue of the lower mind with positive food, leads to positive possibility, transmuting feelings of being trapped and repressed, into a harmonized happiness state of authenticity, surrender, freedom, and fluidity. This authenticity liberates the Artist into understanding the truth that he is completely free to be his authentic self so that he can fully express the truth of who he is and create his reality accordingly.

Applying the three steps to master his mind supports the Artist's sense of well-being and connection. He must recognize that his mental fitness is backed up by his choice to practice and nourish his mind with positive, optimistic thinking, eradicating his illusions and defaulting to negative inner dialogue. Applying the three steps to master his emotions provides the tools and practices that he needs to liberate from his old limited conditioning and his habitual patterns so that he can be connected to his essence, his natural state of fully expressing his authentic self, living in open-hearted connection to his natural state and his happiness.

Be vigilant when stressed and challenged, of being more reactive when feeling repressed and unable to be free to be yourself. Pay extra attention to your inner dialogue that may speak loudly or softly and seduce you into the idea that you are not allowed to be yourself. This inner conversation may have originated in a traumatic experience early in your history where you perceived yourself as being trapped, which somehow disallowed you to be yourself and perhaps lead you to feel emotionally overwhelmed and afraid, expanding into the illusion that you are unable to be who you are. At those times, you are being presented with an opportunity for transformation, and it is important to take advantage of that opportunity by being present and awake to your emotions and your consciousness so that you can exercise your power of choice and practice your tools.

Consistently choose to navigate your thinking and your emotions back to their actual harmonized happy state. You are invited to remove all wounds related to your sense of repression, feeling suffocated and trapped, enabling you to be fully expressive so that you can realize your full potential. This skill supports you in cultivating a strong sense of expression and authenticity, allowing you to release all protections and defenses around the throat and the neck area, transforming fear-based energy into love-based energy. The transmutation of fear into love happening in the fifth chakra makes this area vulnerable to over activity that can weaken your physical system to the point of illness. This area is the bridge to the higher chakras and the higher consciousness. Expressing your compassionate, authentic truth is one of the benefits of this path liberating you into a new relationship with truth. Balancing control issues and mastering the art of surrender are achieved. This path is physically related to the throat, thyroid, and mouth cancer. Working with the tools and practices for rebalancing the fifth chakra will support you in transforming these vulnerabilities into your strengths.

6

Gareth The Guru

The Guru walks the deep blue path of clarity

When balanced, the Guru is insightful, intuitive, visionary, clear, wise, and certain. You have the gift of intuition, sight, and knowingness. You have a sharp mind and are intelligent, able to strike a balance brilliantly between intellectual and intuitive knowledge. You can be ambitious and may desire prestige; you can demonstrate gentle strength and consistency. You can have great mental strength and clarity, vision, and sight. You are easily capable of great positivity and optimism and know how to work with your thoughts to support your desires and your manifestations. You are easily inspired and very capable of originality.

You desire intensity and to have a full experience of life. When balanced, you are easily able to see mental images both from your past and your future, which gifts you with a strong clairvoyant ability. You are capable of generating great ideas and accessing great intuitive knowledge, marrying these two aspects most positively.

When out of balance doubt, confusion and indecision are the traps you need to liberate from to claim your ability to see clearly and take ownership of your intuitive capacity. Stress can cause you to sit on fences and refuse to have any strong or clear opinion about anything along with an active inner dialogue that can convince you that you don't really know anything for sure. Second-guessing yourself and taking two sides on a topic can cause you and those around you much frustration and disconnect you from who you really are and the wisdom that you innately have. Being confused and residing in the purgatory of an inner dialogue of "I don't know" is your greatest challenge and your greatest opportunity. Stress causes you to have difficulty with finding clarity and making choices, which can easily lead to stagnation or slow moving changes in your life. Your opportunity arises from nourishing your thoughts with positive certain language and affirmations, which support you in being decisive and clear even if you have to fake it till you make it until you arrive at a place of certainty.

These thoughts and feelings can lead you into challenging behaviors like being crippled by doubt and confusion and a lack of certainty about everything. When out of balance you can easily stagnate and become paralyzed by your life choices. You have a great intuitive and telepathic capacity, but when out of balance, it is hard for you to see the truth or know what is right. When out of balance, you may be tempted to play mind games with others or yourself. When you live your truth and are clear, this expands your integrity and your happiness. If you live in denial about things or if you harbor secrets, creating a happy life will not be easy. Happiness thrives on open, clean air, and clear open communication. You dilute your happiness opportunities if you are always wondering if a secret has slipped out the back door. Keep your mind in the higher altitudes, try always to choose the high road, and resist the temptation to indulge in gossip and rumor spreading.

Don't dwell in fear, and if fears are controlling you, then do something about that. Everyone experiences fear. Don't let fears control your mind or your life. They can seep into your mind, and then your cells are saturated with fear, illusions, and misperceptions. Imagine for a minute that you have no fear of being fully yourself and all of who you are. How does that feel? Keep your mind focused on that feeling and you will create that reality. It serves you to illuminate your wounds fully and know with certainty what they are constructed of regarding thought and emotion. Identify your fears and inner dialogue in relationship to your own inner knowing and your intuitive capacity. Make meaningful choices when you need to make them. Have the courage to be certain about what you know and what you want and go for it.

Being vigilant, when stressed and challenged of being more doubtful and feeling confused and unclear. Pay extra attention to your inner dialogue that may speak loudly or softly and seduce you into the idea that you don't know anything. This inner conversation originated in a traumatic experience early in your history where you felt overwhelmed and confused, perhaps even stupid for not understanding. Perhaps being afraid inside this experience expanded into the illusion that you are unable to be who you are. At those times, you are being presented with an opportunity for awakening, and it is important to take advantage of that opportunity by being present and aware of your emotions and your consciousness so that you can exercise your power of choice and practice your tools.

You benefit from choosing consistently to navigate your thinking and your emotions back to their actual harmonized happy state. You are invited to remove all wounds related to your sense of confusion, doubt, and indecision, enabling you to be fully clear so that you can realize your full potential. This clearing supports you in cultivating a strong sense of certainty and knowingness. As you to release all protections and defenses around the third eye and forehead area, you transform fear-based energy into love-based energy. The transmutation of fear based consciousness into love-based consciousness here supports you arriving at the truth that you already know everything there is to know to have a happy experience of life.

Your gifts open up as you trust your intuitive information and balance that with your intellectual knowledge. In rebalancing all injuries and wounds associated with intuition and divine guidance, you arrive into your intuitive birthright, liberating you from overactive thinking and negative mental patterns. This balance will support you in re-establishing right relationship and balance with clear and direct insight and intelligence. Your happiness is established through your cultivation of mental fitness, positive thinking, and optimism. This path is physically related to stroke, brain tumors blindness, deafness, and neurological disturbance. Using the tools and practices suggested for sixth chakra rebalancing transforms these vulnerabilities into strengths. You have an opportunity to reclaim lost inspiration caused by the experience of confusion and doubt by expanding into certainty and faith. The choice to be certain and the extension of loving kindness towards yourself and the resulting reclamation of lost energy support this expansion.

Z

Marlin The Master

The Master walks the violet path of enlightenment

When balanced and in your strength, you are a highly spiritual person and find it easy to stay connected to the truth of who you are as a spiritual being. You have a strong faith and understand how it feels to trust yourself, those that you love and the universe. At times of clarity and health, you can feel your connection to all things. Your greatest gift is faith, and through the practice of choosing trust, you expand into your highest self. When you are expansive and connected to the highest expression of who you are, you can choose trust even in the face of others demonstrating their lower self and acting out in untrustworthy ways. Your ability to see the highest possibility in others holds the space for them to rise to be the best that they can be. When happy and balanced, you are connected to faith, joy, trust, and seem to be connected to everything around you.

The Master learned to fortify his emotional vulnerability of not trusting and isolation by strengthening his crown chakra. Pushing more chi though his system allows him to digest his feelings of isolation and distrust by meeting them with awareness breath and compassion. Using positive memory or imagination connecting to times when feelings of trust, a sense of deep connection, and an awareness of his light and divinity are strong. Working with positive affirmations nourishes the inner-dialogue of the lower mind with positive food, leading to positive possibility and the transmuting of his isolation and distrust into his harmonized happiness state of trust and connection. This liberates him into understanding the truth that he is completely free to fully awaken his light and be connected with his own divine nature and the divinity of others and the universe. He realizes that he is free to be trusting and connected even when those around are not free or able to trust.

He recognizes that his mental fitness is supported by his choice to practice and nourish his mind with positive, optimistic thinking, eradicating his illusions and default negative inner-dialogue. This along, with applying the three steps to master his emotions, provide the tools and practices that he needs to liberate from his old limited conditioning and his habitual pattern. Now he can be connected to his essence, his natural state of being fully connected, and engaged with everything around him, living in open-hearted connection to his happiness. This practice also liberates any trapped inspirational energy so that he can connect to his motivation to create an experience and reality in his life that is rooted in faith and expanded by choosing to trust himself, the ones that he loves and the universe.

The negative thoughts and feelings can lead you into challenging behaviors like being cynical, skeptical, suspicious or a naysayer. Happiness requires that you have an inner theology or spirituality that can withstand the storms of life. It does not matter what tradition it comes from, what is important is that your inner spiritual truth, in fact, is a genuine spiritual truth that actually nurtures you. You benefit from consistently attending to your spiritual life, not just visit it when things go wrong.

The Divine light in you can be ignited by using the tools provided here and by the audio and video practices. The Sacred is in every breath of life, yours included, and it's simply a question of finding it and practicing it. Otherwise, when out of balance, you are vulnerable to feeling disconnected, isolated, alone even feeling outcast. I call the crown chakra "the key to happiness," because when it opens, one's experiences of expansion and joy is fully activated. When the crown chakra is open, the feeling that life is good naturally occurs, and depression and other painful emotions are reduced. There exists a sense of trust that experiences have value and purpose – even painful ones and that one's life is a part of a larger evolutionary plan. Inspiration, trust, devotion, and spontaneity all open the crown chakra creating a feeling of spiritual connection.

Be vigilant when stressed and challenged of being more reactive and feeling distrustful and suspicious and disconnected from both yourself and others. Pay extra attention to the inner dialogue that may speak loudly or softly and seduce you into the idea that you are untrustworthy or that it is not safe for you to trust others, compromising your faith and pushing you into doubt and skepticism. This inner conversation originated in a traumatic experience early in your history where you perceived yourself as being disconnected and perhaps lead to feeling emotionally overwhelmed and afraid inside this experience, expanding into the illusion that you actually are isolated and not connected, not where you belong. At those times you are being presented with an opportunity for transformation, and it is important to take advantage of that opportunity by being present and awake to your emotions and your consciousness so that you can exercise your power of choice and practice your tools. Consistently choose to navigate your thinking and your emotions back to their actual harmonized happy state. You are invited to clear all wounds related to your sense of isolation, disconnection and not belonging, enabling you to be fully open-hearted and surrendered into trusting and connecting so that you can realize your full potential.

This rebalancing supports you in cultivating a strong sense of belonging, connection, and trust, allowing you to release all protections and defenses around the ideas of not trusting, being suspicious and skeptical, which is what isolates and separates us. Rebalancing the wounds of the seventh chakra supports your deeply surrendered trust in relationships both with yourself and with others. You can reclaim your lost motivation to create and your inspiration returns as you rebalance all injuries and wounds associated with your relationship with spirituality and your relationship with the highest power of the universe. Here you are invited to clear and rebalance all wounds and misperceptions related to how you perceive God, spirituality, and trust, infusing you with faith and courage and inspiration. This path is physically related to depression, exhaustion, energy, and skin disorders. Working with the tools and practices for rebalancing the seventh chakra will support you in transforming these vulnerabilities into your strengths.

Summary of the seven sacred paths of happiness

Mostly 1.) You are walking the first chakra red path

CHAKRA ONE MULADHARA, THE PATH OF ALIGNING WITH SAFETY

This transformative journey clears all wounds related to your sense of safety, security, stability, and belonging; liberating you from the wounds of the past; supporting you in feeling grounded, safe, and connected. It rebalances and aligns this area. It is physically related to symptoms of low back pain, immune disorders, sciatic problems, and depression. Establishing your foundation of strength, stability, and support reclaims your inspiration. The first chakra is the foundation of your happiness scale, as your well-being is secured by your connection to the earth and your innate stability and strength.

USING THE TOOLS AND PRACTICES FOR THE FIRST CHAKRA SUPPORTS YOU IN TRANSFORMING FROM INSECURITY INTO SECURITY, STABILITY, AND STRENGTH

Mostly 2.) You are walking the second chakra orange path

CHAKRA 2 Svadhisthana, EXPAND INTO THE GIFT OF CREATING UNION

These tools clear wounds surrounding abandonment fears, betrayals, addictions, and experiences of scarcity; rebalancing sexual and creative energy, supporting you in connecting with abundance and creative expression. This practice rebalances all desires and appetites and addictive patterns and is physically related to arthritis, potency and desire problems, fibroids, and menopause issues. You can reclaim the spark of your inspiration that could have been lost inside the experience abandonment as you rebalance this chakra. Your creativity can be restored as you recover your energy here and you can reconnect to your pleasure center. The experience of deep connection with the self and others opens you up to pleasure on the happiness scale.

USING THE TOOLS AND PRACTICES FOR THE SECOND CHAKRA SUPPORTS YOU IN TRANSFORMING FROM DISCONNECTION TO THE EXPERIENCE OF CONNECTION

Mostly 3.) You are walking the third chakra yellow path

CHAKRA 3 Manipura EXPAND INTO THE GIFTS OF CONFIDENCE AND SELF LOVE

These transformative tools clear all wounds related to your sense of self-esteem and personal power, enabling you to be fully empowered so that you can realize your full potential. This practice supports you in cultivating a strong sense of confidence. It is physically related to stomach disorders, ulcers, liver dysfunction, bulimia, and hepatitis. You can reclaim your inspiration by connecting to your personal power, and your self-love, which fuels the establishment of your confidence and opens you up to the experience of arriving at self-satisfaction on the happiness scale.

USING THE TOOLS AND PRACTICES FOR THE THIRD CHAKRA SUPPORTS YOU IN TRANSFORMING FROM POWERLESSNESS AND LACK OF WORTHINESS INTO SELF-LOVE

Mostly 4.) You are walking the fourth chakra green path

CHAKRA 4 ANAHATA, EXPAND INTO THE GIFT OF UNCONDITIONAL LOVE

This transformative journey clears all wounds related to your heart. As you let go of grief, anger, and hatred, you release all protections and defenses around the heart that can cause isolation and separation. This letting go supports your open-hearted compassion in relationship with yourself and others and is physically related to all heart issues, asthma, allergies, and lung and breast cancer. As you heal the experiences in your history that caused heartbreak, you expand into the reclamation of your inspiration to love again. Loving with an undefended heart enhances your well-being and puts you inside the experience of love as you vibrate in this healing frequency of love.

USING THE TOOLS AND PRACTICES FOR THE FOURTH CHAKRA SUPPORTS YOU IN TRANSFORMING FROM FEELING UNLOVEABLE TO THE EXPERIENCE OF UNCONDITIONAL LOVE FOR SELF AND OTHERS

Mostly 5.) You are walking the fifth chakra light blue path

CHAKRA 5 Visshudha, EXPAND INTO THE GIFTS OF EXPRESSION AND TRUTH

These tools help you in surrendering your will and releasing control, which allows you to cultivate the skill of letting go and letting God. This practice liberates you into expressing your truth. Expressing your authentic, compassionate truth is one of the benefits of these tools, which liberate you into a new relationship with truth. Balancing control issues and mastering the art of surrender are achieved. This chakra is physically related to throat, thyroid, mouth cancer, and jaw problems.

USING THE TOOLS AND PRACTICES FOR THE FIFTH CHAKRA SUPPORTS YOU IN TRANSFORMING FROM REPRESSION TO SELF EXPRESSION

Mostly 6.) You are walking the sixth chakra deep blue path

CHAKRA 6 Ajna

EXPAND INTO THE GIFTS OF INTUITION AND CLARITY

These tools help you in rebalancing all injuries and wounds associated with intuition and divine guidance, liberating you from overactive thinking and negative mental patterns; supporting you in re-establishing right relationship and balance with clear and direct insight and intelligence. It is physically related to stroke, brain tumors, blindness, deafness, and neurological disturbances.

USING THE TOOLS AND PRACTICES FOR THE SIXTH CHAKRA SUPPORTS YOU IN TRANSFORMING FROM CONFUSION TO CLARITY.

Mostly 7.) You are walking the seventh chakra violet path

CHAKRA 7 Sahasrara, EXPAND INTO THE GIFTS OF TRUST AND ONENESS

These tools help you in rebalancing all injuries and wounds associated with your relationship with spirituality and the highest power of the universe. Here you are invited to clear and rebalance all wounds and misperceptions related to how you perceive God, spirituality, and trust, infusing you with faith and courage and inspiration. It is physically related to depression, exhaustion, energy, and skin disorders.

USING THE TOOLS AND PRACTICES FOR THE SEVENTH CHAKRA SUPPORTS YOU IN TRANSFORMING FROM ISOLATION TO INCLUSION.

MY PRIVATE SESSIONS

People often ask me to explain how I work, and you would think that would be a relatively easy question to answer, but it isn't. This difficulty may be because my work is continuously evolving, or perhaps because the way that I work is slightly different with everyone. When I examine what is consistent and what remains the same for everyone, I see that I am able to meet you wherever you are and at the same time, see and hold the space for where it is that you can go. I can see you in your highest possibility, in your true spiritual nature and relate to that part of you until you can see and relate to that part of yourself. I support you in identifying and removing the obstacles that stand between you and your highest happiness potential, the highest expression of yourself.

I have discovered that we all have an urge to be that potential and some of us know consciously that we want it and have a strong drive to connect to it, and others are less aware and have greater difficulty and may have more obstacles in striving to achieve it. Independently of where you are, I can see it and support you in finding it for yourself. So I am different with everyone, and the words that I choose and the tools that I use are up to you.

Sometimes we move really quickly through the program and other times we move more slowly. Your higher self determines the timing. I created the book, the toolkits, training programs, and the e-courses online to be able to reach more people and support those who, for whatever reason, are unable to work with me directly while maintaining the integrity of the elements that have proven to be effective. I can also enhance the support I can offer to those who do work with me directly with these toolkits to work with, which provides step-by-step guidance through the process.

The guiding principles are the agreements you have with reality and the core values that are capable of keeping you on track. These values are capable of keeping your compass pointing true north so that when you become stressed and challenged you can reconnect with your inner standards, your core values, and keep everything in perspective so that you can continue to have positive forward movement on your path and in your life. You are invited to evaluate for yourself what your core values are. Sometimes we know what these values are without any need for further consideration and sometimes there is less certainty, sometimes we have always had the same core values and agreements, and sometimes they change. If this is something you haven't put a lot of thought into then now is a good time to consider this question for yourself. These core values also mirror the agreements you have either consciously or unconsciously made with reality. I have outlined here my core values and agreements to illustrate what I mean by this invitation. You can agree with and adopt these values if they resonate with you or if you are clear about your own values, then use them. By feeding your mind with the affirmations that reflect your inner values and agreements you are allowing them to be strengthened and reinforced by your time, energy and focus.

For us to fully understand how we can make friends with our stress and navigate skillfully through our difficulties (so that they can be utilized as opportunities) we benefit from understanding the true nature of our emotions and our moods. The most important thing to know is that they are passing and temporary and not fixed and permanent. This understanding enables us to be present with the discomfort of the negative emotions long enough to use them as portals to reconnect with our deeper nature and our inner values. These values are already well established deeper in our psyche. (You will be taught how to do this in the emotional healing chapter.) We can then lean into those inner values and use them as your guiding principles at times of difficulty and work with them as sources of strength and opportunity. When we practice this successfully, we will armor ourselves with the capacity to endure our challenges so skillfully so that they can open us up to newer, softer, higher vibrations within us that support the full illumination of our essence and connect us to the truth of who we are. This practice can permanently raise our happiness set point and provide greater stability in our lives.

We benefit greatly from fully illuminating into consciousness what is residing just beneath the surface, and by exposing the patterns of thought and emotions that are obstructing us we can remove those obstacles. In the 20 years of working with clients, I have discovered that to navigate successfully through transitions, it is beneficial to be anchored in some guiding principles that support you in coming back to clarity when things become challenged so that you can sustain positive forward movement. This book is intended to duplicate as closely as possible the journey I guide my clients through, in our one-on-one sessions, from their unhappy lower self to their happy higher self. We start with rewriting their inner story through the lens of the perspective of purposefulness, recognizing and valuing the challenges and difficulties that we find in our lives as experiences that actually contain gifts, lessons, and opportunities. We identify the perceptions that were created as a consequence of trauma and evaluate if they are indeed true and if they really serve us, and question if they are helpful to us in creating the reality we want. If these perceptions are not helpful, then we rewrite them so that they are.

Then together we move on to evaluate our agreements with reality, focusing on what are the roles we agree to play in our relationships, in our work, in our family, and in our lives. You are encouraged to do the same and ask yourself are you satisfied with who you are being and if not what is it that there needs to more of from you and what is it that there needs to be less of from you for you to feel satisfied with who you are being.

Choosing to establish and practice new healthy habits strengthens us with the mental, emotional, physical and spiritual nourishment that we all need to connect us to the essence of who we are. When these places are starved we do not know ourselves; we suffer from amnesia as we forget who we really are, we lose sight of our light and strength and gifts. I believe that our guiding principles are the benefits of insight and wisdom that we have earned through the trials that we have successfully navigated in our history. Reaching into and connecting with these principles enables you to benefit from the wisdom that may have been hard won, that you have earned in your history. Imagine how your life would be if your stress were consistently skillfully navigated so that the time of discomfort was compressed and you were free to gain this art of skillfully navigating your stress, so that you actually benefitted from the difficulties you would prefer not to have.

GUIDING PRINCIPLES
THE PATHWAY TO HAPPINESS

This being human is a guesthouse.
Every morning a new arrival.
A joy, a depression, a meanness,
some momentary awareness comes
as an unexpected visitor.
Welcome and entertain them all!
Even if they're a crowd of sorrows,
who violently sweep your house
empty of its furniture,
still, treat each guest honorably.
He may be clearing you out
for some new delight.
The dark thought, the shame, the malice,
meet them at the door laughing,
and invite them in.
Be grateful for whoever comes,
because each has been sent
as a guide from beyond.
~ Rumi ~

*All the guiding principles that follow support us in anchoring in
a perspective of purposefulness that strengthens and nourishes us
to connect to our highest self.
These are my top ten guiding principles that you can
use until you get connected to your own*

1.) *YOU ARE ALREADY PERFECT, WHOLE, AND COMPLETE.*

Our job in the Lifeguides Transformation Program is to remove any illusion, misperception, or fear that stands in the way of the truth of your divine nature. This is not true for some of us it is true for everyone. It is true for you. Just as Michelangelo chips away the excess marble to reveal the already perfect David underneath, we chip away at illusions and fears that were created by misperceptions (ideas that were created by the mind to explain why a trauma happened, why someone hurt you or offended you, ideas that may have nothing to do with reality) and ideas that are no longer serving you and came as a consequence of trauma. Everyone already has, within them, everything they need to change into the person they want to be.

There is already a pathway to walk to awaken to your highest self with tools designed to support you on that path. One day in class, while I was doing my yoga teacher training in the Bahamas, the teacher was instructing us to breathe in and feel the joy expand in your body, and on each exhale, to visualize letting go of all negativity on the flow of the outward breath. And I could actually feel my body responding to his suggestion. Something in the way he was communicating the information, something in his vibe was getting through to me. I actually felt joyful at that moment, without a care in the world.

I allowed my body to follow his instructions to feel as light as a feather as I rose up into my shoulder stand, and magically it was. I was able to glide up into the pose with minimal effort and great comfort. It's incredible, I thought truly magical, why? What magical combinations of ingredients were present to make that moment so perfect for me by allowing me to connect to my essence. Did everyone have the same experience as me, or had I arrived at some magical new level that would be forever present from this moment forward? This was a moment where I truly knew, honestly felt, the wholeness of whom I am. There was no doubt of the connection to the divine, the all, that actually ran through my body so that I knew that I was already perfect, whole and complete (and lifted me up into the most beautiful asana I've ever done.)

This was my first glimpse of the divine practicing yoga through me. This was when I decided I wanted to create the opportunity for others to have that same magical experience and committed to creating that container for others, both inside and outside of yoga class. Have you ever felt like that? Have you had a moment when you just knew that you were more than this physical body? Where you could actually feel your spirit, your divinity? If you have, I encourage you to recollect that moment in time so that you can relive that feeling and choose to reside in it whenever you remember to, as this will create the correct vibration for you to be connected to the magic that is your highest potential. My mind had expanded enough to remember my divinity and my perception had shifted.

"The moment you change your perception is the moment you rewrite your chemistry of your body." Bruce Lipton

How many times have we looked at other people in our lives and thought, 'If only you would take all your best qualities and do more of them, be more of that, and take all your negative qualities and be less of that or better yet, just stop acting out in those negative ugly and unattractive way…. How much better your life and everyone else's around you would be?' How many divorces would be prevented and how many disputes would be averted if we came from the best part of ourselves all the time. Have you ever wondered what the world would be like if all the husbands in the world followed their wives' requests for improvement and all the wives fulfilled their husbands' requests? Not to create a Stepford husband/wife universe but to arrive at our highest potential and come from a place of complete and utter trust. How much peace would that bring? How much love would be possible?

I think we all can agree that the world would be a better place if we all consistently came from a loving, light, and kind place and that we would actually feel good about ourselves if we were able to stay calm and relaxed and be free of fear and stress. So why isn't it happening?

Perhaps it's not supposed to... Perhaps we are not meant to reject our shadows... Perhaps the truth is that we all have a unique combination of positive and negative qualities and that is what makes us who we are. That is what makes us human and perhaps what was happening in that yoga practice is that I was fully embodied, fully present, fully accepting myself, and that is when we find peace and lightness (and the most perfect asanas). There is no judgment, just complete presence and acceptance of who we are in our wholeness our darkness and our light and finally, we can rest in the truth of our own perfection.

> *"Life can be touched only in the present moment, the past*
> *is gone, the future is not yet here, and if we do not go back*
> *to ourselves in the present moment then we cannot be in*
> *touch with life" Thich Nhat Hanh*

The practice of presence is learning how to reside fully with and abide with ourselves no matter what is there with us. No matter what difficulty, what discomfort, what fear, what negative emotion or thought or trait or habit. Just a choice to be here now, to feel fully who we are, and rest in the peace of the truth of whatever that is. This way we can get to know and become fully acquainted with what prevents us from being our best loving and kind selves? From here, we can be the creators of ourselves. The point is we have a choice about who we want to be. We are our own best creation, and if we decide we want to be free of our habitual patterns of negative feelings and thoughts, we can learn here how to do that. The happiest people have a natural tendency towards optimism and a sense that everything will work out well, but the rest of us can cultivate this quality using the three steps to master the mind and master the emotions. One of the foundational pillars of happiness is to know the truth of the perfection of your highest self and implementing the choice to feed the development of this self until it is alive within us.

> *"Live quietly in the moment and see the beauty of all before*
> *you.... the future will take care of itself." Yogananda*

The problem is that obstacles disconnect us from ourselves: obstacles of thought and emotion that feel too uncomfortable to bear, so we tend to distract ourselves from our own selves, and ironically from our intrinsic healing mechanisms, which want us to feel everything and simply be present with it. Instead, we use things to help us not feel.

What has become apparent to me about addictions is that they are actually an issue stemming from our sense of separation and disconnection from source and our own essence. When you think about it, our first experience of connection happens with our mother when breastfeeding or bottle-feeding, and milk is sweet, so we have an unconscious association with sweetness and connection. So it stands to reason that when we are feeling disconnected, we are naturally drawn to sweetness in the form of sugar. Obviously, the sweetness we are actually seeking is the sweetness of connection, but that has been replaced with the instant gratification of sugar.

We will be drawn to alcohol that has sugar and chocolate, cake, and sweets because the need that has become confused in the mind is the need for connection, not sweetness. If you ask people why they take drugs, most will respond that it takes away the pain and it makes them feel good. We are seeking that good feeling of love and connection. This is how most addictions start: trying to satisfy a spiritual or emotional longing with a material substance or object.

Developing the habit of gravitating towards the incorrect solution then exacerbates this problem. This is a self-forgetting of the truth of our inevitable connection to all things, a falling into the illusion that we are alone and disconnected; finding ourselves and judging ourselves to be wrong or inadequate somehow.

In the early 1990s, the Dali Lama was presenting a talk on Maître, the art of extending loving kindness to all sentient beings. The definition of which is to feel an authentic sense of caring about the well being of others and having the ability to show it. During the talk, someone asked him a question about whether or not it is wise to extend that energy and that emotion towards the self first. He seemed a little perplexed by the question, so the asker went on to explain further that in the West, a lot of people suffer from low self-esteem and experience self-loathing. He had difficulty understanding this concept because he had never heard of it before. So he asked his audience, made up of about 50% Westerners if they understood what this was, and they all said, yes, of course, they knew what it was. He then asked a group of Tibetan monks, who meditated regularly, if they knew what it was, and their answer was no. This is very revealing. Does it mean if we live in the East, we do not hate ourselves so much or does it mean if we train the mind to drop beneath or rise above the discursive thoughts, we can maintain a deep and authentic connection to the truth of our innate nature. That we are already perfect whole and complete, and we are always connected to the divine.

EXERCISE

Take a deep breath and hold it as long as you comfortably can, now slowly blow out the breath through a closed mouth as though you are blowing out a candle. Take a moment to remember a time and if you cannot remember a time imagine a time when you felt deeply connected to your essence, your divinity and your innate perfection. Start to feel how it feels in your body, in your heart, and in your mind when you occupying this memory and this vision. You know with certainty that you are already perfect and whole and complete. Allow all of your cells to be bathed and soaked in this feeling so that your body can become so familiar with how this feels you can recall it at will. Allow this feeling to be well established in your memory and ingrained in your mind and your emotions that whenever you feel challenged or stressed in your life, you can recall this experience and embody this vibration and then easily attract more of this experience in your life.

PRACTICE

As you go through your day today see if you can find the opportunities where you can apply this principle and start practicing.

AFFIRMATION

You are now easily, and effortlessly able to embrace the truth of your own perfection.

You embrace the gift of being fully yourself, knowing that this who the universe needs and knowing that who you are is perfect. There is no one else who can be more fully you than you. You are wanted and embraced as you are.

2.) RESPONSIBILITY EQUALS FREEDOM

You are wholly responsible for yourself, the life you've created, and the quality and the content of your experiences. We will support you in becoming fully responsible (having the ability to respond), empowered, and free.

Responsibility equals freedom. Many of us function under the illusion that the opposite is true, that the more we avoid taking on responsibility, the freer we are. When you examine this concept, it falls apart. Most of us have got to the point that we know that when we decide to be fully responsible for our finances, for example, we actually gain strength and power in that area of our lives and the more we show up and attend to making it work, the more it does. That same principle applies to everything. Whatever we attend to and choose to focus on, to the point that we see ourselves as responsible to make it work, the more it does and the freer we are in that area.

> *"There are two primary choices in life: To accept conditions*
> *as they exist or accept the responsibility for changing them."*
> Denis Waitley

Responsibility is actually the ability to respond, having the capacity to stay present with all the seductions and temptations to leave. To grow and progress along the path, it is essential to expand into your greatest capacity for responsibility to confront and remove all the obstacles that exist that prevent you from being able to face this expansion. Freedom is not about running around in denial and irresponsibility; in fact, that is one of the biggest traps there is, to be caught up in this illusion. What looks like carefree freedom diminishes into a lack of choices and careless self-abandonment if we follow that to its logical conclusion, the only way out is through. There is no growth in avoidance. By gathering strength and fortifying ourselves and our ability to confront, we become able to endure difficulty with full presence, which enables us to navigate through life's challenges without flinching, escaping, or collapsing. We just have to look at our lives to find examples of friends and family members who feel overwhelmed, unable to handle one problem or another in their lives.

Imagine what life would be like if there was an emotional gym we could go to flex the muscle that allows us to experience acts of betrayal, disappointment, and grief fully and skillfully. A place where we could see our emotional muscles getting bigger so that we felt like we could take life on its own terms and be victorious. Expanding in responsibility is the route to gather the strength needed to benefit from what is offered here in this program entirely, and you will arrive there. At that place of knowing that you really are strong, that you really can endure, that you really do have strength and you really can take responsibility for all things that show up in your life, responsibility then becomes a choice that you can willingly embrace.

> *"Taking responsibility for being exactly where you are*
> *gives you the power to be exactly where you want to be."*
> *Unknown*

Learn how to cultivate the healthy habits of integrating and digesting negative emotional states and transmuting them into healthy positive ones, so that we overcome the urges to react and then we are free to act. Here, we are meeting and transforming negative, fearful thinking and transforming it, in the moment, into positive thinking and high frequencies. This way, you expand your responsibility for your thoughts and emotions to know how to respond to life's problems in the most effective way, so then you become responsible for creating your best life.

"I've decided to be happy because it is good for my health"
Voltaire

EXERCISE

Take a deep breath and hold it as long as you comfortably can, now slowly blow out the breath through a closed mouth as though you are blowing out a candle. Take a moment to remember a time and if you cannot remember a time imagine a time when you felt completely in charge of your life and able to easily and skillfully navigate the challenges that life presented to you. When you were aware of choosing your thoughts so that you could create what you want. When you were in charge of your thinking and using your mind as a creative tool. When you knew with certainty that you were responsible for the life, you were creating, and this felt good to you. Start to feel how it feels in your body, in your heart, and in your mind when you are occupying this memory and this vision. You know with certainty that you are capable and responsible for your life as it is and this feels positive and strengthening for you. Allow all of your cells to be bathed and soaked in this feeling so that your body can become so familiar with how this feels you can recall it at will. Allow this feeling to be well established in your memory and ingrained in your mind and your emotions that whenever you feel challenged or stressed in your life, you can recall this experience and embody this vibration and then easily attract more of this experience in your life.

PRACTICE

As you go through your day today see if you can find the opportunities where you can apply this principle and start practicing.

AFFIRMATION

You expand into embracing responsibility for creating everything in your life. You have now acquired the ability to respond to life on your terms, and you embrace greater and greater freedom each step of the way.

3.) EVERYTHING IS PERFECT

Everything and everyone in your life are there for a reason: to support you in your growth and evolution on your path to empowerment, purity, and truth. Everything that has happened was supposed to have happened to provide you with the opportunity to make choices. Every challenge was co created with you so that you could reach within you and bring forth your virtues. All of your circumstances are your teachers; bless them, learn from them, and move forward. Your circumstances do not define you they simply reveal you.

It always helps to hold the broader perspective and choose to have faith in this truth. Holding that perspective of purposefulness, allows you to work with life as a mirror, externally reflecting everything that is happening for you internally, and empowers you to act with awareness and choice. When you liberate from the idea that life is making you struggle, that you are having a harder time than anyone else, and you examine your life circumstances from the perspective that everything is valuable, useful, and necessary, your life will become more dynamic, more creative, intentional, and fun. Life truly can become like a prayer, a meditation of creation, once you hold that possibility. Then you will see the lessons, the synchronicities, and the brilliance of the true nature of reality.

This gives you the freedom to appreciate and love truly all the people in your family, your tribe, your circle, and you could even expand into the Buddhist perspective that the ones who irritate you the most, in fact, are your greatest teachers, your holy gurus. You can then stop trying to escape and turn and face, with strength, the source of pain and trouble, and respond with conscious choice rather than knee jerk reactivity. When faced with difficulty, we have three options, accept it, change it, or leave it.

You have the influence to change your own perspective, your own mindset. Seeing the opportunity for your growth inside your challenges gives you latitude inside a shift in attitude. Attitude and perspective are areas that we can truly practice alchemy and wield our magical wands of transformation. I encourage you to expand your capacity on this level using the tools provided here and any other tools you may have in your own personal toolkits, as this is what being alive is about. I know that it is easy to forget these simple truths. I recommend doing whatever you can to stay connected to the ideas and information that keeps you connected to the truth of your own capacity, your own magic, and your essence.

EXERCISE.

Take a deep breath and hold it as long as you comfortably can, now slowly blow out the breath through a closed mouth as though you are blowing out a candle. Take a moment to remember a time and if you cannot remember a time imagine a time when you felt completely in charge of your life and able to easily and skillfully navigate the challenges that life presented to you. Start to feel how it feels in your body, in your heart, and in your mind when you are occupying this memory and this vision. You know with certainty that you are capable and responsible for your life as it is and this feels positive and strengthening for you. Allow all of your cells to be bathed and soaked in this feeling so that your body can become so familiar with how this feels you can recall it at will. You are now embracing more and more freedom in your life. Allow this feeling to be well established in your memory and ingrained in your mind and your emotions that whenever you feel challenged or stressed in your life, you can recall this experience and embody this vibration and then easily attract more of this experience in your life.

PRACTICE

As you go through your day today see if you can find the opportunities where you can apply this principle and start practicing.

AFFIRMATION

You surrender to accepting that all people, experiences, and events that are present in your life right now are present for the purpose of your growth. You expand into the perspective of purposefulness and easily embrace everything as it is. Even the challenges and difficulties serve a very high purpose for you to create the life of your choice.

4.) YOU CREATE YOUR REALITY BASED ON WHAT YOU BELIEVE

Manifestation is actually a co-creative process, a negotiation between you and the universe. It is your responsibility to do your end of this creative process as consciously and effectively as you can. By having clarity, a made up mind, a knowingness, and a certainty of what you want, you will cleanly manifest what you want. You create from where your energy is most highly charged, so if your energy is charged by your shadow, your fear, your wounds, your past traumas, you will create from there and most likely end up with something that you don't want. This is why you benefit from committing to your inner work. I created the transformational program so that you can be sure you will create and live the life that you want. We will support you creating what you consciously choose, not what you are afraid of.

> *"It starts with a dream. Add faith, and it becomes a belief.*
> *Add action, and it becomes a part of life. Add perseverance,*
> *and it becomes a goal in sight. Add patience and time, and*
> *it ends with a dream come true." Doe Zantamata*

Working with your inner energetic system is the path to your emotional well-being, increased happiness and reclaimed inspiration. Clearing the chakras of their illusions and low emotional vibrations is a necessary step to empowering yourself to create your life by design. Each chakra contains a masculine and feminine aspect, an obstacle and an opportunity. When you know how to navigate through the chakras consciously and powerfully, working with the anatomy of inspiration (using the positive affirmations for each of the chakras) effectively using visualizations, and intention, married with the correct emotional frequency for each chakra, then it is possible to enjoy this journey of creation. This is all explained in the manifesting chapter and in greater detail in the manifesting toolkit. When you learn how to apply that information effectively, you will be living the life that you want, the life that you consciously created. Understanding and improving your relationship with your own energetic system connecting you with your chakras empowers you to live your life by design.

As you journey through this program, be vigilant about identifying your areas of strength and your areas of vulnerability. Take some time to look at the explanation for each chakra so that you can see if the information resonates with you and if it does, it is likely that this is the chakra for you to focus on. I suggest you dedicate a month to rebalance and align this chakra, purifying it and clearing it of all negative thoughts and emotions, then reconnect with yourself and proceed from there. You do not have to worry about going in any particular order, just allow your energy and your intuition to guide you. Any choice that you make to overcome those loud and subtle voices of fear, negativity, and pain and transmute those lower frequencies into happier higher ones, is an empowering and transformative choice for you to make.

> *"Everything is energy, and that's all there is to it. Match the frequency of what you want and you cannot but get that reality. It can be no other way. This is not philosophy; this is physics."* Albert Einstein

Recognize the fearful thoughts that seduce you into contracted states of consciousness and know how to transform them. Recognize the emotional frequency that you are habitually residing in and if it does not match the frequency that you want to manifest, then transmute it by meeting it with your awareness, your breath, and your compassion to transmute it into its opposite positive frequency that matches what you want to create. Each lower emotion has its predictable opposite positive frequency so that it has the possibility of transmuting when met with awareness breath and compassion.

For example, if you want to bring more love into your life and you are feeling anything but loving, because you have been betrayed and you feel angry about it, find out where that anger lives in the body. Raise your awareness to the point where you can inhabit that space with your presence, with your acceptance of what is, and then bring your breath into that space. Saturate that space with awareness and breath until that contraction starts to dissipate and then bring in a feeling of love, kindness, and compassion by visualizing someone that you love simply and effectively. Feel that feeling arise from the heart center and feel it move in circles, like ripples on a pond, allowing it to bathe all your cells inside that frequency until you are entirely saturated in that vibration. Then visualize yourself having or being the thing that you want to create, igniting the power of your imagination here to support you in creating something that you may not yet have experienced. If all this feels too complicated, like some mathematical formula, you may do better working with the actual practice so that you can be guided through this process in the audio or video options that you have available to you. I encourage you to check these options out on my website.

"Any thought of love uplifts the vibration of the universe."
Marianne Williamson

Matching your thoughts with the vibration of what you want is essential for this mechanism to work. By being hyper vigilant of the thoughts you are infusing with your attention, time, and energy will ensure your correct manifestation. If you want to experience an unconditionally loving relationship and you are holding thoughts of resentment or revenge, you are not going to magnetize an experience of unconditional love, no matter how much you want to. Your energy needs to be reflected, and those thoughts of revenge will play out in your reality in a way that you will probably not like. Choosing thoughts is a practice of noticing and deciding do you want to see them show up in your reality and then deciding if you want to feed them with your time, attention, and energy; if not, change them as they arise to match with your desired manifestation.

> *"The universe is not punishing you or blessing you, the universe is responding to the vibrational attitude you are emitting." Unknown*

> *"The most powerful thing that you can do to change the world is to change your own beliefs and the nature of life, people and reality into something more positive and begin to act accordingly." Shakti Gawain*

EXERCISE

Take a deep breath and hold it as long as you comfortably can, now slowly blow out the breath through a closed mouth as though you are blowing out a candle. Take a moment to remember a time and if you cannot remember a time imagine a time when you felt completely in charge of your life and able to easily and skillfully navigate the challenges that life presented to you. When you were aware of choosing your thoughts so that you could create what you want. When you were in charge of your thinking and using your mind as a creative tool. Start to feel how it feels in your body, in your heart, and in your mind when you are occupying this memory and this vision. You know with certainty that you are capable and responsible for your life as it is and this feels positive and strengthening for you. You know you can use your mind to create your reality. Allow all of your cells now to be bathed and soaked in this feeling so that your body can become so familiar with how this feels you can recall it at will. Allow this feeling to be well established in your memory and ingrained in your mind and your emotions, that whenever you feel challenged or stressed in your life, you can recall this experience and embody this vibration and then easily attract more of this experience in your life.

PRACTICE

As you go through your day today see if you can find the opportunities where you can apply this principle and start practicing.

AFFIRMATION

You are now committed to aligning your thoughts and your emotions with what you choose to magnetize effortlessly to you.

5.) *LOVE IS THE ANSWER*

Whatever the question, whatever the circumstances, whatever the challenge, choose to do the loving, compassionate, kind thing, over the controlling, punishing, perceived right thing (I'll teach you a lesson on this). The ego will continually seduce you to maintain the status quo and to protect yourself, which may not result in a loving action. Choosing love over power, expansion over protection, and new choices over repetition is an excellent practice to expand into. Love is always, always, the answer, no buts. The mind cannot conjure up a winning strategy that is more potent than a clear open-hearted love. When the mind is free and clear of negative thoughts then love becomes possible. When involved in a romantic relationship challenge, you can rely on love being a good choice.

> *"Unhappiness doesn't and can't exist on its own. Unhappiness is the feeling that accompanies negative thinking about your life. In the absence of that thinking, the unhappiness or the stress or the jealousy can't exist. There is nothing to hold your negative feelings in place other than your own thinking." Richard Carlson*

We may tend to blame the pain that we experience and the lovelessness that we endure as someone else's fault, but if we are experiencing lovelessness, it is because we are harboring judgment and are disconnected from the love in our own hearts. What we have not given to any situation will be lacking in that situation especially when it comes to the question of love. That which we are withholding can cause us pain. The good news about this, of course, is that we do have an influence over this. We can affect change by opening our hearts and allowing love energy to flow easily and effortlessly throughout our bodies and into our own lives. You will find the tools necessary to practice this within this program. One of my clients went through a break up that required her to continue to live in the same house with her fiancé until she found a new place to live. During that time, she could hear her ex on the phone starting a new relationship with a new girl, which not surprisingly threw her heart into a painful contraction. Her first reaction was to pack her bags and leave and live in the car if she had to. She felt that she just needed to get away from that experience and that pain. But instead, she decided to stop and stay and feel it, experience it, and practice what we had been working on together and chose to navigate through it. As she got deeper and deeper into the contraction, it occurred to her that what she was resisting was the reality of him being happy with someone else, really, she thought I don't want him to be happy?... I don't want him to find love?

Ironically he had developed a heart condition and was suffering from an irregular heartbeat. She intuitively knew that it was related to his resistance to loving with an open heart and his rationalization of emotion. She knew that she wanted him to love with an open heart and at the end of the day, did it matter if he didn't love her, as long as he was loving; that was the priority, not that he loved her but that he loved. As soon as she acknowledged and expanded into that truth, then she was free, the contraction subsided, she communicated her truth, and they were both free to love again.

My point here is that it is not what someone has done to us that harms us so much, it is what we are doing to ourselves, and what we may have done to others that cause us the most harm. Why was she wasting her time loving someone who was not available to her? She shared that if she were really honest with herself, she would see that she knew right from the beginning that he was going to reject her; of course, he would, he always did, as he had rejected everyone he has been relationship with for the last 40 years. As soon as he found the inevitable fatal flaw in her, he would reject her, leave her, and she knew it on some level and did it anyway. She knew when he returned to her life, with his professions of love and his promises that it would be different this time, that it would not, but she went along for the ride anyway. She was seduced by the excitement of the illusion that inevitably had to pop and reveal itself in the reality of their being together. He was not a long haul kind of guy; his track record proved it. It was not a rational, logical choice to partner with him, but it was exciting to the ego to pseudo-conquer his resistance to love and turn his disapproval into temporary approval. So there is no surprise to see how it turned out, she said as she reflected on what had happened.

The real question is not about his antics but about her own... "what was I doing, why was I not yet free of this self-protective mechanism of my own that drove me to choose the unavailable guy?" her own barriers to love were certainly not consciously chosen. Somewhere in her past, she had felt the pain of rejection and humiliation, and in that instant had decided to self –protect and shut down that ability to have open-hearted vulnerability again. She may have cultivated a subtle, expertly hidden, yet healthy contempt for men and at that point, it was seeping out into her reality. The problem with that is that we create what we defend against because that is where the energy is charged.

Here, in this program, you can learn how to melt those defenses and once again love with an open, undefended heart equipped with the wisdom to choose the emotionally available partner. Discovering that the walls exist and knowing what the walls are constructed of is the first step to healing them. The fourth chakra tools and the relationship toolkit take care of these issues.

Breaking free of the habit of looking at how others have wronged us and getting into the practice of honestly examining what we are doing to others and ourselves through the choices that we make, and the thoughts and feeling that we occupy is truly a path to freedom and ultimately, to loving and forgiving the self. Forgiving the self for being armored against being loved for fear of being hurt. Creating that same experience of being hurt by the very armor intended to protect us simply repels any possibility of being embraced, loved, and committed to. Armor when met in a way that melts and transmutes turns into amour.

Coming home to the truth of who we really are, rehabilitating ourselves, and thus knowing ourselves in our own perfection, innocence, and capacity allows us the chance to love and be loved fully. This is not as much about having to be perfectly healed and enlightened before you embark on the experience of relationship, as it is about choosing to focus on and seeing the perfection in ourselves and in others so that we can know our own perfection. Through the experience of loving others, we can further love and heal ourselves. It's simply about doing the best we can to show up from a place of strength when entering into relationship. The moment and the place where the pain is the strongest is the potential portal that you can walk through to arrive home to yourself. I wrote the following in my journal when I was at the height of my own emotional challenges, and I think it may speak to you in a way that resonates with you to support you on your own journey of emotional transmutation.

"I wonder why it is that when I am most connected to love, that I also feel most connected to all that is, and at that moment, all I can do is cry. It's as if this faucet gets switched on and I collapse into the beauty of the feeling of that unlimited possibility. It feels like an overwhelming flood of sensory perception gets turned on, that strips away the defenses. Perhaps some of those defenses need to disappear altogether, and some of them need to soften into their greatest strength. There is some sort of merging that is happening some integrative process that helps me mature into the full potential of my power. The thing that feels like weakness is strength and the thing that feels like strength is weakness. Learning to be fully present with the fullness of that intensity holds open the portal for me to navigate through into liberation. By expanding the bandwidth of the flow of that energy that flows within me, allows me to increase my capacity for love through my own energy body, which allows for the full expansion and expression into loving with an open heart."

"Learn how to see and realize that everything connects to everything else." Leonardo da Vinci

EXERCISE

Take a deep breath and hold it as long as you comfortably can, now slowly blow out the breath through a closed mouth as though you are blowing out a candle. Take a moment to remember a time and if you cannot remember a time imagine a time when you felt love, perhaps for a child or a pet an easy unconditional love feeling. Reconnect with and feel that feeling emanate from the center of chest and feel it expand in circles like ripples on a pond until these ripples touch every cell of your body so that you are giving your body a love bath. This love vibration allows you to easily and skillfully navigate the challenges that life presents to you. Allow all of your cells to be bathed and soaked in this feeling so that your body can become so familiar with how this feels you can recall it at will. Allow this feeling to be so well established in your memory and ingrained in your mind and your emotions that whenever you feel challenged or stressed in your life, you can recall this experience and embody this vibration and then easily attract more of this experience in your life.

PRACTICE

1.) As you go through your day today see if you can find the opportunities where you can apply this principle and start practicing.

2.) Start a gratitude journal to develop this positive heart quality further. Every day for the next 30 days write down three things that you are grateful for so that your mind can be focused on the positive in your life.

3.) Start practicing random act of kindness for strangers and notice how that expands your heart and your experience of love on a regular basis.

AFFIRMATION

You know with certainty that love is the answer and always the best choice that you can make, no matter what the circumstances. Expanding the bandwidth of the flow of that energy that flows within you, allows you to increase your capacity for love through your own energy body, allowing for the full expansion into loving with an open heart.

6.) THE MOST IMPORTANT GIFT IS EMPOWERMENT

Here empowerment simply means to focus on the good, right, and positive in others, seeing them in their highest best selves and being willing to be enthusiastic about reflecting that back to them independently of all conditions. Whenever confronted with the opportunity to empower somebody, always choose it. Even when it's hard to express it, it is more empowering for everyone to share your positive truth than to repress or protect it. Practice focusing on what is right, working, and possible in all people and all circumstances all the time, and notice for yourself how that shifts things in your reality and improves your experience of happiness. This way the door simply keeps opening and all the walls keep melting. Realize what a difference you make and make it. The ego will find endless seductions to make yourself inferior or superior, but accepting yourself and others as they are has the miraculous effect of helping everyone improve. Recognizing and acknowledging the unique gifts and qualities that others possess empowers them to become more themselves. To be free to be yourself and have your gifts seen, utilized, and appreciated allows your spirit to shine its light, something that the world needs for us to be perfectly ourselves.

"He is able who thinks he is able. "Buddha.

Acceptance sets the stage for growth to be possible, and coming from ego evokes the ego in another. Carrying a vibration of love empowers and supports others to arrive at that vibration within themselves and at their highest potential. Dissolving all judgment allows acceptance to be experienced and naturally empowers another to be and do their best. Learning to communicate from love and not from attack, seems obvious enough, but the mastery of that is a subtle and significant skill to master. Life will supply endless opportunities to achieve communication from love, always remembering that those opportunities can come disguised as failures, mistakes, challenges, and powerful seductions to be critical, unkind, and disempowering

Embracing those opportunities to raise up to your best self and your highest potential allows for the growth, healing, and rehabilitation of the spirit's mechanism to work. For communication to happen, there needs to be a speaker and a listener, and it is too easy for the listener to turn off and shut down if the speaker is attacking in any way. I have discovered that it is important to recognize the eternal nature of relationships and not abandon love when you leave someone who you have been involved in a love exchange with. An open-hearted separation is the best way to leave; it is the only way to leave with all of your energy intact. Even in the dissolution of relationships, it is possible to empower the other by sharing everything they did right, rather than talking about all the things that went wrong and all the judgments that you have.

Taking full ownership of your judgments is a path to freedom as it allows your love energy to be fluid and your heart to stay open. Practice purification of the mind and the emotions, meaning being radically honest with yourself, while confronting within yourself all negativity of thought and emotion. Then once confronted, transforming them to their opposite positive form.

There is more information on how to do this as we progress through this book. This choice allows for the opportunity for your heart to be open, which is your benefit, your responsibility, and within your influence. Responsibility for all harmful thoughts and actions allows the space for atonement, correction of wrongs, and miraculous thought correction.

One of the main motivations for me to create this program is to allow you to have a path towards the achievement of these goals as a way to get from where you are to where you will actually be and able to keep your heart open. Now you know how to remove the obstacles that may have prevented this from happening before. It will generate different results because you have changed. From this position, it becomes possible to be kind and loving towards others in a way that supports you in rising to the opportunity to empower them to rise to their best selves.

When we are in pain, it is so easy to become stuck in those lower vibrations and those fear-based thoughts that silently invite others to join you there. It is easy to be seduced into reactivity if we are residing in low vibrations and being in judgment. When expanded in love-based consciousness, it is easy to invite others silently to join you in a place where you can actually like and appreciate yourselves and others.

EXERCISE

Take a deep breath and hold it as long as you comfortably can, now slowly blow out the breath through a closed mouth as though you are blowing out a candle. Take a moment to remember a time and if you cannot remember a time imagine a time when you

were naturally and easily able to see the best in someone else when they could not when you shared with them the truth of their light who they are when they are at their best. At that time you choose to help them see their own beauty and light. Reconnect with and feel that feeling emanate from the center of your chest and feel it expand in circles like ripples on a pond until these ripples touch every cell of your body. Allow all of your cells to be bathed and soaked in this feeling so that your body can become so familiar with how this feels you can recall it at will. Allow this feeling to be so well-established in your memory and ingrained in your mind and your emotions that whenever you feel challenged or stressed in your life, you can recall this experience and embody this vibration and then easily attract more of this experience in your life.

PRACTICE

As you go through your day today see if you can find the opportunities where you can apply this principle and start practicing.

AFFIRMATION

You are now free to choose to empower others and yourself by focusing on what is positive, right, and good in others, in yourself, and in all circumstances. This choice brings you a greater sense of freedom, love, truth, and peace in your body and in your life

7.) ALL FEELINGS FULLY, FELT AND INTEGRATED, TRANSFORM INTO LOVE JOY AND HAPPINESS

The highest truth of healing emotions is all feelings, fully felt and integrated, can be transformed into love, joy, and happiness. In this program, we will show you exactly how to do this. This is one of the themes of this book that will be repeated. These repetitions are intentional, as it is my goal to provide the experience of transformation, and repetition is one of the primary tools of profound and lasting change, as it supports a thorough understanding of the material. The truth is that for us to be free of emotional distress and negativity, we must feel our feelings, thoroughly and completely, until there is nothing left to feel and nothing left untouched or consciously experienced by us. Knowing our inner reality and relating to our emotions fully, by listening and speaking, with them allows us to be masterful in our emotional maturity. When we stay present and connected to the information that our body is constantly attempting to communicate to us, we have the opportunity to heal trauma from the past. We must understand that we are the masters of our emotions and learn how to remain fully connected to and feel our physical sensations so that we can be fully functional and alive. Our body's ability to heal is far greater than we have been lead to believe.

Here, we have the opportunity to learn about how to transmute a vibration of fear by entering into the frequency of love. Replace fear-based consciousness and consequent behaviors with love-based consciousness and consequent behaviors. Fear separates us and love brings us together. This is explained in greater detail in the chapter about the mental level of healing.

Compassion meditation is about seeing and empathizing with others going through the same experiences we go through. The recognition is that everyone is just like us, as they go through the same archetypal experiences as we do, feel the same emotions, and tackle the same challenges. We are all walking through a similar battle, and compassion for others is rooted in recognizing that we are all just doing the best we can.

You can calm fearful energy by neutralizing it. If you are fearful, it's partly because you feel disconnected and see yourself as separate and isolated. It is true that we each walk our spiritual path alone, but that does not mean that we are separate or isolated. We have lots of reasons why we do not choose to feel all our feelings, as many of them are uncomfortable, unpleasant, and associated with trauma and trigger memories of distress, and this distress can feel overwhelming as we regress into feeling our deepest fears. By bringing those feelings into the territory of physical sensation, we can help neutralize and release many of the negative associations that accompany certain emotions. Then we can simply get on with the job of thoroughly feeling and experiencing the intensity of our physical sensations, with the certainty that we really are strong enough to be present with whatever intensity or discomfort exists.

This consistent choice leads to the experience of participating in a life-changing practice that paves the road to freedom. This simple truth contains great power, and it is easy to underestimate its importance because of its simplicity. Being present with the discomforts that exist and raising our awareness of what is happening inside our own energetic system is a necessary first step toward to our healing.

EXERCISE

Take a deep breath and hold it as long as you comfortably can, now slowly blow out the breath through a closed mouth as though you are blowing out a candle. You are now committed to being interested and curious about your inner world choosing to be fully present with all discomfort or contraction, noticing where you feel it most intensely in your body. Bring your breath to this area so that you can fully feel and integrate any and all disturbance in your body. Take a moment to remember a time and if you cannot remember a time imagine a time when you felt love, perhaps for a child or a pet an easy unconditional love feeling. Reconnect with and feel that feeling emanate from the center of chest and feel it expand in circles like ripples on a pond until these ripples touch every cell of your body so that you are giving your body a love bath. This love vibration allows you to easily and skillfully navigate the challenges that life presents to you. Allow all of your cells to be bathed and soaked in this feeling so that your body can become so familiar with how this feels you can recall it at will. Healing all your feelings with awareness, breath, and compassion. Allow this feeling to be so well established in your memory and ingrained in your mind and your emotions that whenever you feel challenged or stressed in your life, you can recall this experience and embody this vibration and then easily attract more of this experience in your life.

PRACTICE

As you go through your day today see if you can find the opportunities where you can apply this principle and start practicing.

AFFIRMATION

You now choose to be fully present with all your physical sensations fully feeling them until there is nothing left to feel. You know that all a feeling wants is to be felt. As you now relate to your emotions as energy in motion you feel all of them as physical sensations, breath into them, saturate them with compassion and allow them to transmute into their highest possibility to strengthen you.

8.) SURRENDERING THE EGO AND TRUSTING OUR SPIRIT EQUALS FAITH AND TRUST

Faith and trust are essential to our development and growth. To achieve these qualities successfully, we must surrender our ego. Our ego does not support us on our pathway to peace or authentic power. In fact, it deters us and leads us in a negative direction. Once we can trust in the truth that the universe helps us to be creative and strong and is continuously supporting us in realizing our creative potential, we flow more smoothly with life and reap the benefits of an abundant and friendly life. Expanding our connection to our essential nature to the truth of who we are as spiritual beings support us in liberating from the adverse effects of our ego.

Our ego is a fictional character that we created in a time of distress to help us, to defend us against the threat and perhaps perceived annihilation. So we developed this character, this aspect of our personality that we believe is us, to help us get through difficulty and distress, to survive. Often the ego takes on the characteristics of someone who was present in our past traumas, someone who was in a winning role and we perceived them as strong, more capable of survival, and we unconsciously emulate them. These characters are often unkind sometimes cruel and dominating, but we can, quite unintentionally, at times of difficulty, copy the very same character traits that may have caused us harm. This aspect of us is the least attractive part of the self. An impostor that is not us yet runs around pretending they are you.

"He who conquers himself is the mightiest warrior."
Confucius

Our choices can feed into the recreation of this personality or not. We can starve this character of creative juice by making other choices that start by acting as if we are already who we want to become. This choice is not denial; it is creative. Your anger, grief, and disappointment are not you. Love is the way out of these lower emotional states, not only in our processes but also in our lives.

> *"All that we are is the result of what we have thought. The mind is everything, what we think we become." Buddha*

So when confronted with a situation that you usually respond to with anger, wait, give yourself a pause, a space to respond differently, to respond from choice, to think about whom you want to be and who you truly are. Start practicing responding to your internal discomfort with love instead and create the opportunity for a new pathway of responding to be available for you. Our authentic self cannot be uncreated or improved upon; it is something that is pure. And our journey is about removing all impurities to come back home to the self.

To the ego, love is the enemy and forgiveness is a crime as it leads to its own death, so it will work relentlessly to prevent us from being loving and forgiving. It will convince us that if we are loving and kind, then we are doormats and subject to the power of someone else's ego, and that response is a weak choice. The truth is that there is nothing more powerful than love and forgiveness and there is no ego-based move, strategy, or manipulation that can be victorious over or stronger than coming from an unconditionally loving heart. Communication that works is rooted in the intention to join with that other person, to move into alignment and support their goals, their wants, and needs, not attack or stand in opposition to them for the sake of being right or advocating for your needs at the expense of someone else's.

Ninety percent of communication is nonverbal, so be sure before you speak that your true intention will be communicated and trust that the other person is sensitive and brilliant enough to know your true intention. For our intention to be pure, we need to be sure that our perception of the other is free of judgment, illusion, and projection, continually inviting mutual understanding and forgiveness. If we were to honor our relationships truly, we would see them as eternal and know that our conversations will continue on some level until we arrive at purity in communication.

Purity contains forgiveness, understanding, and unconditional love. It may not be easy to create new pathways or cultivate new habits, even if we know they are healthy habits and that is why we may need support in implementing those new habits. So the ingredients that need to exist to create healthy communication are the same elements necessary to create healthy habits, pure intention, pure thoughts, and high vibrations. Purity of consciousness and emotion means only giving attention and energy to positive ideas and feelings about yourself and those that you want to be close to. This choice to be clean and clear and positive allows you to notice each discursive thought that may arise so immediately and thoroughly that you waste no time and energy in feeding and therefore, recreating any negativity in your reality.

That is why I have created this book for you with audio and video connections that allow you to have the actual experience of transformation. We have reached a point in our evolution where only reading the words on a page, gathering more intellectual knowledge not enough; we need to walk through the experience of transformation by including processes and practices. Nothing I could write here would create profound and lasting change in your life, and that is my intention. That is why I created the processes that provide the experience of transformation that will support you in doing that. Faith and trust finally become possible when we remove everything that stands in the way of it, and understanding and conquering the seductions of the ego clear the path for faith to be possible. It may start slowly with small glimpses into what it would feel like to be egoless, but when practiced, it becomes a healthy habit that leads to a life of peace, balance, and well-being. Faith does not make things easy, but it does make them possible. Believe that you are the creator of your reality and that you have the power to create the changes you want in your life, and you will be masterful in this beautiful, magical world that you live in.

> *"Destiny is not a matter of chance it is a matter of choice. It is not a thing to be waited for; it is a thing to be achieved."*
> *William Jennings Bryan*

EXERCISE

Take a deep breath and hold it as long as you comfortably can, now slowly blow out the breath through a closed mouth as though you are blowing out a candle. Take a moment to remember a time and if you cannot remember a time imagine a time when you felt love, perhaps for a child or a pet an easy unconditional love feeling. Reconnect with and feel that feeling emanate from the center of the chest and feel it expand in circles like ripples on a pond until these ripples touch every cell of your body so that you are giving your body a love bath. This love vibration allows you to easily and skillfully navigate the challenges that life presents to you. Let all of your cells to be bathed and soaked in this feeling so that your body can become so familiar with how this feels you can recall it at will. You are expanding your light, and your essence is fully occupying your body now, as you do this you allow your ego that contains your wounds, your fears, and insecurities to be healed and transformed into their highest possibility. Allow this feeling to be so well established in your memory and ingrained in your mind and your emotions that whenever you feel challenged or stressed in your life, you can recall this experience and embody this vibration and then easily attract more of this experience in your life.

PRACTICE

As you go through your day today see if you can find the opportunities where you can apply this principle and start practicing.

AFFIRMATION

You have now surrendered and let go of the ego and expanded into a greater feeling of trust that expands your faith. Faith in all things, faith in yourself, faith in others, faith in the universe. You now expand into choosing trust, knowing this choice allows you to have the experience of living in a benevolent universe that supports you in every way possible.

9.) *KNOWING WE ARE THE MASTER CREATOR OF OUR LIFE.*

The path to our personal empowerment requires us gathering an understanding and experience of the truth that:

1. We are the Masters of our Body

2. We are the Masters of our Mind

3. We are the Masters of our Emotions.

This mastery is how we can know that we are the creators of our reality and finally go about the real work that we are here to do, expressing and bringing forth into reality what is within us. We are the salvation we are seeking. We are the ones who can purify our thoughts, our minds our, souls; no one else can save us. We are the ones who can create our lives by design.

Ironically, it is when we are most stressed and most seduced into our lower selves, that the part of us that is negative, angry, and wounded, and we are least able to be our best selves when we can most efficiently birth the highest aspect of who we are. Our own consciousness, our own presence, our own awareness of who we really are, and our connection to our spirit, when squeezed by life, are the holy spirit or the universal energy of light sent to keep us on the path of righteousness. The path of right and appropriate choice is to be free of fear, limitation, and entrapment. Knowing through experience leads to certainty, and certainty is the necessary vibration to occupy to create change in your life and the correct conditions for the growth of your spirit. Any vision that you can infuse with a vibration of certainty becomes your reality. Knowing ourselves for who we really are and the abilities that we possess is essential for our growth. We may start by having small insights and little experiences in less significant areas of our lives, but practice cultivates the healthy habit of knowingness, which improves certainty. This certainty about the truth of your innate nature, your beauty, and your light is essential in knowing and expanding more fully into inhabiting that reality on a more permanent basis.

This program lays out how to become the master of your mind and your emotions so that you can have maximum influence over your body and your physical reality. You can know this through your own experiences of cultivating healthy habits and by occupying positive mental and emotional states. This skill navigates you into the certainty of knowing who you truly are and knowing the abilities that you actually have, which invites, you to be the creator of the life of your choosing. All this will ensure that your vote, the voice of your intention, is as loud as possible when co-creating with the universe the highest expression of the life intended for you.

EXERCISE

Take a deep breath and hold it as long as you comfortably can, now slowly blow out the breath through a closed mouth as though you are blowing out a candle. Take a moment to remember a time and if you cannot remember a time imagine a time when you knew that you were creating your experience and you were in charge of making that experience a positive one. When you knew that you were in charge of your life that you were the creator and the master of your ship, the creator of your life. Allow all of your cells to be bathed and soaked in this feeling so that your body can become so familiar with how this feels you can recall it at will. Allow this feeling to be so well established in your memory and ingrained in your mind and your emotions that whenever you feel challenged or stressed in your life, you can recall this experience and embody this vibration and then easily attract more of this experience in your life.

PRACTICE

As you go through your day today see if you can find the opportunities where you can apply this principle and start practicing.

AFFIRMATION

You are now free to be fully yourself, your real authentic self. You now understand and know how to master your mind, through awareness, transformation, and practice, and your emotions with presence, breath, and compassion, which positively transforms your life now. You are free to be fully yourself.

10.) *ALWAYS CULTIVATE YOUR INTERNAL EMPOWERMENT OVER EXTERNAL POWER*

It is an excellent idea and good spiritual practice to learn to love yourself as unconditionally as your dog does. Our archetypal experiences lead us on a journey of understanding that our circumstances do not define us, they simply reveal us. When we choose to reach within the depths of our character and pull forward our virtues of courage, honesty, integrity, and love to meet our challenges, we set in motion an internal mechanism of empowerment that will serve us well as we progress on our evolutionary journey. When we chase after external pseudo-power in the form of possessions or position, we will inevitably be faced with the opportunity of losing them or losing our virtues and ourselves trying to hold onto them.

This mistake inevitably navigates us back to cultivating that which cannot be lost or taken away from us. By cultivating that which is within us, we invest in our own light and our own power, not in external false gods of pseudo power, accumulation, and materialism. Honestly evaluate for yourself where you are masterful and where you are not, where are you making internal investments, and where you are choosing to invest externally. Can you trace the thoughts that exist behind these choices and behind this reality for you. This expansion into love-based consciousness and the love vibration supports our empowerment, our enlightenment, and our salvation. This program gives you the steps to help you in navigating back to that love vibration in thought and emotion. We all benefit from examining where we are withholding love and where we can broaden and deepen our connection to the flow of love so that we can realize our full potential of giving and receiving love.

An open heart is our instinctive intrinsic response to love; we unlearn that as we get hurt and recoil away from the open-hearted flow of love energy, in the mistaken idea that it was the openness that causes the pain, the problem. The open-hearted response to love never was the problem; all love problems stem from a withdrawal and shut down of this mechanism, a disconnection of love flow from the self, and you do not get hurt if that flow remains intact. Therefore, consistently making choices that support and enhance our capacity to be loving, kind, and yes even vulnerable (meaning being undefended), empower us in our authenticity, our peace, and our freedom. The most highly treasured qualities that we could acquire.

EXERCISE

Take a deep breath and hold it as long as you comfortably can, now slowly blow out the breath through a closed mouth as though you are blowing out a candle. Take a moment to remember a time and if you cannot remember a time imagine a time when you knew that your happiness was an inside job and that you had the power to be happy, independent of your circumstances. This practice is you standing in your internal power and investing in gaining strength in this experience and in this reality. Allow all of your cells to be bathed and soaked in this feeling so that your body can become so familiar with how this feels you can recall it at will. Allow this feeling to be so well-established in your memory and ingrained in your mind and your emotions that whenever you feel challenged or stressed in your life, you can recall this experience and embody this vibration and then easily attract more of this experience in your life.

PRACTICE

As you go through your day today, see if you can find the opportunities where you can apply this principle and start practicing.

AFFIRMATION

You are now committed to cultivating your internal virtues of courage, integrity, honor, and truth. When challenged and stressed, you stay present enough to be able to make the highest quality choices for yourself. You expand your capacity to make decisions that are courageous, kind, considerate, and loving. This option allows you to develop your internal empowerment and supports you in cultivating the qualities and virtues within you that can never be lost.

These guiding principles are truths that support you coming back into balance. When installed into the subconscious, they can become the compass that points you back home, to your true north. You are invited to work with these guiding principles until you find your own.

The top 10 healthy habits that make up "The Happiness Habit"

Knowing how to establish healthy habits is so essential to increasing your happiness set point, that I have laid it out in simple-to-follow steps how to form new healthy habits on a deep subconscious level.

You need to access Alpha consciousness by lying down with your eyes closed. (Listen to the meditation.) This step is essential if you want to create change at a deep subconscious level. Without this step, you will only affect ten percent of your mind.

1.) Create your script by following the guidelines for how to heal mental patterns using positive affirmations that are the opposite positive form of the negative inner dialogue. They elevate to the level of antidotes when installed into the subconscious.

2.) Listen to the antidotes repeatedly every day for 30 days minimum. This practice nourishes the mind with the exact right food to cause the dendrites to clump together and create new trenches, new superhighways of gray matter that are capable of establishing the new healthy habits of your choice.

3.) These habits become the new default patterns, and you can then practice building these new habits by making the healthy choices that reflect the habits you want to establish.

4.) Practice these new choices until they become your natural behaviors and a part of your character.

If you are interested in looking at some research on happiness, I highly encourage you to look at Happiness 101 on You Tube to have a fuller understanding of what the science says about what contributes to a happier life. Here are my top ten healthy habits that become the skills you can acquire to be the artist of your happy life. What follows is a list of the top ten healthy habits that support you along with the affirmations and tools that elevate these healthy habits to the level of transformation practices.

10.) ***Nurturing your relationships,*** Choose to focus on what you admire, appreciate and respect about your partner and to expand that with time, energy, focus, and gratitude. Start with your relationship with yourself, know how to love yourself, be positive and achieve your goals.

Affirmation

10.) You are now committed to nurturing all your relationships by focusing your time energy and attention on the thoughts, emotions, and deeds that feed the things that you admire, love and appreciate in all those you are close to. Your nurture your relationship with yourself by making yourself and your needs and goals a priority in your life. You know that practicing the act of self-love is essential to your well-being and the happiness of yourself and all those around you. Closing your eyes and visualizing someone or something you love allows you to feel those feelings emanate from the center of your chest and bathes your body in this healing vibration. You now choose to practice this whenever you feel stressed or challenged by those that you love.

Tools

Relationship toolkit
Relationship Bookio
Relationship mp3

2nd chakra mp3, yoga practice, and toolkit

Online courses

9.) ***Aligning with your purpose***: Achieved by consistently staying on track with cultivating the skills that reflect your present time agreements, gifts, and talents.

Affirmation

9.) You now imagine what it would feel like to be your best self all the time, owning your gifts and talents and having clarity and certainty about what they are, making choices every day to express those gifts with the world in a way that adds value to you and everyone you touch in life. Remember what you felt like when you fell in love, can you remember how good it feels to see magic and wonderment everywhere when you feel your happiest most confident self. You know how great this feels and how great it is to feel like that all the time. Feeling truly alive feeling inspired and creative, being free to be fully yourself and expressing the truth of your gifts. The experience that we are all seeking is the experience of aliveness, fulfillment, and happiness.

Tools

Chakra clearing mp3
Chakra Balancing mp3
Chakra Empowerment

Fulfilling your purpose mp3 and toolkit.

Online courses

8.) **_Exercise:_** for me it's yoga, but it could be anything, knowing that when you get moving your life gets moving.

Affirmation

8.) You now choose to include exercise with your other healthy habits so that your body can be supported in being in peak condition. You choose an exercise regime that fits with your lifestyle, weight training, running, cycling or other fun activities contribute to your happiness habit. Yoga is an excellent way to include several healthy habits in one activity you can practice presence, master your mind and master your emotions as your exercise your physical body this way, which helps you to reconnect with your essence.

Tools

Chakra 1-7 daily yoga practice
Chakra 1-7 Yoga workshops All yoga toolkit

Online courses

7.) **_Meditation_**: Presence, consistently, consciously inviting your energy to be here and now.

Affirmation

7.) Presence: You make being present a priority and practice presence by being curious and interested in what is occurring in your body on the level of physical sensations, you embrace everything that is present with acceptance and awareness choosing to accept yourself and all arising conditions as they are fully. You attend to your breath with this same awareness allowing yourself to breathe deeply and fully and you extend kindness and compassion towards yourself. You have cultivated the meditation habit and know that using the guided meditations helps you be happier in your life.

Tools

Presence practice mp3
Presence practice yoga practice
Presence meditation toolkit

Online courses

6.) **_Diet_**: For me, it's Juice Plus, good nutrition is at the foundation of a happy life and establishing doable healthy habits in the diet is essential for establishing a happy, healthy life.

6.) You now choose to make healthy, wise choices in relationship to your food selecting a diet that is full of fruits and vegetables that allow you to detox, reduce inflammation and stabilize your blood sugar. Juice Plus is an easy, convenient way for you to get the excellent nutrition that you need.

Tools

Healthy habits mp3
Detox yoga
Detox toolkit

Online courses

Juice plus nutrition link to website to order from www.m-bradshaw.juiceplus.com

5.) **_Establishing your guiding principles:_** that reflect your values and agreements that you can enthusiastically, consistently participate in present time.

Affirmation

5.) These guiding principles support you in keeping your compass true north and helps you finding the gifts and opportunities that lie inside all of your difficulties and challenges. You now choose to maintain a high frequency and positive mind set at all times, supporting yourself in working in right relationship with your thinking, so that you can easily create the things you want in your life.

Tools

Guiding principles mp3
Guiding principles yoga
Guiding principles toolkit

Online courses

4.) **_Holding a perspective of purposefulness_**: seeing that everything is happening just as it should for the benefit of your growth and being able to find the gifts in the center of your challenges. Practice finding the meaning inside your difficulties.

Affirmation

4.) You are now occupying a perspective of purposefulness that allows you to find your clarity, strength, and foundation when you feel stressed or challenged by the circumstances and events that life is presenting to you. "You now surrender to accepting that all people, experiences, and events that are present in your life right now are present for the purpose of your growth. You expand into the perspective of purposefulness and easily embrace everything as it is. Even the challenges and difficulties serve a very high purpose for you to create the life of your choice."

Tools

Perspective of purposefulness mp3
Guiding principles Toolkit

Online workshops and courses

3.) **_Skill_**: Know that happiness is a skill and practicing the skills to arrive at a greater experience of well being and increasing your happiness quotient.

Affirmation

3.) You are now free to be fully yourself, your real authentic self. You now understand and know how to master your mind, through awareness transformation and practice, and your emotions with presence, breath, and compassion, which positively transforms your life now. You are free to be fully yourself. You practice the skills of happiness by mastering your mind and emotions and by practicing presence. You establish and practice your guiding principles and consistently choose to have a perspective of purposefulness. You have healthy eating and exercise habits and nourish your body as consistently as you nourish your mind. You know that practicing nourishing your relationships is as important as nourishing your body. You know that happiness is the skill set that is worth investing in.

Tools

Happiness Habit mp3
Awakening inner lite toolkit

Online courses

2.) ***Mastering the emotions***: is critical knowing how to navigate through a negative emotional experience into its opposite positive possibility is life changing.

Affirmation

"You now choose to be fully present with all your physical sensations fully feeling them until there is nothing left to feel. You know that all a feeling wants is to be felt. As you now relate to your emotions as energy in motion, you feel all of them as physical sensations, breath into them, saturate them with compassion and allow them to transmute into their highest possibility to strengthen you."

Tools

All Yoga toolkit

Online courses and personal coaching

1.) ***Mastering the mind***: thoughts are creative they create our reality, and they can be brought within the sphere of our influence. This mastery is the most important choice you can make in creating your life by design.

Affirmations

1.) You are now free to be fully yourself, your real authentic self. You now understand and know how to master your mind, through awareness transformation and practice, and your emotions with presence, breath, and compassion, which positively transforms your life now. You are free to be fully yourself." You nourish your mind with positive thoughts and ideas until you arrive at the reality that is created clearly from your positive thinking.

Tools

Awakening intuition toolkit
Manifesting toolkit

Online courses

INVITATION TO BE AGENTS OF CHANGE

You are invited here to be agents of change, to assist in whatever way you feel called and able to, in this shift from fear-based consciousness to love-based consciousness. Today, fulfilling our potential becomes more urgent than ever, not only for us but also in assisting others in becoming themselves fully too. As we each evolve to the place where we can live out our potential, we assist the world to live out its own. Since negative thinking and emotions lead to a negative and small reality, supporting others to shift their thoughts and emotions helps the whole universal shift in consciousness and supports the world in moving forward.

If you find benefit in this program at all, please share it with others and support them in creating these changes in themselves. I have created an opportunity for you to benefit financially in sharing this program so that you can gain an extra motivation to help your fellow man evolve forward and free themselves of the limited trap of negativity, illusion, and lies. When we support the emergence of greatness in others, we are doing our part to help in this universal shift in consciousness and help heal the world, bringing about greater peace, balance, and well-being. By generously supporting others, you generate more generosity from the universe that which you give away, you keep. Affirming the goodness and rightness and innocence in others offers them the opportunity to rise to that place in themselves, and this program offers them a big hand up to that part of themselves. Please share it. If you want to know more about how to be agents of change, please email for more details.

Lifeguides@att.net

Please consider this invitation seriously; it contains a great opportunity for you to offer some valuable help to all those you love that could benefit from this program.

If you are already a healing practitioner and have a client or patient based practice and you see how these practices may be helpful, please visit my website for special programs to support you to support others.

MENTAL HEALING
AND CLEARING

Where Your Mind Goes, Your Energy Flows...
Keep Asking Yourself
'What Do You Want To Build?'
And Build It By Putting Your Energy There

Learn how to master the thoughts so that
you can transform fear into love

The Importance of Thoughts

(UNDERSTANDING HOW CONSCIOUSNESS WORKS)

All behavior begins with a thought, and thoughts can be changed. They reside within the realm of our influence, and you can choose the thoughts that occupy your head, by selecting what you feed with your energy time and attention, as long as you remember that you get what you feed. Thoughts can then produce feelings, choices, and behaviors. When we change our thoughts, it affects everything, our feelings, our behaviors, our habits and our choices. All our experiences reveal what we are thinking, what we are choosing, and we can enhance our power of choice by raising our awareness around what we are thinking. Therefore, if you don't like what you are experiencing then practice your power of choice and change what you are thinking and witness how that shifts things in your life.

> *"Any situation that you find yourself is in is an outward reflection of your inner state of beingness." El Monja*

To manifest what you want, it is essential that you only entertain and allow the thoughts that reflect what you want, not what you believe is right because your fears and your illusions contaminated those thoughts. Have an experiment with yourself, where you become vigilant over what you are thinking, recognizing where your mental energy is running, and making a conscious choice only to entertain the thoughts that reflect what you want. See your life change in front of your eyes, reflecting the change occurring behind your eyes. Whatever happens out there mirrors what is happening inside.

If you find yourself saying things like "this always happens to me" or "men always do this" or "women always do that"? These are significant clues about your habitual choices, your patterns. Some thoughts, ideas, and beliefs in you may attract others who exhibit behaviors that reflect your unconscious habitual patterns of thinking. This reflection will keep occurring until you transform those thoughts. The universe is a big Xerox machine that just reflects what is happening inside. This simple concept carries huge weight once we realize this truth. We are powerful creators, and it is essential we do not forget this truth. Once we embrace and accept this to be true and we finally practice harnessing the power of our thinking on both a conscious and subconscious level, we can fully use our minds to manifest our life by design.

If you find yourself stuck in some habit of complaining or if you find your life is filled with strife or conflict, it is revealing some conflict or fault in your thinking. A thought that is faulty can be changed. We simply have to identify that particular idea and transform it, shifting the energy away from feeding the negativity of it into feeding the opposite positive, even if we do not yet believe it. When it comes to transforming thoughts, sometimes we have to fake it until we make it. The faulty perception may be right in the center of your conscious mind, in which case it may be easy to locate and transform it. Or it may be buried so deeply in the subconscious that we may be surprised that we ever entertained such a thought, not to mention empowered it with our energy so powerfully and consistently that it had the ability to create our reality, a reality that we don't want. Take a moment to look at what you are presented with in your life that you don't like or want, and this will provide the greatest clues to what is happening between the ears.

Practice becoming more aware and conscious of the content of your mind and practice discernment in choosing only to breathe life into those thoughts that can create the reality that you want to experience, which may or may not correlate with what you believe is right or true or even possible. For example, you may think it's true that men are difficult and be frustrated about why you can't find a relationship with someone who is cooperative and easy. Obviously, it is because your consciousness is wounded and imbalanced around this belief, and therefore you have to keep recreating this experience in your life so that you can raise your awareness to the point where you can transform and resolve that belief on both a subconscious and a conscious level. Looking at what consistently happens in your life gives you the greatest insight into what your subconscious mind is doing.

As a group consciousness, we are now more aware than ever of the importance of positive thinking. Movies like "What the Bleep do we Know" and "The Secret" are affirming and confirming the need for us to shift to positive thoughts and feelings to manifest and work successfully with the Law of Attraction and create our life by design. We remain uncertain and frustrated about how actually to do this. We can practice the techniques and technologies included here, to become fully realized as a magician, the creator of our reality. This practice is how we can participate in the practice of the Law of Attraction. This skill is the secret that successful people of the past actually understood and practiced in their lives. What follows are the three simple, yet, not necessarily easy steps to transforming your thoughts, the instructions for how to change fear-based thinking into love-based thinking. Please don't be fooled by the simplicity of these steps, and don't imagine that means that they don't have power understanding that, because they are simple, does not say that they are easy.

THE THREE-STEP FORMULA FOR TRANSFORMING MENTAL PATTERNS

STEP 1: DISCOVERY OF NEGATIVE CYCLE OF THOUGHT

To transform negative mental patterns into positive mental patterns, we first have to become aware of what all of our voices of fear, doubt, and illusion are saying to us silently in our heads. What negative, self-misperceptions are you holding on a subconscious level? Remember whatever you are saying to yourself on a subconscious level will inevitably be created in your reality. (This happens to show you what your patterns are, giving you the opportunity to become aware of your own subconscious, empowering you with choice, in the moment, to change your thinking.) It is quite easy to gain access into this information because it resides just beneath the surface and is continuously reflected back in your experiences of life. Look at the patterns that keep repeating themselves. Think about the issue that challenges you most in life, the issue that you wish you never had to experience again, and this will reveal where you are out of balance and wounded. If we scratch just beneath the surface by practicing awareness, we can find this information. By asking skillful questions, we can reveal this valuable information. Sometimes people know what their wounds are; they will tell you straight away things like "I've always been afraid of being alone." or "I don't feel like I deserve to be loved" or "I don't feel like I am enough" or "I have never been very smart." We are always revealing ourselves by the statements we express about who we believe ourselves to be. When you are most stressed, afraid, and challenged, your patterns are most evident and most readily available to you.

Step one is all about capturing this valuable information on paper, as this gives you something positive and useful to do when in stress, difficulty, or struggling. Get it out of the mind and out of the body and get it down on paper. Thinking of yourself as separate from your mind (as in your thought patterns, which are not you) and allowing yourself to witness your thinking is a valuable practice to support bringing the light of consciousness to this shadowy information.

Often this information is blind to us, so you can ask friends to support you in this discovery process. Ask them what you seem to be repeating in the form of a challenge, a lesson, or a frustration, or a place that you seem stuck. Ask them if they know what your patterns are, and you will be surprised at how much they see and how consistent that feedback will be. Try to be open and grateful for their support in this process. Of course, your higher self is the greatest support for your growth, so always filter feedback through that channel and arrive at your own truth.

If this doesn't feel like an option for you don't worry, we have other many potent tools to share with you on this journey. I recommend you work with the chakra clearing meditation available online to go through this process as it builds a bridge between your subconscious and conscious mind so that you are supported in illuminating all your illusions and misperceptions with awareness. In your journal, record everything that comes up for you in the self-discovery process. It is essential that lots of time and care be put into this process. Keep asking yourself what is not working in your life and what the reason is and pay attention to the first response that arises. Do not allow yourself to answer "I don't know", sit with a question until a reply comes to you. Even if the answer doesn't make sense to you or you can't see why you said it or wrote it down. Do not stay stuck, work the tools or call me to ensure your positive forward movement.

Simply trust that whatever comes up and is revealed in this process is valuable, accurate, and necessary. This information is extremely valuable and is currently creating your reality for you, which could create an experience of exactly what you don't want. There may be some resistance to knowing this information, some denial as to its value or importance. You may not even recognize yourself as you answer the questions. Just practice surrendering to the truth of what is coming up and trust that it is valuable, meaningful, and accurate. Record in the journal the answers to the question. The thing that keeps repeating in my life is? Then ask the thing that isn't working in my life is? Then keep asking the reason why? Then ask what is the thing I am most afraid of? This is the exercise that you can do, if you want more support and want to work with the chakra clearing meditation go to my website.

When listening to the Chakra Clearing meditation treat this process as sacred and make sure that you prepare yourself appropriately for it. Give yourself time to be alone without interruption. Create a safe nurturing environment for yourself, making sure that you are comfortable and relaxed with your journal close by and ready to write in. Please follow the breathing instructions very carefully, as the breathing technique is potent and transformative. It is not necessary to do the breathing every time that you listen. It is advised that you listen to the meditation every day for thirty days, with the breathing two to three times per week. I encourage you to set intentions in your dreams and ask them to reveal everything that you are able and ready to know about this to your conscious awareness, I recommend sleeping with a journal under your pillow.

A second process can reinforce this chakra clearing process, and it's straightforward. Do not underestimate the power of this tool shrouded in its simplicity.

EXERCISE

Start by visualizing a bridge illuminating and connecting the subconscious mind to the conscious mind. See the energy flowing easily and effortlessly across the bridge allowing the light of awareness to illuminate the conscious mind with the information that you are now ready and able to see. Now take a deep breath and hold it as long as you comfortably can. When you have to let the breath go and only when you have to let it go, blow it out through pursed lips like you are blowing out a candle. Now answer the following questions as quickly as you can, blurting out the first idea that comes up for you.

1.) The thing that isn't working in my life is?

2.) The reason is...?

3.) The thing that keeps repeating in my life is?

4.) The reason is...?

5.) The thing that I am most afraid of is?

6.) The reason is....?

Keep going with the questions until you uncover the CORE CRY, which will be the foundational wounded belief of the chakra that is out of balance. The core cry is a short statement that contains the bottom line idea at the root of the problem. All patterns rotate around one of the chakras, and each chakra has a core cry. This will indicate where your karmic wound is, and what your karmic contracts will be in terms of evolving your consciousness. It usually sounds like "I'm afraid to be alone" or "I'm not good enough" or "I don't deserve to be loved." One of these statements will express the fear that is ready to be healed and transformed in this lifetime.

Spend some time inviting the truth of your fears to reveal themselves. Take the time to write down everything you know about the voices of fear that attempt to limit you by seducing you into believing you are something other than your divinity. When tired or stressed, the voices rise to the surface and cause a disturbance. When you invite the voices to surface when aware and relaxed, this is time to capture those voices on paper and work with them effectively. Any voice in your mind that tells you that you can't or that something is not possible or is an obstacle, in thinking that, you now have the opportunity to transform into an empowering belief that will propel you forward into the future of your choosing.

When you put energy into the thoughts that are reflective of and consistent with what you are wanting, then you can't help but be successful. You empower yourself to become the creator you were supposed to be. This allows you to create the future of your choosing.

STEP 2: CREATING A POSITIVE CYCLE OF THOUGHT

Now that you have your negative cycles of thought written down on paper take comfort in the truth that they are beginning to lose their power and their hold over you. Simply by having the light of consciousness shine on them, their power starts to dissipate. The first thing to do is discern which of these thoughts serve you and which do not. You decide this simply by asking the question: "DOES THIS THOUGHT CREATE THE REALITY THAT I WANT" (do not worry whether you believe it is possible or true or not.) Simply ask yourself, does it create the reality that I want in my life by investing my mental energy in this direction. Positive statements do; negative statements do not.

Knowing the difference between a positive and a negative statement is essential when cultivating the happiness habit. Some negative statements are obvious and easily recognized; others are more subtle and shrouded in positive intentions, yet still negative in their nature.

THE SUBCONSCIOUS MIND CAN ONLY FOLLOW WHAT IT IS DIRECTED TOWARDS AND DOES NOT RECOGNIZE THE WORDS NO OR NOT.

So we need to invest some time in fully understanding some of the mechanisms of the subconscious so that we have the opportunity of using it as a tool to help us create the reality that we choose. For example, if you wanted to lose weight and eliminate chocolate from your diet, you would not create a statement that said: "I want to lose weight and stop eating chocolate." Although that seems the most obvious opposite positive statement, it is incorrect and confusing to the subconscious mind for two reasons:

You are directing the attention, and therefore, the energy into the thing that you don't want, the weight, and the chocolate. Remember, when you are redirecting the subconscious with nutritious thoughts, it is essential that you only direct energy into what it is that you want. Just as if you were programming a computer, you would only tell it what you wanted it to do, not what you didn't want it to do. Therefore, you always create a statement that is positive and directed towards what you want. (I am aware that I have repeated this idea many times and that by now, you have intellectually understood. Don't be surprised if when you enter into your own process, it suddenly becomes difficult to remember this. We all have the amnesia habit when it comes to our patterns, so be gentle and forgiving with the self. I have repeated these concepts so that they can override our amnesia and permeate deeply into your subconscious, so that as you enter into an imbalanced and potentially wounded emotional vibration, you may still have access to this understanding. The correct way to create the opposite positive statement is....

"You choose to eat the fruit and vegetables that you enjoy."

Life (the universe) is just like a great big Xerox machine that simply reproduces whatever it is that you are putting energy into. I can't emphasize enough how essential it is to direct your energy into what it is you want to create even if you don't believe it is true. You always create your statements in the present tense as if it already is. What is present in that statement is wanting to lose weight; therefore, the subconscious will always create the experience of "wanting to" lose weight not the goal itself. Even if you don't yet believe a statement is true, it is essential that it be created as if you do. This is particularly the case when it comes to overcoming fears. It is sometimes necessary to take a leap of faith into the direction of what you want, but do not allow the statement to reflect the truth of the lack of faith. Here is an example of a statement that does not work for a flying phobia: "I want to be able to enjoy the experience of flying instead of being afraid."

This statement doesn't work for the following reasons

1.) You create the experience of "wanting to be able to."

2.) It emphasizes the mental energy around the idea of being afraid, which naturally attracts that experience.

The correct a way to state this is: "You now enjoy the experience of flying."

It is possible that if you had this fear, every part of you would be screaming no, no, no. Don't get overly concerned about that; simply take that leap of faith and state the new antidote in the direction of where you want to go. You will then navigate the energy into the direction that you want to go, not what you believe is true. Other, more deeply rooted fears may be more challenging because of the depth of the emotional charge that can shroud the simplicity of applying the same principle. Simply apply the same principle anyway.

I will take the three top fears that people have and state them in their opposite positive <u>form as a guide for you to follow:</u>

1.) <u>"I'm afraid I'll be alone"</u>

Examples of incorrect antidotes:

"I'm not afraid to be alone"

"I am not alone"

These examples continue to put energy into the experience of being alone and would reinforce the experience of being alone and the experience of being afraid.

Example of correct antidotes:

<u>"You are always connected to your higher power, to the highest power of the universe, and to all of the people in your life."</u>

> *"Be careful how you are talking to yourself because you are listening."* Lisa M. Hayes

2.) <u>"I am not loved or lovable."</u>

Examples of incorrect antidotes:

"I know that I could be lovable one day."

"I am trying to love myself more so that others will love me."

Examples of correct antidotes:

<u>"You are perfectly loved and lovable just as you are."</u>

'You deserve love. You now experience love in your life."

"You easily give and receive love."

3.) "It is dangerous to trust"

Examples of incorrect antidotes:

"It is not dangerous to trust"

"I now want to be trusting everything."

In your self-discovery process, you may have discovered a core-lie that states that it is dangerous to trust, and you may believe that it is true. But recognize that this belief does not serve you. It just continues to recreate the experience of not trusting. This experience is obviously limiting and perhaps even toxic in your life and in your body. Therefore, it is in your highest good to overcome this illusion and put your energy into a statement that creates the quality of experience that comes from trusting in the benevolence of a friendly and abundant universe.

CORRECT ANTIDOTE

"YOU NOW SURRENDER TO DIVINE LOVE AND TRUST IN YOURSELF AND IN OTHERS"

Surrender is a key factor in learning the lesson of trusting and therefore, it is appropriate it is included as an example of a positive statement. You may have noticed that in the positive statement, the language I have chosen is a little embellished and exaggerated. This is intentional because the subconscious loves to be stroked and likes the flavor of this language. Feel free to go to town and pump up the language of your statements, making them juicier and more exaggerated and inviting. I will now go through the list of examples for each chakra so that you can see the process of transforming negative statements into positive ones.

FIRST CHAKRA

Example: "I do not feel safe."

"YOU ARE SAFE AND SECURE IN THE WORLD. YOU NOW KNOW THE TRUTH THAT IT IS SAFE FOR YOU TO BE IN THE WORLD"

Example: "I need security."

"YOU ARE SAFE AND SECURE RIGHT HERE RIGHT NOW. YOU HAVE ALL THE SECURITY THAT YOU NEED"

Example: "I feel disconnected."

"YOU KNOW THAT YOU ARE ALWAYS CONNECTED. YOU ARE ALWAYS CONNECTED TO YOUR HIGHER POWER AND THE HIGHEST POWER OF THE UNIVERSE. YOU ARE ALWAYS CONNECTED TO EVERYONE IN YOUR LIFE"

Example: "I cannot forgive."

"YOU NOW FORGIVE EVERYONE IN YOUR LIFE. YOU ALLOW YOURSELF TO LET GO OF THE PAST AND RECLAIM YOUR ENERGY IN THE PRESENT MOMENT"

SECOND CHAKRA

Example: "I can't find a partner."

"YOU NOW FIND A PARTNER TO SHARE YOUR LIFE WITH"

Example: "All my relationships are difficult."

"YOUR RELATIONSHIPS ARE NOW EASY AND EFFORTLESS. THEY ARE FILLED WITH COMMUNICATION SO THAT IT IS EASY FOR YOU TO GET YOUR NEEDS MET"

Example: "I'm not creative."

"YOU NOW CHOOSE TO REALIZE YOUR FULL CREATIVE POTENTIAL. YOU ARE CREATIVE. YOU CREATE EASILY AND EFFORTLESSLY, AS YOU EXPRESS ALL OF YOUR CREATIVE TALENTS."

Example: "I don't have enough money."

"YOUR LIFE IS ABUNDANT. YOU HAVE MORE THAN ENOUGH MONEY"

Example: "I never get what I want."

"YOUR LIFE IS ABUNDANT. YOU ATTRACT EVERYTHING THAT YOU WANT"

Example: "I never get my needs met"

"YOU EXPRESS YOURSELF CLEARLY AND ASK FOR WHAT YOU WANT AND NEED. YOUR NEEDS ARE ALWAYS MET"

Example: "I have repressed my sexual energy."

"YOU NOW CHOOSE TO EXPRESS YOUR SEXUAL ENERGY APPROPRIATELY AND CLAIM YOUR RIGHT TO YOUR SEXUALITY.

"Nothing positive came out of negative thinking." Ramon Price

THIRD CHAKRA

Example: "I don't deserve to have what I want."

"YOU NOW DESERVE TO HAVE ALL YOUR WANTS AND NEEDS MET"

Example: "I am not worthy of love."

"YOU NOW DESERVE TO BE LOVED. YOU DESERVE TO GIVE AND RECEIVE LOVE AND YOU DO THIS NOW."

Example: "I'm not good enough."

"YOU ARE PERFECT, WHOLE AND COMPLETE. YOU ARE PERFECTLY LOVED AND LOVABLE JUST AS YOU ARE. YOU ARE ENOUGH"

Example: "I can't do what I want."

"YOU DESERVE TO HAVE AND DO WHAT YOU WANT. YOU ARE RESPONSIBLE AND DESERVE TO REAP THE BENEFITS OF BEING AN ADULT.

YOU DESERVE TO HAVE THE LIFE THAT YOU WANT"

Example: "I'm powerless."

"YOU ARE POWERFUL AND STRONG. YOU DESERVE TO FULLY STEP INTO AND CLAIM THE FULL POTENCY OF YOUR POWER"

Example: "Everyone is against me."

"EVERYONE SUPPORTS YOU IN CLAIMING YOUR POWER. PEOPLE LIKE AND APPROVE OF YOU"

Michelle Bradshaw Kanti

FOURTH CHAKRA

Example: "I am jealous and envious."

"YOU NOW SHOW LOVE AND APPRECIATION FOR
EVERYONE AND YOU RECOGNIZE THEIR UNIQUE GIFTS.
YOU KNOW THAT YOU ARE AS VALUABLE AND IMPORTANT
AS EVERYONE ELSE. YOU KNOW THAT YOU ARE LOVED"

Example: "I'm not loved."

"YOU ARE PERFECTLY LOVED AND LOVABLE JUST AS
YOU ARE"

Example: "I don't know what love is."

"YOU NOW SEE ALL THE LOVE THAT IS IN THE WORLD. YOU
SEE IT EXPRESSED IN ACTIONS OF KINDNESS, COMPASSION,
AND APPRECIATION. YOU NOW EXPRESS THIS IN YOUR
LIFE. IT IS SAFE TO LOVE. YOU KNOW WHAT LOVE IS"

Example: "I am afraid to love."

"IT IS SAFE FOR YOU TO SHOW THE BEAUTY OF YOUR
HEART AND YOUR LOVE AND SHARE IT WITH OTHERS.
THE MORE YOU SHARE YOUR LOVE AND GIVE IT AWAY,
THE MORE YOU KEEP. IT IS A WISE CHOICE TO SHOW
LOVE, COMPASSION, AND CONSIDERATION. THE BEST
WAY TO PROTECT YOUR HEART IS TO USE IT"

FIFTH CHAKRA

Example: "I can't express myself."

"YOU EASILY AND EFFORTLESSLY EXPRESS YOURSELF.
YOU EASILY EXPRESS YOUR FEELINGS AND SPEAK

COMPASSIONATELY EXPRESSING YOUR AUTHENTIC TRUTH"

Example: "People don't understand me."

"WHEN YOU TALK FROM THE HEART, AND YOU EXPRESS YOUR FEELINGS YOU ARE UNDERSTOOD AND APPRECIATED"

Example: "I feel fake."

"YOU CHOOSE TO SHOW YOUR TRUE AUTHENTIC SELF. YOU ARE EXPRESSING YOUR TRUTH EASILY AND EFFORTLESSLY"

SIXTH CHAKRA

Example: "I'm stupid."

"YOU ARE BRILLIANT. YOU HAVE CLARITY AND INSIGHT. YOU ARE CONNECTED TO YOUR INTUITION THAT KNOWS EVERYTHING"

Example: "I don't know."

Example: "I'm not smart. I'm not educated."

"YOU HAVE ACCESS TO ALL THE INFORMATION THAT YOU NEED. USING AND TRUSTING YOUR INTUITION GIVES YOU ALL THE GUIDANCE AND SUPPORT THAT YOU NEED"

SEVENTH CHAKRA

Example: "I don't trust."

"YOU NOW SURRENDER TO DIVINE LOVE AND TRUST IN YOURSELF AND IN OTHERS"

Example: "I am alone."

"YOU ARE ONE WITH THE DIVINE WHOLENESS AND INTEGRITY OF AN ABUNDANT AND FRIENDLY UNIVERSE"

Example: "I don't know God."

"YOU CHOOSE TO HAVE FAITH IN A HIGHER INTELLIGENCE AND CELEBRATE THE MANY BENEFITS THIS CHOICE BRINGS YOU"

Example: "I have no purpose"

"YOU ARE NOW ALIGNED WITH YOUR DIVINE PURPOSE. YOU ARE VALUABLE. YOU ARE NEEDED IN THIS WORLD. YOUR UNIQUE GIFTS ARE WANTED AND CHERISHED BY THE WORLD AROUND YOU"

N.B. All negative statements can be addressed with the five positive statements I have created for each of the chakras that create the anatomy of inspiration.

When creating your positive cycles of thought, it is important that you use your language. Your subconscious will resonate much more readily with your language than mine. What preceded is a guideline to support you in understanding how to create positive statements for yourself, feel free to paraphrase. If you know that you are unlikely to create your own antidotes, you can email me, and we can create them together, or you can use the ones provided in this book. What is important is that your mind has an opportunity to be nourished with positive thoughts rather than stagnating in the same pattern of consciousness that created and continue to repeat the problem.

You now have the chance to plant the seeds of thought that will be created in your reality, the reality that you choose to nurture and grow for yourself. Anything that you put here will be reflected in your life. Be sure to include everything that you want to address. But not all at once, the subconscious appreciates working on one issue at a time. This is your opportunity to write the creative script of your future and ultimately rewrite your story. Embrace and enjoy this process; it will cultivate the habit of happiness. When you have completed the process of stating each of your negative statements in their opposite positive form, you are left with your script.

POSITIVE CYCLE OF THOUGHT (ANATOMY OF INSPIRATION)

If this is not clear or you feel like you need more support you are invited to work with me in two half-hour private sessions; you can use these sessions in any way that you want. Email me @ thehabitofhappiness.org

STEP 3: PRACTICE AND NOURISHMENT

This third and final step is probably the most important step, and without it, step one and two have little healing value. Perhaps the most important thing I have learned is the necessity to cultivate a strong level of awareness, meaning having a high degree of attention units available to you when developing new healthy habits and practicing positive choices when rebalancing the mental and emotional patterns that reside within the chakras. The presence practice guided meditation, available for free in the audio section of my website helps with this, by arriving into the healthy habit of being present with yourself, your body, your emotions, your consciousness, and you increase the attention units that you have available to you. We acquire these attention units by reclaiming our energy from any place they may have been distracted in a lost life force that traps them in times of trauma and moments of suppressed awareness in the past. Reclaiming those units of energy allows you be more fully present so that you can practice a high level of vigilance to what's happening inside your mind and your emotions inside each moment. Being attentive enough to notice and change the first moment a discursive (similar to the benefits received in mindfulness meditation practices) thought and emotion arrives and being able to change it at that very moment, is the practice of heightened awareness and learned in the Presence Practice.

This is the final and perhaps the most important step. As a group consciousness, we have grasped the benefits of a positive mental attitude. Many of us have worked with positive affirmations before, but what we may have neglected is the essential nature of the subconscious. For transformation to happen, we have to be working with both relaxation and heightened states of consciousness so that we can gain access into the subconscious and use the subconscious mind as a tool for positive chosen change. The Buddhists refer to this state as relaxed wakefulness. When creating change around subconscious mental patterns, it is essential and necessary that we work with our witness consciousness that resides in our expanded capacity for observation. Knowing that we can feel the breath enter in and out of our bodies, but we are not the breath; that we can notice all of our physical sensations, but we are not those sensations; that we can notice our thoughts rise and fall, but we are not those thoughts; we are the witness of those experiences. This gives us the opportunity to know that we can positively influence and take charge of these things and ultimately, of ourselves. This is how we use the mind as a tool that helps us create the reality that we choose.

"New thoughts lead to a new story which leads to a new life." Jennifer Gayle

There are four different levels of brain wave functioning: Beta, Alpha, Delta, and Theta. It used to be believed that to create change, we needed to access the deeper states of consciousness of Delta and Theta. Now we know that to create change, all we need to do is access Alpha. I describe this state as relaxed wakefulness. The body is relaxed, and the mind is in a higher state of awareness with more energy, life force units available to it. To gain access to this healing state of Alpha, all we need to do is lie down and relax the body, wake up the mind with the Presence Practice. Then we are in Alpha and able to work with the mind as a support system to invite in the positive changes we want to see happening in our lives. This state can be achieved through the

Presence Practice meditation, through the yoga practices, and through the chakra meditations.

In addition, as we are falling asleep at night, we naturally go into these different brain wave cycles. Simply lying down and relaxing is a way for us to access Alpha. Using the presence practice ensures that we have all our attention units available to us to direct our mind into inhabiting the thoughts that reflect what we actually want to achieve. Cultivating the witness aspect of your consciousness allows you to be fully aware of and feel the breath and know that you are not your breath. That allows you to be fully aware of and feel all your physical sensations and know that you are not those sensations that you are fully aware of. That is fully aware of and knows the thoughts, but it is not those thoughts. That is the witness of those things that is your essence, your spirit, the witness of all things.

When in Alpha, we use this state to cultivate heightened awareness so we can free ourselves from old negative cycles and create positive new change by choosing nourishing affirmations and thoughts that reflect the habits and behaviors we want to cultivate while the mind is open, alert, and active. These positive ideas are allowed to soak through and permeate through the subconscious and arrive deeply into our essence.

This process allows the dendrites in the brain to join and literally form a new trench in the brain ingrained with these new ideas. This allows the mind the opportunity to reproduce these thoughts into energetic vibrations that create behaviors and choices that reflect in reality. The subconscious loves repetition and will respond well to the nourishing ideas contained in the meditations and yoga practices I created or the ones you can create yourself and listen to at home. Or if you feel like you want my assistance in this process, I can work with you at whatever level you determine you need. You can email me the negative cycle, and I will do the rest, or you can email the positive cycle, and I will give you feedback to prepare it for you to work with. Or I can make you your own personalized meditation… You decide.

If you feel ready to work independently, I have provided the presence practice script that cultivates the correct level of attention, and then in your own language and that follows: your own voice, you can read the positive cycle of thought (to cultivate the habit of happiness) that you have created for yourself using the three steps. Finish by reading the completion section:

Presence Practice

Begin with slow gentle inhales through the nose and soft easy exhales out of the mouth, each inhale inviting you to arrive at the home of the body. Each inhale invites you deeper and deeper inward, home to yourself. Each time you exhale you release and let go of everything that you no longer need. Everything that isn't yours.

As you inhale, now invite all of your energy to enter through the crown of the head, reclaiming your energy from any place where it may have been distracted throughout the day, throughout the week, so that you can be fully present fully here, residing inside your body.

Each time you exhale, release all energy that you no longer need, release anyone else's energy that you may have been holding onto. Let go of everything that is not yours, everything that you no longer need. Release and let it go on the flow of the outward breath, notice the breath without changing the breath at all right now.

Notice how it flows, where it chooses to touch, where it chooses to arrive, and the ease with which it flows. Feeling the breath staying present and connected to the flow of breath in and out of the body.

Ujai breath

Gently invite your breath to the ujai breath, which is an inhale and exhale through the nose into the back of a constricted throat, making the sound of the ocean in your face. Invite your inward breath now to descend through the central channel until it arrives in the home of the belly, bringing your awareness to the area of the naval, placing the hands on either side of the naval to support you in energetically residing here.

Be fully connected and fully present with the breath residing in the home of your body, notice how it feels to breathe into this space. Cultivate that inward awareness and that sense of ease and acceptance for how things are.

Repeat the mantra: **"You fully and completely accept yourself as you are."**

Connect to the witness consciousness that can feel and move the breath, but is not the breath that you can feel. Notice all your physical sensations, but you are not those sensations that can notice and be aware of thoughts rising and falling but is not those thoughts.

Allow a slight pause at the bottom of the inhale and the bottom of the exhale.

Notice the effects of this pause on the body and the mind, inviting you deeper and deeper into peace into presence.

Anchor yourself in the principles of awareness and acceptance so that your body can carry forth that memory into your practice and into your life today. Healing happens inside this experience of presence.

On the next inhale, invite your awareness and your hands to rise up into the area of your heart, cultivating an inward tone of kindness and compassion towards yourself. Take a moment to connect with your witness and discover what you are feeling on the level of physical sensations, choosing to feel all of your feeling as physical sensations.

Relating to your emotions as e-motions, energy in motion flowing up and down the central channel moving towards any areas of stagnation, blockage, or discomfort, gather any and all information that may want to be communicated, repeating the mantra to yourself: **You are willing to fully feel all of your feelings**

Choose to be aware and accepting of what is. Recognize the perfection at this moment that all is well, right here, right now.

Allow the breath to flow into any place of contraction or discomfort, extending an inward tone of kindness and compassion to yourself.

To support you in this practice of loving the self, take a moment to visualize someone or something that you love. Perhaps a child or pet, a natural unconditional love. Now visualize that being and start to literally feel that feeling of love emanate from the center of your chest and feel it moving in circles, like ripples on a pond, to include more and more of your body, until your entire torso is vibrating inside this energy of love. Allow it to continue to expand until it includes your legs, your feet, and your head so that the entire body is bathed and soaked in this love vibration. All the time, maintain that inward tone of kindness. This is how we can allow the idea of loving ourselves to be elevated into an act, a practice.

The highest truth of healing our emotions is "all feelings fully felt and integrated can transform into love, joy, and happiness." Cultivating this practice of breath, awareness, and compassion establishes the foundation for healing our emotions.

The way that we fully feel our feelings is to relate to them as physical sensations. Notice where our fear and our anger and our sadness reside inside our bodies. Cultivate the courage and the willingness to move towards those sensations with our awareness with our breath and with our compassion. Allow the breath to be directed towards those tight or contracted places so that space can be created and we can reclaim that energy and have it available in our practice and in our lives.

As you connect with that witness aspect of your being, become like a curious investigator interested in discovering what is happening inside your body in each moment. Feel all of your physical sensations, allow the space for them all to exist, the comfortable and the uncomfortable sensations. Learn how to abide with whatever is, cultivating the habit of being with your pain and discomfort. Meet all of those sensations with that inward tone of kindness, bathing them with that love vibration. Allow the breath to flow easily and effortlessly so that you can actually transmute that energy with your presence your breath and your compassion.

This is how presence allows healing: <u>Anchoring you in the principles of kindness and compassion towards yourself, so that your body can carry forth that memory into your practice today, taking the idea of loving the self and breaking it down and elevating it into an act, a practice.</u>

Notice now what is happening in the mind. Allow your mind to be free of thoughts, free of thinking, entirely clear. If your mind is full and busy, you can liberate from the thoughts by simply giving the thoughts a title like:

Worry,

To do list

Relationship problems

Drama

If you want further assistance in letting go, visualize a beautiful white healing light entering through the center of the forehead. Feel it washing through to the back of the brain, cleansing and clearing the mind as it moves through, and as you exhale, this light exits through the center of the forehead in a gray smoke. Allow it to take all thoughts with it. Using this tool each time you notice the thoughts distracting you and taking you away from simply being present, being awake. Repeat the mantra to yourself:

You are willing to be awake and present*. Allow the mind to be clear and free. During this practice, we are training the mind to be of service to you and any and all requests you make. Cultivate within this practice that sense of presence and peace that is the starting place for all healing to be possible for you to find that profound and intimate connection with yourself. For you to practice the art of loving yourself.*

Take a moment to allow your body to become very familiar with how this feels, establishing a memory in your body of this vibration so that you can bring it back into conscious awareness and reconnect with this healing vibration in your practice today and anytime that you choose.

Return to the breath: Continue to relax for another moment in silence, integrating all the benefits you received in the practice. Allow your body to become very familiar with how this feels, bringing these benefits and this feeling back to present time, maintaining your full consciousness, feeling energized, and empowered and filled with inspiration and motivation. You will find that you have more energy to do what you have to do.

Take in a nice deep breath, now feel your body filling with energy and vitality. Now, exhale slowly, roll onto your right side, pausing for a moment. Give yourself a hug, extending gratitude and appreciation towards yourself for showing up for yourself, maintaining this vibration of gratitude and rise to sitting.

You can record this script and listen to it every day to help you cultivate presence.

EMOTIONAL HEALING AND CLEARING

All Feelings Fully Felt and Integrated Can Transform into Love, Joy, and Happiness

Introduction

One of the highest truths of emotional healing is that all feelings fully felt and integrated can transform into love, joy, and happiness. For us to feel our feeling fully, it is necessary to relate to our emotions as e-motions, energy in motion through the chakra system. It is important to feel the feelings fully on the level of physical sensations. For us to integrate our feelings, it is necessary to bring our presence, our awareness, and our breath to those sensations no matter how uncomfortable, intense, or overwhelming we may perceive them to be. For us to establish our emotional mastery, it is necessary for us to inhabit our bodies and our energy fully in a way that allows us to be unafraid of our own emotional intensity. Once we accept and understand our body's attempts to communicate with us all the time, we can embrace the brilliance and the beauty and the gift of our own emotional energy and our intensity. When we finally learn how to relax into high states of emotional intensity, unafraid of being emotionally overwhelmed, then finally we can fully understand and embrace emotional mastery.

Our bodies communicate in the language of body. It is through our physical sensations, tightness, tingly sensations, congestion, feelings of fullness or emptiness, butterflies, constrictions, and all our various aches and pains (that our bodies attempt to let us know what's happening with our emotions). Letting us know where our trapped, un-integrated, undigested emotional energy may be residing. This communication is ongoing and happening constantly. There is a very limited range of sensations to choose from through which the information can come forward and let us know that our attention is needed. The signals sent and the messages given for anxiety, excitement, and nervousness are all very similar, purely on the level of physical sensations, leaving us with a large possibility for misinterpreting the signals. When we mature, we tend to misinterpret the language of the body or worse yet, not at all by numbing out to those very subtle, precious and very refined signals, thus disconnecting us from our own intuitive brilliance. We have brilliantly created many strategies of numbing out, addictions, anxieties, and medications, all born from our not understanding the subtle and essential mechanism for healing that naturally already exists in our body within our energetic system.

Often confusion arises when we introduce the mind and all its ingrained patterns of ideas, thoughts, beliefs, and fears that do little in supporting the body in getting its information correctly interpreted and its needs met. We have learned to understand our body's messages through the filter of the mind. We have already seen how the mind is full of misperceptions and fears and this leads to confusion. We benefit greatly from relearning how to be connected to the communications and signals that our body is constantly providing. We do this by letting go of the mind and all its interpretations. Reconnecting to the primal body and giving it its voice back, using presence, breath, and compassion.

For example, we may get a vague sense that we have a discomfort around the heart area. We then tend to interpret that signal through the mind by saying something like, "I have tightness around my heart... I know that it must be heartbreak. I know why I have heartbreak... I'm hurt because my boyfriend betrayed me. All men are untrustworthy anyway; it's not safe to trust anyone." Leading the mental energy towards manifesting this reality. Or worse yet, we are culturally seduced into misinterpreting, suppressing or ignoring our emotions and wisdom entirely, arriving at a determination that we have some physical ailment that arrived mysteriously and unfortunately through no choice or cause of our own. This convinces us that we need to consult an expert (doctor) to tell us what is wrong with us.

This habit disempowers us and brings our focus outside of ourselves into the hands of the trained expert or into our own ideas, thoughts, misperceptions, and illusions, taking us out of our bodies, disconnecting us from the very mechanism designed to heal us. We seem to be able to find countless ways to take our focus away from our bodies, yet this choice does not serve us. We are living inside a medical model that separates our physical symptoms from our emotions and consciousness. Thankfully, we are navigating towards a more holistic and integrated model of health that includes the important influences of our mental and emotional habits, tendencies and preferences. Including these essential elements allows us to arrive finally at a balanced view of medicine and wellness that embraces the brilliance and gifts of each these aspects of who we are.

Why do we continue to make this unhealthy, self-defeating choice of denying and disconnecting from our own emotions? One of the possible reasons is to avoid being emotionally overwhelmed. Most of us have experienced what it was like to feel emotionally overwhelmed when we were children about two or three years old. We discovered very quickly that we did not like this experience, so we decided on a deep level that we did not want to feel that anymore, so we committed to not feeling that feeling ever again. Gradually, we chose to disconnect more and more from our own feelings, our bodies, our energy, and our spirit, apparently not understanding just how disempowering and disabling this choice is. Sometimes our parents' fear of emotion reinforced that decision, and we may have unconsciously been given the message, directly or indirectly that it is somehow wrong and negative to feel our own emotional intensity. This further disconnects us from our emotions, our energy, and our own attention units; leading us into the dysfunctional reality of emotional numbness and disconnection.

The highest truth of healing our emotions is that all feelings fully felt and integrated can transform into love, joy and happiness. For us to heal from emotionally wounding experiences, the first step requires us to stay connected to the body. To stay present with our physical sensations enough to learn that it is safe to feel our physical sensations, to understand our energy. To know that we can master our energy to such a degree that we can navigate our way through any emotional state to find our way to peace, balance, and well-being, to health and to happiness.

It is necessary to stay connected to the body, to connect at the level of physical sensation, to stay at the very first signal and listen to and honor it by feeling it. This is what is meant by fully feeling our feelings. Trust that it is safe for you to stay connected to those feelings that are coming up. Know that you are safe. Know that it is safe for you to feel those sensations. Those sensations cannot do anything to you; they cannot take you anywhere you do not agree to go. Just allow yourself to stay present in your body and feel them; this is the best insurance policy against emotional overwhelm. Being very present and curious and interested empowers us to become the masters of our emotions. Supporting your body in digesting these intense energies is liberating, healing, and empowering because, in this process, we have the opportunity to release the past, reclaiming our ability to be fully available to our present experience. Identify where your body is holding the most energy and choose to be in right relationship with it. This is achieved with your presence, both your awareness and your physical presence, by bringing your hand to it (touch it) and physically attending to yourself.

Once you have mastered this first step of staying present with and connected to your feelings, the next step is to integrate them. Integrating feelings means to bring the breath to them. If, for example, the sensation you are connecting to is tightness in your chest, then bring all of your presence and your awareness and focus (both internally with your awareness and externally by placing your hand in that area) to that tightness in your chest and then create some space here. We start to dissipate the constriction by breathing differently.

The most useful breath at this place is the pant. So start to pant into the tightness. Eventually, as you keep focused and you keep breathing, you will feel the constriction subside and become spacious as the tightness starts to dissipate, and you will feel like some space has been opened up.

The simplest guideline to follow for the breathing pattern is, the heart and above uses the pant. For the area of the heart and below use the deep enthusiastic inhale for a count of four, and the soft surrendered exhale for a count of two, inhaling and exhaling through an open mouth. With the heart, you can use either breath; trust your guidance to determine which breath to use. The breathing allows the energy to move through the chakra system and actually digests the intensity of energy moving through the system. Trust that this mechanism can be utilized no matter what emotion you are dealing with, no matter what the intensity.

At this point, you may feel a constriction in another part of your body, either above or below the original constriction. Simply repeat the process by bringing your awareness internally and externally to that place, following the constriction. This means it may move up or down, so simply follow the energy as it moves. Stay fully present and connected to your physical sensations then bring the breath and the awareness to that area until the constriction expands and opens and moves. Keep repeating until the constriction dissipates.

The moment it dissipates, take a moment to connect with someone or something that you love. A child or a pet, an easy unconditional love connection so that you can connect to and feel that love vibration. Feel it emanate from the center of your heart and feel it expand, like ripples on a pond, until it extends to include the entire torso, the legs, the feet, the arms, the head so that the whole body is bathed and soaked in that healing vibration. Following this process will heighten your sensitivity to your body's signals and enable you to release and let go of constriction.

Emotional energy sits like plaque on your chakra system. It is essential that this plaque is removed so that your emotional energy and physical energy or chi, can flow freely without obstruction. The three elements necessary to ensure the achievement of this is:

1.)   The awareness (both internally and externally)

2.)   The breath (to allow the process of integration)

3.)   The love vibration (by connecting to someone or something that you love)

All these elements are married and brought together in this chakra balancing meditation available on my website. For your practice, it is not necessary to do this breathing every day; three to four times a week will suffice. If you feel able to do it every day, please do. The breathing technique may feel uncomfortable and unnatural at first, but please don't let that stop you, do what you can. Please persevere with it until you feel the benefits of using this potent tool.

At this point, you can add the positive affirmations we talked about in the last chapter, as the body is receptive and the mind is open, and the emotions are soothed. Emotional clearing and healing is centered on the chakra system. A chakra is a center of energy that correlates to an area of your body in alignment with the spine and with an aspect of your life. These centers regulate the flow of physical, emotional, and spiritual vitality through the body. The life force, the chi, and the prana are all connected to the health of the chakra system.

There are seven chakras located in alignment with the spine. These seven chakras represent seven sacred pathways to change, heal, transform and ultimately arrive at happiness. Starting at the base of the spine, the first chakra, the first sacred pathway relates to safety, security, a sense of belonging, and forgiveness. This is the storehouse where all experiences related to this aspect of life are filtered, stored, and interpreted. If there has been a wounding experience in the past related to this aspect of your life, it is stored in the first chakra and physically affects this area in the body.

It may be more accurate to think about a chakra instead of being a storehouse. Rather consider it more like an antenna that connects with the correct frequency for each of the past wounds to be attuned to, and when you intentionally dial into this frequency, you gain access to everything that is related to that frequency.

The Chakra System

PHYSICAL AND EMOTIONAL BODY CONNECTION

Our energetic health is the life force, the prana that makes us alive, and the flow of that life force is critical in the connection between our mind and body. The chakras are both supporters of and/or obstacles to that energetic health. They are the bridge from heaven to earth. There are two directions of movement on the bridge. The shiva consciousness descends from the crown (this is the masculine principle, grounding and manifesting pure consciousness without form). The feminine shakti energy is the primordial power of the universe rising up from the perineum making its way in an ascending current of liberation and realization through the central channel of the body. It is the flow of the awakening energy; a flow of high intensity and great release; an opening of energy that can be both exciting and chaotic. Shiva descending energy has grace and order, and this energy brings peace and impregnates shakti with consciousness. This upward flow is the liberating current that leads to awakening and enlightenment. The downward current is the path of manifestation, creating in the earth the fulfillment of our inspiration. The point is to have a complete journey both there and back.

When bringing the chakras back to balance, it is important that both of these energy directions are flowing unobstructed and finding their free expression. The chakras are portals between the inner and outer world, the place in the body where our physical reality meets our spiritual nature. Allowing this life force energy to flow optimally makes it possible to experience our full aliveness. How does this apply to you? Your body is the vehicle to carry the aspirations of the spirit, the karma, and past lifetime wounds. This programming of your chakras determines the particular challenges and frustrations that you will experience in your life. Here, in this program, you are presented with the opportunity to go into your chakras and write the programs that work and help you reclaim your inspiration and manifest the life that you want which supports your personal growth, your healing, and your recovery.

The chakras provide a context for understanding how to progress along our path and journey of healing. Seven steps or healing pathways are given to us for our growth and evolution, and all steps and paths are equally necessary for arriving at our destination. To align our inner space with the outer journey is crucial to understand. We benefit greatly by being aware of, confronting, transforming, and removing all obstacles to our positive forward movement along this path. By nourishing our consciousness and our emotions with truth, love, and positivity, we clear up our internal limitations and activate our external movement.

To successfully heal the emotions, it is valuable to know how to occupy our physical and energetic body fully, to become fully embodied. The development of our emotional mastery is intimately connected to how we occupy our physical and energetic body. How present you are affects your ability to be connected to your physical sensations, independently of how uncomfortable, intense, or constricted you may feel. Our capacity to be present with and confront our discomforts dictates how skillfully we will manifest and develops our courage and our ability to face with presence, and awareness everything that is here. This courage is what determines how masterful we will be in relation to our emotions.

Choosing to be fully connected, fully present with yourself is the most courageous, transformative, and healing choice you can make. Consistently making this choice is the key to transformation and liberation. Issues, disturbances, and illnesses manifest themselves in the mental, spiritual, and emotional body before they even start showing up in the physical body, so it is possible to resolve issues before they even manifest on the physical plane, preventing the need for a lot of physical discomfort and disease. It is extremely valuable to practice sensitizing your connection to your physical body so that you can heighten your sensitivity to your energetic body, your chakras, and heal any constriction or energetic build up before it becomes a physical problem or condition.

Your spiritual energy can become, frozen, or trapped in these areas of contraction and until we reclaim that life force, we may be limited within our energetic system and our creative, intuitive, and sensual capacity, our inspiration could be obstructed causing us to be unable to fulfill our potential. It is also valuable to establish a physical practice, such as yoga, that allows you to be connected to your body in a way that supports greater physical and energy body awareness. Moving into shapes that tug on the connective tissue of the body opens up the pranic channels and the nadis so that the breath can move throughout the body, freeing the trapped physical, mental, emotional, and spiritual energy in a way that liberates, nourishes, and energizes your essence.

As we bring our presence and our awareness to our discomfort, we begin the job of releasing the enturbulated spiritual energy that contains some psychological toxins, supporting us in letting go of the issues in the tissues. Once these pathways are flowing without constriction, we lighten up to having a greater opportunity to embrace our enlightenment. The path of enlightenment is related to raising our energetic vibration. Each of our emotions carries an energetic vibration. Emotions, such as anger, revenge, jealousy, and shame carry such a low energetic vibration that inform the cells to die; whereas emotions, such as love, gratitude, and bliss send signals to the cells, to heal, grow, and flourish. As we free up this energy, we naturally raise our emotional tone, becoming happier, lighter, and more peaceful within. This supports us in our ability to know how to create our own internal emotional vibration. In this program, we are practicing emotional mastery and creating an emotional guidance system that can lead us into inspiring our health, our creativity, and our happiness. The mood management method shared in the meditations, and the yoga practices support us in mastering our emotions to the point that we can choose the emotional state that we want to occupy.

This program is designed to provide you with the tools and technologies for achieving the habit of happiness. One of the most important skills to acquire is to know how to create the emotional state of your choice, and sometimes the most potent tools are shrouded in simplicity. Achieving this state change is very simple. All we need to do is use the power of our memory, our imagination, and visualization. We can connect to the frequency of love, for example, by connecting with someone or something that we love or appreciate until we can feel that feeling emanate from the center of our heart and soak every cell of our body with this feeling frequency. As we practice this, we develop our confidence in ourselves and in our capacity to be powerful creators. We also learn how to create the perfect internal environment to support us in having an optimum experience of life.

Each of the chakras vibrates at a different frequency. The colors of each of the chakras correlate with their vibrational frequency, and the thoughts and emotions of each chakra can be invited and connected to and created to balance and align that chakra. The meditations and the videos available via my website can guide you through this experience. The exercises in this book can show you exactly how to do this by supporting you in creating healthy habits. It is our personal responsibility to come back to our own internal wholeness, balance, and integrity, which in turn helps us in coming back together as a group, as a society to balance and wholeness. Restoring ourselves by connecting with our own divine nature, can then invite wholeness and healing into our communities, our societies, and our world. The chakra system is both a map and a system for personal growth, a manual for the rehabilitation of the spirit, and a profound formula for wholeness, marrying the immortal to the mortal.

The happiness yoga practice helps to allow this unobstructed flow of energy as it is an amplified holistic practice that includes the mental, emotional and physical body, but for those who are not yoga practitioners, there is enormous transformation possible with the meditations and the practices described and provided here with this book. The understanding and development of the chakras evolved mainly through personal experience and the intuitive information accessed by the ancient seers. This is a context for you to understand your own patterning, your own issues. The goal is to create clarity and opening in the chakras to balance and align them. The prana awakens the rainbow bridge and allows us to learn how to manage our energy through life.

Issues that happen along your path externally impact your charkas internally and they can support or block the awakening of the chakras. We have a descending manifesting current and an ascending liberating current. When confronted with trauma, we can either increase or decrease our energy to deal with a threat. Increasing means gathering more information or support, or we can decrease our energy, which means going into conservation mode, withdrawal and conserving our energy by going into retreat (which compares with our basic survival mechanism of fight or flight response).

The challenge is in childhood flight meant disassociation from the body; fight means increased energy as stress. We can fixate with increased energy or avoid with decreased energy. So if our past trauma was neglected, for example, and the response was to increase energy, the way that shows up as a pattern in adulthood is a fixation on getting love and support by being overly social perhaps too concerned with the opinion of friends. If the choice was to avoid, then you may become unconcerned with friends and support and be more of a loner. This can create an internal conversation about not being loved. So we employ a deficient energy response that leads to a roadblock (what I call a karmic lump). Or we could apply an excessive response, which means we become fixated and become stuck. These programs direct how we run energy that becomes grooved into the nervous system and hardwired as patterns in our energetic system and our behavior.

If you are excessive, you need to dispel energy; if you are deficient, you need to charge and open. The amount of energy available in the environment that you grow up in indicates whether you go deficient or excessive (remembering that whatever happened in a past life reflects itself in the circumstance in your present life somewhere) in your response to trauma. If you had lots of energy around you in childhood then you most likely go excessive; if there was not enough, you go deficient in your response to challenges and stress.

One chakra could be deficient and one excessive, and even with the same chakra, you can have different coping strategies. This creates blockages. The answer is to create balance and allow energy to flow. Look at where the energy is coming from and where it wants to go. If deficient, you need to charge; if excessive, you need to discharge. Working with energy rebalancing is the solution. We do have conscious influence over our energetic balance. We have influence here when we have conscious awareness here. We are always functioning in all of the chakras all the time. The journey is about rising up through the chakras to realize our own enlightenment and then bring the energy back down into the world to share the gift of our light with others in a grounded and practical way through creation and manifestation.

My yoga practices described

Yin yoga is a passive contemplative practice of long holds that target the connective tissue with the intention of lubricating the joints, calming the mind and emotions to open a portal to the spirit. This opening provides us with an opportunity to remember the truth of who we are in our essential nature. Maintaining a posture for at least three minutes at an edge of slight discomfort allows a healing mechanism to be triggered and enhances our ability to abide with whatever arises. This fortifies us on many levels, cultivating our capacity to feel our real strength and our ability to confront and successfully navigate through whatever comes up in practice and ultimately in life. My practice chooses the asanas that best target each of the chakras. We intentionally invite attention towards each of the chakras using specific breathing practices, visualizations, and affirmations with the intention of healing and rebalancing each of the chakras.

Yin yoga targets the yin tissues, the ligaments, joints, and the bones to maintain their healthy capacity. Yin yoga is a chi enhancement practice, amplifying the quality of our energy and supporting a smooth mobility in the connective tissue. Yin tissues need to be pulled and compressed to maintain pliancy (when stressed appropriately, they grow back a little stronger and more pliant) and nourish the meridians coursing through them. Yin refers to the feminine aspect of our nature, which is cooler, less mobile, more hidden, and mainly stationary. This is a practice of steady stress. By stimulating the circulation of chi through the meridians and the ligaments, this allows us to maintain elasticity in the joints, which allows muscle groups to soften and exposes joints to pressure as it pulls the skeleton apart concentrating chi in deeper yin tissues (bones and ligaments). We target the ligaments with the purpose of loading the ligaments with chi (we are not stretching them), stimulating the healing of degenerative tissue as it is the chi that heals. This passive practice encourages the development of the more feminine, passive, receptive side of our nature, which gives us the opportunity to be more balanced and enhance our overall well being.

This practice is truly physically and spiritually therapeutic and ensures a harmonious balance of the body, mind, and spirit by providing stable strength and smooth mobility in the connective tissue, which houses a liquid rich and highly sensitive energetic system that is the portal between the physical and spiritual aspects of our being. Our state of mind is directly related to our energy body. With the invitation both mentally and physically of focusing the energy in the center of the body, we fortify ourselves in our ability to overcome the distractions of emotional disturbance and overactive thoughts.

Yin yoga can best be described as like an acupressure session, by applying intentional pressure through the asanas and enhancing and restoring energy that flows through the meridians. This practice ensures healthy distribution of chi (life force energy) by increasing the flow of prana into more balanced patterns. This activating energy flows through the meridians (invisible rivers of energy) that flow through all tissues and bones, moistening the joints and revitalizing the energy body. Pulling and pressurizing the tissue triggers the body's natural healing repair response, inviting chi and blood to flow to these areas, making them more lubricated and stronger and more usable. As you are introduced to your energetic system this way, you gather more body intelligence and deepen the connection to your emotional world, putting you more in the driver seat, empowering you with the ability to choose the emotional state you want to occupy, allowing you to be the master of your emotions.

Each chakra offers the opportunity to meet and transform a lower emotional frequency into its opposite positive higher emotional state when we meet these energies with our awareness, our breath, and our compassion. In the first chakra, we can meet anger and transform it to courage. In the second chakra, we meet fear and transform it into wisdom. The third chakra allows us to meet and transmute anxiety into equanimity and peace, and in the fourth chakra, we meet grief and transform it into joy. In the fifth, we release control and arrive into surrender. The sixth allows us to let go of confusion and doubt and rise to clarity, and the seventh makes it possible to remember the truth of our divine nature.

The Anatomy of Inspiration

I have created five affirmations for each of the seven chakras that allow you to rebalance and align the main chakras. The affirmations provide the correct mind nutrition to release trapped energy and reclaim our inspiration. The visualizations, the breathing practices, and positive memory provide you with a connection to the correct emotional frequency and healing vibrations to rebalance the chakras to the point where you can create the healing state that can support you in magnetizing the life experiences of your choice. The breathing practices that target each of the chakras accelerate your ability to master your emotions. Through the correct use of the tools and the practices provided here, we target the root of each of the chakras to activate, rebalance, and nourish the thoughts and the emotions associated with the particular part of your anatomy and the associated area of your life. As your biology relates to your biography, we can guide you on a healing journey back to balance, wholeness, and peace.

When you establish a clear and strong relationship with your happiness archetypes, they become capable of reclaiming any lost inspiration and becoming the architect of your future happiness. By making friends with and shaking hands with your happiness archetypes you will be supported in establishing a strong connection with your inner energetic system that contains the map that can navigate you into your highest happiest self. This ignites the divine spark of motivation that arises from the spirit that carries the desire to express itself in the fulfillment of your purpose authentically.

Inspiration is the upward flow of awakening spiritual energy, that has both a masculine and feminine aspect, an obstacle and an opportunity. When the journey of awakening your inspiration is intentionally participated in, you holistically support and strengthen yourself in igniting the power of your awakened inspirational energy that holds power to support you in fulfilling your purpose. I know that purpose is most often viewed as the work we do in the world, yet our purpose actually answers the question of what we are doing here in a body and applies to every area of our lives.

It starts in the first chakra by creating a stable foundation by engaging the masculine principle by choosing to reside in the positive mental antidotes that affirm your safety, security, and stability. Occupying the feminine aspect by raising the emotional vibration from anger to compassion, cultivating the courage necessary to ignite a solid sense of grounded manifestation. This removes the obstacle of insecurity and transforms it into the opportunity of strong, stable connection to the earth that supports the experience of materialization.

This energy then gathers strength as it rises into the second chakra by engaging the masculine principle of choosing to reside in the positive mental antidotes that affirm deep connection to yourself and all those you are close to. Occupying the feminine aspect by raising the emotional vibration from fear to wisdom, cultivating the clarity necessary to ignite a solid sense of connection. This removes the obstacle of disconnection and transforms it into the opportunity of creative expression.

As this energy center then gathers strength and invites the energy to rise and rest in the third chakra, it ignites the masculine principle by choosing to reside in the positive mental antidotes that affirm your worthiness and your value. Occupying the feminine aspect by raising the emotional vibration from anxiety to equanimity cultivating the inner peace necessary to ignite a solid sense of confidence and power that awakens the willpower to take the actions necessary to support your awakening. This removes the obstacle of self-loathing and transforms it into the opportunity of connecting to and asserting one's will.

The energy then gathers and rises to the heart, the fourth chakra energy center, by engaging the masculine principle, by choosing to reside in the positive mental antidotes that affirm your choice to give and receive love freely. Occupying the feminine aspect by raising the emotional vibration from hatred to love cultivating the loving frequency necessary to ignite an open, loving heart. This removes the obstacles of ingratitude and jealousy and transforms it into the opportunity of appreciation, gratitude, and love. This supports the upward flow by freeing your trapped spiritual energy that got stuck inside the experience of heartbreak and lost love and reclaims it back as a creative motivational force towards your reclamation of your inspiration and the fulfillment of your purpose.

As the energy gathers and rises into the throat, the fifth chakra, by engaging the masculine principle by choosing to reside inside the positive mental antidotes that affirm your freedom to express your authentic truth. Occupying the feminine aspect by raising the emotional vibration from fear to love, cultivating the surrender necessary to ignite free flowing expression. This removes the obstacle of silence and transforms it into the opportunity of communication and the expression of truth.

This energy then gathers and rises to the center of the forehead resting in the sixth chakra engaging the masculine principle by choosing to reside in the positive mental antidotes that affirm your certainty and clarity. Occupying the feminine aspect by raising the emotional vibration from doubt to clarity, cultivating the intuition necessary to ignite a clear channel of intuitive flow. This removes the obstacle of confusion that comes from negative thoughts and transforms it into the opportunity of certainty and clarity of vision.

As this energy then gathers and rises by engaging the masculine principle, by choosing to reside in the positive mental antidotes, that affirms your choice to trust that you reside in a friendly universe.

Occupying the feminine aspect by raising the emotional vibration from isolation to connectedness, cultivating the faith necessary to ignite an experience of unobstructed trust. This removes the obstacle of distrust and transforms it into the opportunity of faith. This final step fully ignites your spark of divine inspiration for you to begin the descending chakra journey of manifesting your purpose. This whole mechanism is outlined in great detail throughout the book and is present in all the tools and all the practices.

Research has revealed that those who feel inspired and are happy have greater experiences of joy, peace, and well-being. When we occupy these emotional states more consistently, we have greater health and overall wellness. Optimists and positive thinkers see challenging and arduous experiences in their life as impersonal, temporary, and specific and positive experiences as more pervasive, personal, and permanent. Pessimists see negative experiences as personal, pervasive, and permanent and positive experiences impersonal, temporary, and specific. Establishing a perspective of purposefulness through the inclusion of the guiding principles in your internal reality and embracing the affirmations and the healing states for each of the chakras establishes this anatomy of inspiration that leads to experiencing all the benefits that optimists enjoy. What follows is a deeper journey through each of the chakras, outlining how you can establish this internal anatomy of inspiration.

PART 2:

The Anatomy of Inspiration
(and the seven paths of happiness)

FIRST CHAKRA

The Red Path of the First Chakra

from insecurity to stability

Alchemizing anger to courage

First chakra

SAFETY, SECURITY, BELONGING, FORGIVENESS

<u>*AFFIRMATIONS (for the anatomy of inspiration at the base of spine).*</u>

1.) All of your needs are constantly and continuously taken care of by an abundant and friendly universe. You are perfectly protected in all ways.

2.) You now choose to release the past into the forgiving arms of the universe. You surrender to letting go and trusting the process of life.

3.) You are safe and secure in the world that you lovingly co create for yourself. You are completely safe right here right now.

4.) You are connected to all life. You are connected to your higher power and the highest power of the universe.

5.) You are the master of your life

You are the master of your body

You are the master of your mind

You are the master of your emotions

You now embrace the truth that you have the power within you to be the master of your life.

Emotionally transmutes from anger to courage

Transforming the vulnerabilities of the 1ˢᵗ chakra into your strengths

Physically associated with Base of spine, legs, feet, bones sciatica, rectum, bowel, colon, varicose veins, immune system, liver imbalances (liver meridian runs through it.)

Vulnerability. Chronic low back pain, rectal and immune disorders, depression, multiple personality disorder, obsessive compulsive disorders,

Mental vulnerability, When stressed or challenged the inner dialogue tone is

"I am not safe."

"I am not supported."

"I don't feel secure."

"I don't trust life."

Strengthens into the opposite positive form to,

"You are safe and supported right here and right now in this body at this time."

"You are constantly supported in getting all of yours needs met."

"You now feel secure and supported in being protected and getting all your needs met."

"You now choose to trust life and all those in your life."

Emotional Vulnerability, When stressed or challenged the tendency is Agitation Irritation, Anger, Insecurity, Unsafe, Terror, Unsupported.

**Strengthens, when met with awareness, breath, and compassion..
into** Compassion, Groundedness, Stability, Strength

Spiritually This path invites you to walk through the reactivity of anger
into the expanded state of open hearted compassion, feeling grounded
enough to choose the vibration and frequency of security, stability, and
support, by remembering or imagining how that feels until you can
choose it, any time you want to. Arriving at a place of knowing that
you live in a friendly, benevolent universe.

LOCATION AND FUNCTION

Located at the base of your spine, the first chakra houses the hips,
the perineum, and the groin area, including the entire lower part of
your body, your legs, and your feet. The first chakra is the foundation
of the whole chakra system. It is the root of your body and the root
and foundation of your life. This is where we have the opportunity to
build a strong foundation fortified with a sense of safety, stability, and
security. Like all foundations, it is necessary to ensure the stability and
strength of this foundation so that you can build a strong and reliable
home for the self. Our sense of connection to the world, to nature, and
to ourselves is established by having a balanced and aligned first chakra.
This state of coherence allows you to connect with your happiness by
residing in an emotional vibration of security and the mental habit of
affirming your safety, security, and support. You can reclaim any lost
inspiration, lost to an overwhelming experience of feeling unsafe.

This is the supporting structure for your body, and your experience
of life is affected by how well-established you are in this chakra. If the
wounds from your past, both the past of your present life and past life
experiences, made you feel unsafe and challenged your sense of security
and belonging, those experiences are stored in, (energetically connected
to) the area of your first chakra. This affects your ability to find peace
and happiness because it affects your ability to feel secure, safe, and
supported. I just want to clarify here what I mean when I say that this
is where the energy is stored. It is more like the antenna— the receptor

site—to receive the energetic signal that connects to the memories of these experiences. Just as Jerry Seinfeld is not stored inside your television, but you do need a connection to this particular signal to receive that program, in order to see him on your TV.

MISPERCEPTIONS OF FIRST CHAKRA

It is a common experience, when we are traumatized, to believe that we are not safe; as such, first chakra issues and challenges are quite common. The severity of those wounds is proportionate to the perceptions created as a consequence of the experience of not feeling safe in the past. It is not necessarily dependent upon the degree of trauma that was present, but rather how the mind interpreted the event itself. Obviously, if a child had its parents taken away from them, the potential for that experience to be wounding is very high, but it is not inevitable that this experience creates a greater wound than a sensitive child's interpretation of a thunder storm, for example. If the mind perceived the experience of the thunderstorm as life threatening, then the energetic contraction that comes from the breath lock down, creates a wound that profoundly affects the level of emotional security this person achieves. Obviously, this wound requires healing and releasing.

The degree of trauma is dependent upon where the mind goes with its interpretation of the experience and what the perceptions are that the mind created, rather than the event itself. Most likely, the event itself, the thunderstorm, is a reminder of something that happened before, in the past of this present life or a past life, that re-stimulates the original trauma. The energetic constriction is relative to what the mind has invited regarding its interpretation of the events that can create fear, doubt, illusion, and misperception, which has a connection to past life experiences; the yogis believe that we reincarnate with every illusion, misperception, and unresolved wound that we ever experienced. These wounds contain all our internal dialogue that is filled with illusions and misperceptions and all the associated lower emotional vibrations. We bring this into the present life in the form of karma (which resides at the root of the chakra), not with the intention of making us suffer, but with the intention of recreating and fully illuminating its contents, offering us the opportunity to heal and remove this blockage.

Now with the information contained here, you can know exactly how to do this. Some yoga traditions postulate that it is the role of the parents to inflict the sacred wound onto the child. This reveals itself in the experiences of trauma that we go through within our family dynamics, and these experiences are containers through which we bring forth, our past-life wounds so that we can see them so that they can be healed. Bringing the light of consciousness to this energy is liberating and empowering because now we can begin the sacred journey of healing. This journey involves raising the awareness and consciousness to a point where transforming mental and emotional patterns is possible. If for example, our parents were filled with fear and insecurities, they may energetically pass them down to us, usually in a way that impacts our first chakra and makes us feel unsafe and insecure. This creates an energetic blockage and constriction that may be difficult to put into language, but it can be healed energetically by using the breath to clear this energetic vortex. It is healed in creating the opposite antidote of affirming your continued safety, security, and support.

Karmic Wounds of the First Chakra

Many first chakra wounds may have transpired in past-life experiences. Probable past-life experiences include lifetimes in which you may have lost your life early, often tragically. Having lost your life in battle is one of the many ways in which we may have had our sense of security shattered. Shocks that came in through the experience of having our sense of security shaken to the core affect the first chakra. Experiences that made you feel weak as though you didn't have a leg to stand on for example or literally losing your legs in a war or an accident affect your first chakra. Healers often have first chakra issues as a result of being tortured, hanged and burned in past life experiences; it isn't hard to imagine how these experiences create wounds and perceptions around the beliefs and feelings of not being safe. This experience can happen even if the person has what looks like a high level of safety.

Because of the power that possessing healing gifts brings, it can evoke jealousy and insecurity from those around you including those in authority and political power, creating the experience of witch-hunts and persecution and the inevitable tortures that follow such imbalanced fear-based group consciousness. It is natural to experience fear as a response to these experiences, yet when the survival mechanism is engaged to such an extent that it goes into overdrive, we can have an adrenal response that becomes destructive. This pushes us into our sympathetic nervous system response, which is reactive and protective and leads us into patterns of thinking and feelings that are based on fear, worry, doubt, and anxiety.

Anxiety is rooted in an over-extended fight/flight response, in which the fearful thinking fuels the continued release of adrenaline. This can explain why some people seem to come into this lifetime with an anxious predisposition; even before life has a chance to make them anxious or afraid, it's already there! This explains why some talk therapies may be limited in their ability to heal anxiety, because the anxiety may not be directly connected to experiences in childhood, and the emotional trauma is more effectively cleared by the breath, the body, and the physical sensations.

Do you believe in, or even know, about past-life traumas that may be currently affecting you? If so, write them out here as a way of lifting the charge off them. If not, write about some traumas in the past of your present life that you feel may have an energetic charge to them and may be affecting you. The writing will invite you to review the experience with your awareness opening up the possibility of releasing from the effects of it. The experience of losing your home, and/or your family, or being outcast can wound your first chakra. Anything that shakes your foundation has the potential to injure your first chakra. It could be played out in the present life by perhaps not having your parents available because they were working, or because they were participating in their own addictions. Or they may have been lost in their own emotions, feeling overwhelmed or anxious or afraid, something that disabled them from showing up for you in a way that allowed you to feel safe. Most often what has happened in a past-life has played out in the present life in some form. Sometimes the expressions they take on in this present life are so subtle that it's hard to fully grasp how that experience could have created the wound and anxiety of not feeling safe.

KARMIC CONTRACTS

It is important to re-emphasize not to lose yourself in the story of what happened when evaluating past trauma, but step back and ask yourself what the potential perceptions and misperceptions that you created as a consequence of this experience are. Awareness of the energetic charge and where it's manifesting in the body, and the associated inner dialogue in the voices of fear is the most important thing. As you get connected to that, you will also have a portal to walk through to connect, to know what your karmic contracts may be. As you connect to your contracts or your agreements, it is important to understand that they do not limit you. We live in a container of free will and choice, and once we become aware of what our karmic contracts are, we then have the opportunity to renegotiate and rewrite them to reflect what we want to create. If for example, you reveal in your self-discovery process that you were burned at the stake because you were practicing as a healer or a midwife, it is possible the misperception that you created was "it is not safe for me to use my intuitive gifts, so I will disconnect from them." It is not difficult to imagine that your karmic contract in this life was to reconnect to that power of intuition, heal that illusion and misperception and get rebalanced and resolved around that wound in consciousness. It would, therefore, be necessary to renegotiate the agreement to disconnect from your gifts so that you could stay safe and create a new contract that states it is safe and appropriate for you to use the power of your intuition fully. Creating new karmic contracts is as easy as creating the intention around what it is you want to create; obviously, in order to do this, we, first of all, need the awareness of what the karmic contract is.

It is easy to imagine why there would be issues around feeling safe and secure with such experiences in the biography and the biology. Remember, whatever has happened in a past life finds a way to come forward in the present life somehow. It is the role of the parents to inflict the sacred wound onto the child; often these injuries are brought into this lifetime by having a chaotic, abusive, or alcoholic experience in childhood, which created the feeling of deep insecurity and instability, fueling the illusion and feeling of not being safe. Also, the first chakra is one of the areas where issues around trust reside. This may now seem more evident as it is related to safety, security, and stability. If an experience damages our sense of safety then, not surprisingly, we are going to have great difficulty trusting anything or anybody. Trust may not always be a function of others demonstrating trustworthy behavior, but rather choosing to trust the way things and other people are; making this choice can then achieve the experience of trusting.

When exploring your karmic contracts, it is essential to look at roles that you have played in relationships. Then ask yourself, what is it that there needs to be more of from me, and what is it that there needs to be less of from me, for me to feel fulfilled and satisfied with who I am being? Know that this information can form the foundation of your new karmic contract.

FIRST CHAKRA IMBALANCES

The first chakra is related to our survival instinct our will to live and therefore, affects our basic health and vitality. When an imbalance exists in this chakra, we have difficulty letting go, which can manifest itself in many different forms, like holding on to clutter in the home or weight in the body, or be constipated leading to issues with the colon and bowel. We may also be overly fixated on the material plane and material concerns and functioning in survival mode. We could become workaholics or shopaholics, overspending or we could have a polar response to that which manifests in the opposite form of hoarding. We may find ourselves to be fearful of change or resistant to structure. When this chakra is balanced, the benefits we receive are a sense of groundedness and connection to ourselves, others, nature and the highest power of the universe, leading us into an experience of safety and security. We would enjoy greater physical health and feel very comfortable and at home in our bodies, and most importantly, we could start to reap the benefits that a sense of safety and security would bring.

There are seven pathways to grow and evolve; all steps build upon each other and have equal importance in supporting our arriving at our destination. Understanding how to align our inner space with the outer journey is critically important to understand and is achieved by following these sacred pathways of balancing and aligning each of the chakras. Understanding our subtle energy body, to the degree that we establish a relationship with it, liberates us to a life of health and balance.

When I started working on creating the Lifeguides Transformation Program, and I made the first chakra meditation, I started confronting first chakra issues in my own life. The home I had bought a couple of years earlier with a friend suddenly became unstable and threatened, as the co-owner of the property decided that the agreement that we had made did not work for her any longer and she wanted to change the agreement so that it better supported her financial benefit. This inevitably brought lots of instability into my life, as I was confronted with meeting all the unresolved issues that had been, sitting in my Muladhara, waiting for me to meet and rebalance and align all the illusions and misperceptions that I had brought into this lifetime with me.

I knew this mechanism was triggered with the intention of supporting my growth to the next level of my capacity. I discovered a pattern of deficiency in this chakra, as when I was confronted with this challenge, I lost all of my energy. I felt like I had been hit by a truck and all I wanted to do was sit down, lie down, go to sleep so that I could conserve and gather more energy. This response is typical when dealing with a deficient response in any chakra. I had to make an effort to charge my energy up to confront and deal with the impending battle to fight for my rights.

Instinctively I knew that I needed to rest and gather more energy to deal with what was coming. I needed to get more information, get support, talk to friends, talk to a lawyer and charge my energy up, which was the opposite to my default pattern. I needed a victory here, so I had to break free of my programming. This was not easy or natural for me to do, and at times, I felt that I was walking through molasses, as I became aware that I was rebalancing a deficient response pattern in my first chakra about stability. Interestingly enough, I noticed within the same chakra an excessive response of anger that needed to find a way to be discharged for there to be a balanced response by me.

BALANCING AND HEALING FIRST CHAKRA

When we surrender to trusting that we are safe, our whole reality shifts and the world appears stable and safe; it becomes brighter and more beautiful and pregnant with possibility. The experience of feeling safe naturally follows the belief that you are safe. The knowledge that you are safe comes from a consciousness that is charged in that direction, by that thought, this thought contributes to the state of coherence that brings us to the habit of happiness.

The belief that we are safe is energized by choosing to think on both the subconscious as well as conscious level the beliefs and ideas that reinforce and strengthen us with messages about our safety and security. This then invites the possibility of that experience, which then, in turn, creates the reality of that experience which reinforces the belief in that reality. We have already seen the steps in the mental clearing section how to strengthen the lower self with these beliefs. The emotions also need to be vibrating at a clear level. Clearing and healing all the energetic, vibration, e-motional (energy in motion) obstacles and blockages that exist in this part of the body create the perfect environment to create new beliefs and emotional vibrations and manifest a new reality. Our energetic clarity is critical for us to realize our full potential and manifest our true creative expression of who we are. Feeling safe and secure, connected and stable is the necessary foundation that we need to establish to build towards our creative expression, which is the territory of the second chakra.

Each time I meet with new clients, the first thing that I invite them to do is to raise their awareness around their internal mental and emotional reality, starting by turning up the volume on their inner dialogue, simply by paying attention to it, moving towards it and illuminating it with awareness. This way they can find out and know for themselves what is going on just beneath the line of awareness. I can support you in gathering some awareness in a private reading, or you can simply use the tools that we provide and increase your awareness for yourself. Rather than me telling others my insights, I prefer to support them in discovering for themselves the workings of their internal reality, as it is only valid if it is real for the person, themselves. I prefer the idea of teaching a man to fish over giving him a fish.

All of the tools are designed to support you in discovering what is true for yourself. This way a bridge can be built to raise your awareness of your patterns and tendencies, which empowers you to arrive at a heightened state of awareness, a deeper knowing and a point of liberation from habitual patterns. I then invite my clients to set intentions for their dreams, to reveal whatever it is that they are ready and able to see, to know and be connected to. They begin with the chakra clearing meditation (available in the audio section), which raises a series of skillful questions for each of the chakras that you can journal every day. Then my clients are invited to attend the yoga classes that enhance their connection to their inner mental and emotional world. (which you can attend with the videos).

By turning up the volume and deepening their connection with their internal voices, especially when stressed, there is the opportunity to know consciously what is happening with the thoughts and feelings on an automatic level. The yoga practice connects them to their internal investigator, who is curious about all of their thoughts and their physical sensations that connect them to their emotions, feeling their feelings as physical sensations, allowing them to gather information from the body that provides data for deeper evaluation and understanding.

The yin asanas invite them to create intentional discomfort, a dull achy sensation by tugging on the connective tissue, which creates an internal template, that learns, until it knows, that they have a capacity to feel, and breathe and bring compassion to the self even when uncomfortable. This practice cultivates a knowing, through experience, that you really are strong, that you really can endure, even in times of stress and discomfort. Which in turn creates the space needed to make wise choices, under uncomfortable conditions, that allows for the full digestion and integration of the lower emotional frequencies to the point of instant transmutation into the higher frequency of love or above. After these practices are included for a few weeks, (if you are working with yoga as a tool or with the guided meditation if not), we open up the space to communicate with the subconscious mind, if it is necessary, and if it is helpful. Here I have included case studies, which included that element, but it is not always necessary depending upon the level of access that the individual gathers. These stories are archetypal in nature and represent a compilation of several different clients' experiences thus everyone's privacy is protected.

Mandy's journey walking the first chakra red path, arriving at security

Mandy is an attractive, vivacious married mother of two. She has a daughter in her mid-twenties and a son in his late teens. Her marriage works well; her husband is a successful businessman who has worked hard to build his own company from nothing. They share the same sense of humor and have managed to successfully navigate their way through the many challenges their marriage has invited them towards healing. Mandy grew up with working class parents who have retired and are living comfortably. Her father drank throughout the marriage, and her mother remains unhappy about his choice to continue to drink. She was never supported in having balance in her first chakra, so she was plagued with a sense of insecurity and fear throughout her life, which led her to constantly question his fidelity, a fact that irritated him until he decided to work with the energy and flirt outrageously with every attractive woman he met. This obviously deepened her insecurity, and the wound festered.

Although he never strayed, she lived in fear of his abandonment his entire life. He never physically abandoned her but, of course, his choice to consistently drink himself unconscious, and to withhold his affections towards her, provided her with the consistent experience of his emotional abandonment. She never felt safe, she never trusted him and lived her life with this constant sense of fear and insecurity.

Mandy loves her father; he's a very likable man and has always been challenged by her mother's emotional enmeshment, suffocation, and fearful energy. Mandy has expressed her frustration with these issues with her mother with the guidance of her therapist, but this has done little to alleviate the problems she is currently dealing with. The silent unspoken message from her mother is "Nothing is safe" and "You are not strong enough." Of course, there was also lots of love and affection and fun in their family dynamic, so Mandy functions within the standard range of psychological health. She struggles greatly with her fears and worries about her children's ability to make it in the world. She's concerned about their capacity to make wise and appropriate choices for themselves and is not at all convinced that they will "get their act together" and be successful. As we know, these fears and this consciousness serve in assuring the likelihood of her fear being right and becoming a self-fulfilling prophecy, leading her into the frustrating reality of her children's struggle with life.

Beneath the top layer of functionality in her relationship, Mandy doesn't have any financial control, and her husband makes all the choices about where their money goes. She justifies this by saying, 'he probably makes better choices than I do anyway.' They have a very intense and volatile communication style, and some would say that he's a bully or abusive. She doesn't experience it that way; for her it's normal. Mandy often gets sick, which renders her incapable of contributing to the family finances. She has chosen a job that doesn't allow her to generate a significant, consistent income. She recognizes that in the past she has used sickness as a way to lighten up the intensity from her husband, pushing him into a more nurturing and nourishing role rather than a demanding, receiving one. She approached me with a request to guide and support her in breaking free of this cycle of using sickness to get nourishment and to stop worrying about her children. She was not happy and wanted to get there.

So we started with the first step of mental healing and clearing by identifying the fixed beliefs within the subconscious, and after her work with the self-discovery process, we talked directly to her lower self and revealed the negative cycle of thought. So the question that we ask is: "The thing that isn't working in my life is?" followed by "the reason is" (This is what transpired in that session.)

Health and happiness! "the reason is..."

I'm not well nor happy

Not Strong not healthy no energy

I'M NOT STRONG ENOUGH

I fear everything... danger

The world is dangerous everything can go wrong

IT'S NOT SAFE

FEAR... (it's normal for these sessions to go in circles and often what arises makes no sense to the conscious mind)

Mandy's bottom line or core cry is "IT'S NOT SAFE" and "I'M NOT STRONG ENOUGH." This could combine to "It's not safe for me to be strong." It's not too difficult to see how these illusions could be installed through the modeling provided by her parents. Remember that it is the role of the parents to inflict the sacred wound, which in this case, was the misperception that Mandy was not safe and not strong enough. What may be more interesting is to look at and explore what may have happened in the karma, in past lifetimes, to get to the cause, the original experience that created this illusion that is still currently believed. When I explore past-lives with clients, I am reluctant to say the information that arises in a reading or a regression is absolute and definitive I prefer to offer openings for exploration for their own guidance and intuition to review.

The process I provide will support you in this essential journey of self-discovery. It is not useful to blame the parents or imagine that they may have done something wrong, or that there were mistakes in what happened in the history. What is useful is to use this valuable information that has been excavated in the self-discovery process and transform it, so there can be liberation from the illusion and the emotional, energetic charge so that there can be an opening into the truth. In Mandy's case, the truth that is escaping her subconscious is "You are brave enough and strong enough to confront and overcome life's challenges." (The weight of the emotional intensity that comes as a consequence of feeling unsafe, can be lifted through the self-discovery process, allowing you to reclaim that trapped spiritual energy so that you can be more vital, alive, and happy. The breath work that you are guided through in the processes that I provide allows you to lift this energetic charge.) We then created a script together that represented Mandy's new happiness story that she could work with both as a practice and nourishment for her lower-self to transform her negativity into positivity and inspiration. Follow step two, which contains the opposite positive of everything she stated and combined it with the affirmations for the first chakra and I repeated it twice.

Mandy's new happy success story

If you resonate with Mandy's story, you can use this story as a template for and an inspiration for you to write your own new success story to nourish your lower self to transform to your higher happy self.

You are healthy and strong, your health is vibrant and fortified, and you are now enjoying excellent health in your body, mind, and spirit. You are now connected to your inner physician, and you can enjoy optimum health at all times. You are now well, peaceful and balanced on every level. You have unlimited energy that allows you to accomplish everything that you need to get done. You are safe and supported; you are completely safe right here, right now. All of your needs are constantly and continuously taken care of. You are protected by your positive energy, and all negativity bounces off and away from you. You are the one who creates your safety, your security, your protection, your health and your happiness in your life. You are your best insurance policy to ensure that everything goes right in your life so that you have all the things that you want in your life. You are safe and supported; you are at peace with high confidence that your life is going exactly the way that you want it. You are ensured to have the best possible future. (I added these first chakra affirmations from the anatomy of inspiration to the Success story).

1) ALL OF YOUR NEEDS ARE CONSTANTLY AND CONTINUOUSLY TAKEN CARE OF BY AN ABUNDANT AND FRIENDLY UNIVERSE. YOU ARE PERFECTLY PROTECTED IN ALL WAYS

2) YOU ARE CONNECTED TO ALL LIFE. YOU ARE CONNECTED TO YOUR HIGHER POWER AND THE HIGHEST POWER OF THE UNIVERSE.

3) YOU ARE SAFE AND SECURE IN THE WORLD THAT YOU LOVINGLY CREATE FOR YOURSELF. YOU ARE COMPLETELY SAFE RIGHT HERE AND NOW.

4) YOU NOW CHOOSE TO RELEASE ALL WOUNDS AND OBSTACLES BOTH MENTALLY AND EMOTIONALLY, THAT COME FROM THE PAST TO THE FORGIVING ARMS OF THE UNIVERSE. YOU SURRENDER TO LETTING GO AND TRUSTING THE PROCESS OF LIFE.

5) YOU ARE THE MASTER OF YOUR LIFE. YOU ARE THE MASTER OF YOUR BODY. YOU ARE THE MASTER OF YOUR MIND. YOU ARE THE MASTER OF YOUR EMOTIONS. YOU NOW EMBRACE THE TRUTH THAT YOU HAVE THE POWER WITHIN YOU TO BE THE MASTER OF YOUR LIFE.

Each player in Mandy's story is playing their role perfectly to support Mandy in healing these illusions. This support often comes in the guise of a challenge. For example, her mother brilliantly introduced her to the illusion so successfully that she believed it. Her daughter's various escapades into chaos, further invite her to believe the story and the illusions and this is very often what karmic contracts look like. Our tribes, the people who are closest to us, confirm our worst fears. They do not do this to make us suffer; they do this so that we can be free. So they help us by placing us inside our insanity, the illusions and misperceptions our minds seduce us into until it becomes clear and apparent that what we are thinking is not accurate or correct.

Mandy is doing well, She got a slight cold last winter, but other than that has not been ill or used illness to get the attention that she needs. She simply asks for her need for connection to be met from a strong place of worthiness, that she now energetically embodies as a result of doing the practices. She still comes to my yoga practice and uses the practice that I designed for her and others with a first chakra wound, which you can find on You Tube. Mandy was dealing with a deficiency in her first chakra response, so after working with the first chakra toolkit, she came back to a place of balance. I can design a personalized yoga practice for you that works with the karmic path that you are working with in this lifetime and also any secondary challenges that you may be facing. I feel that we all have a primary and secondary path of karmic rebalancing that we are walking to bring back into balance in this lifetime. I can support you in finding this path and provide you the tools necessary to allow you to grow into your own highest potential.

The first step is about identifying for yourself what your path is, if that is too obscure for you, email me, and we can determine that together. The most important thing is to take a step, do not stagnate, as that allows a continuation of the past pattern, the most important thing is to move, make a movement, grow, evolve and make progress. Establishing an optimistic perspective in the first chakra brings your anatomy back to balance and supports you in creating the habit of happiness and ignites your inspiration.

First Chakra Toolkit.

This toolkit contains everything you need to rebalance and align your first chakra, bringing about a state of coherence that feeds your well-being. You are supported in cultivating the habit of happiness through the establishment of a positive, optimistic attitude and emotional frequency in this area of your anatomy. This transformative journey clears all wounds related to your sense of safety, security, stability, and belonging, liberating you from the wounds of the past, supporting you in feeling grounded, safe, and connected. Here you can reclaim any inspirational energy lost to insecurity, instability, anger, and agitation and regenerate it as passion.

The toolkit rebalances and aligns the area physically related to symptoms of low back pain, immune disorders, sciatic problems, and depression. If you relate to anything that I have I mentioned here and identify yourself as someone who is walking the first chakra path, and feel that you would benefit from having this chakra rebalanced to support you in cultivating the habit of happiness, I have designed some tools to help you as you go. You can practice these tools whether you do yoga or not. Firstly I have summarized a daily morning yoga practice available on You Tube. It contains the visualizations and the correct emotional frequency to occupy as you repeat the affirmations. Lastly, I have listed the tools you can use to support you in the alchemical process of turning your vulnerabilities into strengths. Please check in with your intuition and follow its guidance towards which tools and what timing may work best for you. Everyone is different and in the interests of honoring those differences I defer to the wisdom of your guidance.

If you are interested in my recommendation, I suggest you work with the tools in the order listed. If you prefer to work with me in person at your own pace, then please find my contact information on my website. My intention in this book is to empower you to connect to your inner guru and activate your inner physician so that you can best support your body, mind, and spirit to heal and nourish itself. I also know that we can get stuck behind our obstacles sometimes and we may benefit from a strong external reflection to give us a helping hand along the path. You can use the visualization, positive memory, and affirmation every morning in bed. The other tools are to be worked with your eyes closed lying down every day for 30 days.

Top ten techniques for the red path.

I have provided the information that you need to work on your own at home, to increase your happiness, reconnect with your inspiration and navigate from your lower to your higher self. All this information is contained in the You Tube videos, so if you find it easier to work with that tool or the mediations, it not necessary to learn this.

1.) State of relaxed wakefulness, (PRESENCE PRACTICE MP3) Awareness

A.) Notice for yourself, with curious investigation, all your physical sensations B.) Feel all of your feelings, emotions, energy in motion, C.) Notice the monkey mind, let go of thinking, so that you can connect to the witness aspect of consciousness.

2.) Breath

3.) Compassion

4.) Visualizations

5.) Positive memory

6.) Raised emotional frequency

7.) Skillful questions

8.) Affirmations

9.) Behavior changes after nourishment and practice

10.) Yoga poses

ORIENTATION TO THE YOGA POSES

Take your time to find your edge of sweet discomfort to inner thigh groin area where you can reside in stillness, take your time to find a place where you can comfortably reside inside your edge of sweet discomfort. You know that you have found your appropriate edge when the breath is flowing easily and effortlessly up and down the central channel, and the muscles in your face remain relaxed. It is important that you are feeling the physical discomfort and the stimulation most intensely in the area that I am inviting you to feel it. Which in this case are the inner thigh and groin area. We do not want to have any pain and discomfort in the knee joint the neck or the low back. You are encouraged here just to relax and let go. If you feel a sharp electrical sensation, then you need to back off, to the point in the raised illustration, or come out altogether.

2.) _Breathing technique_ Visualize your inhale enter into your body through the crown of your head inviting the breath to descend through the central channel of the body until it arrives at the very bottom of your spine. Bring the awareness to the pelvic floor suspend the breath, and keep the throat open, contract all of the muscles on the pelvic floor doing what's called a muhlabanda lift here and invite the prana to come to the coccyx, the very last bone in the tailbone. You may not feel this invitation in your physical body, but trust that we have set the intention and created the space for your body to respond appropriately to this instruction, exhale and release the breath up the central channel and allow it to rest in the area of the heart.

3.) _Visualization_ Visualize a beautiful ruby red wheel of light circulating like a fan in a clockwise direction and as it moves it heals, and it clears removing all obstacles and blockages allowing you to create space so that you can remember the truth of who you are as a spirit and as a soul.

4.) Positive memory and 5.) Raised emotional frequency

Recall now a memory of a time when you felt completely safe and supported and protected. Recall that moment in time in your mind and remember all of the details around that time when you felt safe and supported and protected and secure. Feel how that felt in your body, now allow every cell in your body to be soaked in that beautiful feeling soaking and saturating all of your cells with that healthy healing vibration. Allow yourself to fully connect to and feel all of your feelings

6.) *1ˢᵗ chakra questions. (Record and play these questions while in the pose)*

1.) *List any and all fears that are associated with the past connected to ideas and beliefs about safety or security, the family, authority, and your home, The fears that you are and able to see and integrate are allowed to surface into your consciousness now.*

2.) *List all your beliefs and perceptions about your relationship with your mother, and how you think that has affected your sense of safety and security and support?*

And your relationship with your father?

And your brother, your sister?

3.) *What was the role that you played and the identity you carried within your family in your childhood? Is that role still agreeable to you now?*

4.) *What are you ready to let go of now in the form of a role, a way of being a pseudo identity that may have become a habit or a pattern? What aspects of your personality are you ready to relinquish, to dismantle, and let go of?*

5.) *How safe and secure and supported did you feel in childhood?*

6.) *Do you feel safe in your life now in your community, in your world right now?*

7.) *Were you made to feel safe and supported by your family, did you get reassurance and positive, clear and pure reflection of your essence?*

8.) *Were you able to establish a deep and intimate connection with yourself, with your truth?*

9.) *Do you feel safe enough to be all of who you truly are?*

10.) *Do you feel like is it safe for you to be you?*

11.) *What structure and support were present for you in childhood in your home in your school in your community?*

12.) *Did you feel supported in your family, in your school, in your community?*

9.) *Affirmations.* Record and play these affirmations while in the pose.

First chakra yoga practice

Wide kneed child's pose (inner thigh and groin area) Meridian affected- liver, kidney, spleen, gall bladder. Emotionally transmuting anger to compassion, instability to stability Mental affirmation " You are perfectly safe and supported" Core cry " I do not feel safe."

WE ARE SEEKING OUT AN ACHY SENSATION IN THE AREA TARGETED

ONLY (any discomfort in other areas requires adjusting

1ST CHAKRA WIDE KNEED CHILDS POSE (raised)

1st chakra photo 1 and 2 Wide kneed child's pose forward

1. Start on all fours.

2. Bring your big toes together and take your knees a bit wider than hip width apart.

3. Sit back on the heels and relax the forehead down onto (or towards) the floor. You may find your edge as you are sitting up or you may be able to come all the way forward. You decide if you want to find it with or without the bolster, it is easier with the support and comfort of the bolster beneath you, just find the shape that best works with your body.

4. Rest the arms where they feel most comfortable.

5. Breathe with ease, inhaling as much breath as feels pleasurable and allowing each exhale to fall out of the body completely. Imagine that the exhales empty out of the forehead and flow into the ear

1st Chakra forward fold

1. Sit up on a folded blanket. Straighten the legs in front of you. Remove flesh from the sits bones. You may want to sit up straight or have the arms straight, or you can fold over the bolster. You want to feel the stimulation in the hamstrings and inner thighs, not the back. If the back is achy and uncomfortable, then come to the wall and allow the legs to rest up the wall in the same shape.

2. Lengthen the spine by raising the arms up above the head and then extend forward from the low back into the chest.

3. Drape the spine down, allowing the back to round.

4. Support your forehead with a bolster, either under or over your knees.

5. Enjoy a few soft breaths and then turn your awareness towards the sensations in your body

AFFIRMATIONS

1.) All of your needs are constantly and continuously taken care of by an abundant and friendly universe. You are perfectly protected in all ways

2.) You are connected to all life. You are connected to your higher power and the highest power of the universe.

3.) You are safe and secure in the world that you lovingly create for yourself. You are completely safe right here and now.

4.) You now choose to release all wounds and obstacles both mentally and emotionally, that come from the past into the forgiving arms of the universe. You surrender to letting go and trusting the process of life

5.) You are the master of your life.

You are the master of your body.

You are the master of your mind.

You are the master of your emotions.

You now embrace the truth that you have the power within you to be the master of your life.

Expected behavior change

Wide Legged Forward Fold

Opens groin, ankles, hip flexors

1. Sit up on a folded blanket.

2. Widen the legs 90 degrees or more apart and allow them to relax. If you are feeling the discomfort in your low back, then come to the wall and allow the legs to come up the wall in the same shape, so you feel the sensations in the inner thigh groin area.

3. Lengthen the spine up and then extend forward from the low back into the chest.

4. Drape the spine down and position your prop(s) so that the forehead can sink into the support easily.

    1.) Feeling a sense of security and stability, giving you the opportunity to think and feel yourself to be more solid and grounded. So that now, you find yourself behaving in ways that reflect that reality and truth. Freeing you to be your authentic self.

    2.) You can now allow yourself to feel safe enough to be more vulnerable, seeing emotional vulnerability as a strength, as it removes all barriers between you and those you love. Because you can trust in your continued safety and security, you know and act so that you will always be protected and provided with opportunities to grow and learn and evolve.

    3.) You can trust that all of your physical needs will be taken care of and you will be provided for, which allows you to be free to relax and be more yourself.

    4.) You notice a greater sense of confidence and self - assurance that allows you to live your life more fully in the present.

    5.) You allow yourself to be large living your life fully with every aspect of yourself fully awakened.

6.) *Fully expressing your creativity, allowing yourself to be fully seen and heard.*

7.) *You are free to fully occupy and express your own identity.*

8.) *You are free to be fully all of who you are, you are creative and wise and powerful*

9.) *You are free to bring forward all of your gifts and all of your talents and make your contribution to the world.*

10.) *You now act with confidence, and you stand fully in the truth of who you are.*

SECOND CHAKRA

The Orange Path of the Second Chakra from Isolation to Connection Alchemizing fear to wisdom

Second Chakra

(abundance, creativity, sexuality, relationships)

1.) You trust in the abundance of the universe. You are blessed with a never-ending supply of everything that you need.

2.) You honor everyone in your life and trust that their presence is in your highest good. You now choose to bless everyone in your life.

3.) All of your relationships are loving and harmonious filled with love, respect and honor.

4.) You are the creative power in your world. You now celebrate your own creative ideas and express your unique gifts and contribution.

5.) You allow all of your desires and appetites to be perfectly balanced and aligned.

Emotionally from fear and aloneness, to
Wisdom and connectedness

Transforming the vulnerabilities of the 2nd chakra into your strength

Physically associated with Lower abdomen to the naval area, sexual, reproductive organs, Large intestine, lower vertebrae, Pelvis, Appendix, Bladder, Kidney, Hip area.

Vulnerability. Arthritis, Chronic low back pain, sexual potency and urinary problems, prostate and ovarian problems, uterine illness, fibroids, menopause severity.

Mental vulnerability, When stressed or challenged the inner dialogue tone is

"I am alone."

"I feel disconnected."

"I feel isolated."

"Everything is chaotic."

"It's all going to hell in a hand basket."

Strengthens into the opposite positive form of "You are always connected to your higher power, the highest power of the universe and to all those you are close to."

"Even when there is no one with you, you are still connected to everything and everyone."

Emotional Vulnerability, When stressed or challenged the tendency of the mood level is fear. Fears overtaking logic, feeling a sense of scarcity, feeling abandoned, overwhelmed, out of balance, unable to cope, and vulnerable to addiction, loss of creative interest, lack of libido.

Strengthens, when met with awareness, breath, and compassion.. into

Wisdom

A sense of interconnectedness, feeling plugged in.

A sense of belonging

Sexually and creatively awake

Prosperous, sense of abundance in all things

Balanced

Spiritually this path invites you to walk through the reactivity of fear into the wisdom of choosing how you want to respond to life, and it's challenges so that you can turn them into opportunities. Learning that fear is truly just false evidence appearing real. Knowing that you belong in this body, in this life in a way that allows you to experience and enjoy it's pleasures fully. Arriving into choosing to fully express your creative and sexual energy, in the most pleasurable and balanced way possible, because you belong here in this body, in this life. That you are always connected to all things at all times.

LOCATION AND FUNCTION

The second chakra is located just behind the naval and houses all of the reproductive and sexual organs. Also, the bladder, the kidneys, and the urinary tract are affected encompassing the entire sacral area of the body. Some of the disturbances include hip joint deterioration, abdominal distension, genital disease, bladder problems, and reproductive issues. The second chakra is a very sensitive and active area of the body representing critical issues that we are invited to resolve in our lives. Water is the element of the second chakra and pleasure is its principal. The second chakra is the home of our sexuality. Once our survival needs are satisfied in the first chakra whose element is earth, our pleasure is considered in the water element of our second chakra. Here we are invited to open up, to connect, to create. There are lots of opportunities for imbalances to be created here as pleasure can seduce us into indulgences that are unhealthy. Thus the second chakra is the home of addictions. Other imbalances include emotional dependency, mood swings, poor boundaries, fear of change, and boredom. The drama of abandonment can be recreated and played out in an attempt to bring forth the original drama that created the imbalance in the first place and thus invites the opportunity to rebalance this chakra by illuminating it into our awareness.

Addiction is a disease of bonding and connection, and perhaps instead of raging a war against addicts, we need to share the happy love meditations and support them in reconnecting with themselves, with their environment and with society. Perhaps we could help them by teaching them about themselves, their gifts and support them in finding their dignity and their pride and their self –love, then their interests in bonding with drugs, alcohol and other bright shiny things may subside. If we provide a safe, loving environment for them to plug into to discover themselves, their gifts and their creativity, to nourish their minds with positive thoughts and the anatomy of optimism and help establish the habit of happiness, their need for substances and other things to bond to may disappear. Practice looking at those struggling with addiction through eyes of compassion, understanding, that their actions are cries from their spirit to connect. I would love to partner with any program out there willing to test this principle.

The Pleasure Path

The truth is, we all want more pleasure; we are hard wired to seek out, to give and to receive pleasure. I am not talking about a short-term distraction, but rather a sustainable sense of healthy long-term fulfillment, joy, and happiness. Reclaiming a sense of wonder about our sensuality our aesthetic sensibility, our sexuality, our pleasure, and the miracles that love allows. By rebalancing and harmonizing our energetic system, we reinforce our internal wiring to support us in finding our inner peace and fulfillment, affording us the possibility of connecting with our partners, with nature, and with society, in a way that establishes a connection, bonding, satisfaction, and a profound sense of peace. When we expand our internal energetic pleasure container, we reinforce ourselves and strengthen our opportunity to experience more joy, feel more pleasure and embody the benefits of a system flooded with the biochemistry of pleasure. When our system is balanced and harmonized, we arrive into a state of coherence, internal harmony, and alignment that allows us to have clarity, wisdom, inner peace, and pleasure. Romantic love is our strongest drive, yet the biochemistry it produces makes it impossible for us to sustain the emotional benefits we receive when we fall in love, as we would be unable to focus on getting our tasks done.

Our bodies build up a tolerance to this chemistry and then, as we all know, the feelings of passionate love lose strength over time. In the lust stage of romantic connection, we release estrogen and testosterone; in the second attraction stage, dopamine and norepinephrine, the pleasure and excitement chemicals drive romantic love. The attachment stage is powered by Oxytocin (which women produce in higher quantities supported by estrogen), creating this bonding chemical and experience, and Vasopressin, which men produce more readily, causing jealousy and the desire to protect the connection, created by attachment and bonding. Excitement and pleasure remain high in Oxytocin bonded couples. There is a natural bonding and connection that occurs in the giving and receiving of pleasure in partnership, more intensely felt and physically enjoyed in sexuality, but present in all forms of touching, at its best, in a fair exchange of energy in a giving and receiving of touch.

We all seek the satisfaction and pleasure experienced in the times of connection, exchange, and bonding. We are actually capable of recreating this inner state independently any time that we choose, finally freeing us from the slavery of our chemistry. The pleasure path and the practices contained in this Toolkit actually teach you how to do this. It is interesting to note here that, when we have gone through emotional pain, loss, and heartbreak we produce more endorphins which actually lead to a lower production of oxytocin, which compromises our ability to bond perpetuating a negative spiral of loss, hurt, rejection, and the emotional pain of isolation. When we raise this biochemical reactivity up to the level of conscious choice, we are finally able to make our own creative decisions about love, pleasure, and partnership.

As a society we can liberate from the male-dominant model of relating, that built its foundation on the lie that women (Eve) are inherently untrustworthy. And we can expand into a model of equality, where both men and women can be trusted to support and empower each other, then we set the stage for a greater experience of pleasure, connection, and love. Breaking free of the battle of the sexes, we allow for the vulnerability necessary to ask for what we truly want and need so that our deepest needs can be met, by ourselves, our partners and ultimately by the constructs of society that we demand. This vulnerability establishes an opportunity for us to connect in the most satisfying ways, bringing about a state of internal peace that supports that external possibility.

We are living in fascinating times, that contain the exact right conditions for us to transform and break free of the structures that no longer serve us nor reflect where we are in our conscious evolution. I am hopeful that we have finally arrived at a place where we may actually allow ourselves to give and receive more pleasure. Understanding that we can take individual responsibility, and exercise our power of choice, to build and strengthen, the internal container we all already possess for pleasure, aliveness, and satisfaction.

This living, energetic container is already established within our bodies, in our nadis, meridians, and chakras, our energetic system. We can develop a deeper, cleaner, more profound connection with this system; then we support each other and society to realize its highest potential for pleasure. All the tools I have provided in this book and in the toolkits support this deeper connection with our energetic system. Yes, our society may still erotize male domination, but there is an awakening to the fact that this model leaves everyone dissatisfied, and not getting their needs met. The art of exchanging pleasure has a spiritual dimension and a pathway to raising consciousness. If we look at early history, we see that the priestesses were often involved in supporting the kings in arriving at wisdom through the art of sacred sexuality, a pathway of igniting and sustaining the experience of pleasure.

There is no longer need to vilify women as the carnal or dangerous temptress, or men as the aggressor, but an opportunity to appreciate the gifts that each partner brings to the table, in an attempt to heal the illusions and misperceptions propagated by a fearful misguided societal model that just does not work. We are all seeking bonds forged through love and trust rather than through fear or force. Dominator sexuality and pleasure is an obstacle to both personal and social health. The time is now ripe for a new relationship paradigm that is rooted in our true essential nature, that is all about getting our needs for connection, love and pleasure met.

Both sex and spirituality have historically been drastically altered during times of chaos, dislocation, and restructuring. The traditional tantric rite of maithuna is to awaken the kundalini, often identified with Shakti energy (the creative power of the goddess.) In these practices the man connects with this divine feminine energy through giving the female sensual and sexual pleasure, helping to sustain the ecstatic experience for both. In fact, its sole purpose through prolonged and exquisite sensation is the spiritual experience of ecstasy, which awakens the chakras and supports the pathway to enlightenment.

Initially, in India, the infinity symbol represents the equality of the male and female through sexual union, leading to wholeness and infinity. In the animal kingdom, it has been discovered that female coalitions are necessary to avoid male dominance and aggression. It is time for us, as women, to come together in sisterhood to support the rising of the feminine, to allow for a new model of relationship based on pleasure, equality, partnership, and cooperation. Human sexuality is a help, not a hindrance, towards our spiritual evolution and the cultivation and right relationship to pleasure can ignite the chakra system as a pathway to enlightenment, along with ensuring the perpetuation of the species.

I am interested in presenting a holistic perspective and approach to pleasure and vitality and health. By learning to connect to the body's energy centers, you learn how to open your inner channel of light and pleasure, by illuminating and removing any and all obstructions of thought and emotion stored in the chakras. These obstacles can dilute or numb down your own sensation, and your connection to your vitality and aliveness. When awakened you can realize your full pleasure potential, achieving a synergistic combination of sexuality and spirituality. The yoga practices provided in the toolkits support you awakening your energy centers in a way that enlivens you. All the breathing practices and the guided meditations help you in arriving into this sensitized relationship with yourself. By using positive memory and imagination to create the emotional frequency that you want to occupy, creates the biochemistry of your choosing. This skill liberates you to know yourself as the creator of your internal state and your behavior, your physical reality and your life.

Science is useful in showing us the effect of these chemicals, but it is within our spiritual awakening, that we discover how to be at cause to these emotions so that we are then free to choose our behaviors. By consciously and consistently, choosing to occupy this state of pleasure, that supports coherence, we demonstrate our emotional mastery, and finally, come to know the truth of our own creative potential. The second chakra is related to our emotional identity. It is essential that we have a strong, clear, and masterful connection to our emotions to identify and digest them efficiently. If our wounds lead us to be overly identified with our feelings, we can be emotionally reactive, and run the risk of becoming emotionally overwhelmed. This reactivity leads us to be ruled by the feelings and not informed by them. This vulnerability, in fact, is a way of avoiding being fully present and digesting and integrating the emotions and therefore creates emotional imbalance or dysfunction. If our wounds lead us to be under-identified with our emotions, then we become disabled because we cannot gather the essential information that our body is consistently seeking to reveal to us. When this chakra is balanced, we open up the internal rivers of feeling, and we allow ourselves to be moved. Passion arises from this stimulation, to stimulate the will and the action of the third chakra. Through this mechanism, we can reclaim any lost inspiration caused by the experience of rejection, loss, and abandonment. This reclamation motivates us towards relationship and partnership, allowing us to pursue and participate in relationships with enthusiasm for all the gifts that it brings. This energy supports the positive, clear mindset that creates a happy experience of relationship.

HEALING THE WOUNDS OF THE SECOND CHAKRA

As we heal and clear and balance and align the second chakra, the healing focuses on creativity, relationships, abundance, sexuality, along with the resolution of abandonment wounds and addictions. When we finally correct the misperception, the core cry that "we are alone" and align with the truth that we are always connected, we can, at last, create the opportunity to have profound and meaningful intimacy in our lives. Firstly with ourselves and then with those we are closest to. This skill allows us the possibility to fully experience love in a clean and clear way that is healing to us, and all those in our lives. The deeper emotional experiences of loss, grief, mourning, and sadness are integrated inside this area, and the intensity of those emotions can be transformed and transmuted into love energy through the understanding of our innate connectedness. When emotionally balanced here, we can feel deeply, express appropriately, and feel satisfied. The second chakra is related to your emotional identity and oriented towards self-gratification. When out of balance we can act in a selfish, self-serving, self- absorbed, an almost narcissistic way that does nothing to resolve the longing for intimacy and feeds the continued experience of disconnection and aloneness. The balance here enables you to successfully identify your emotions and their source, supporting your opportunity to work through them.

We all have abandonment wounds to some degree because we have all gone through separation anxiety as a part of our developmental process. Also, we all went through the original separation from source, a wound sometimes so deep it could take a lifetime integrating the intensity of that trauma. The question is not, has there been trauma here, rather, to what degree have we been traumatized and is the second chakra, your path of healing. Is this the path you have chosen to walk in this lifetime? Assessing and understanding the territory of the second chakra empowers you with the tools to navigate the inner landscape to arrive at a balance. When imbalanced in an excessive direction we will tend to indulge ourselves in our addictions needing constant stimulation, being susceptible to mood swings, having poor boundaries and emotional dependency. When deficient we can be rigid, numb or insensitive, fearing change and lacking desire, we may even fear sexuality and avoid pleasure altogether. When balanced there is the ability to experience pleasure and sexual satisfaction and ability to embrace change. We can have embodied intelligence and healthy passion and a strong, healthy relationship with abundance, actually allowing ourselves to have the goodness and wealth that we create.

KARMIC WOUNDS OF THE SECOND CHAKRA

The core cry of the second chakra is "I don't want to be alone." It may take other flavors, of fear of loss of friendship, or in its unconscious distorted form, leaving others, while you stay with them, through distancing and disconnecting. Leading to a feeling of dissatisfaction with the people that love us and want to connect with us. We may project onto them the ideas of their inadequacy or lack of worthiness, leading to disconnection and possibly ultimately rejection, a perpetuation of the very thing that we do not want. So to avoid the overwhelming pain of rejection, we reject. There is a high possibility in this wounded pattern of rejecting and judging those that want to connect with so that what motivates us is perpetuating the experience of being alone. As ironic as it sounds, the experience of connection is the thing that is most desired and most feared and, therefore most likely to be created. This unhealthy push/pull can take many forms; we can decide that others are not good enough to perpetuate the disconnected feeling, re-grooving the old familiar, uncomfortable feeling preventing us from connecting with the feelings that we crave. We may carve out a more comfortable role for ourselves, of being more desired and project onto the other a need to be more together, more patient, more kind than they may or may not be able to be.

If this is your path, most likely there is karma around being abandoned, betrayed, and outcast. You may have experienced, in past lives, the terror that arises when we experience ourselves to be rejected, abandoned, outcast and completely alone. You most likely had lifetimes in which your partners left you, while you still loved and wanted them. We all probably have had that experience or lifetimes in which we may have upset an entire community and been outcast and left alone in the wilderness. The degree to which they chose to reject you, and send you out into the wilderness or the desert or some remote location to fend for yourself, is the degree to which you may have been wounded. The depth of trauma that you allowed yourself to perceive and experience reflect the level of healing that may be required. Reflecting the amount of energy that is stored and trapped at the root of the chakra, that is waiting for you to meet, and free from its contracted state.

You may have been outcast as an unjust punishment, or it may even have been justified, according to the laws of the community where you lived. How you interpreted these events, with the perceptions that you created can have a significant karmic imprint on your soul and can determine the path of your healing journey and is actually a greater predictor of the depth of the healing required than the actual event itself. Perhaps you had lifetimes in which you were fortunate enough to find true love, only to have that lover ripped away from you because of war or other circumstance. Or your lover may have simply changed their feelings for you in which case the experience of rejection is intensified. All these experiences can have a profound imprint on your soul and carry forward into this lifetime so that we can recreate the same experience to heal and create a new improved and resolved outcome.

In this lifetime there probably exists an underlying fear that you will be alone or an experience that you don't have family close by, or a partner to share your life with, where your journey of evolution is independent and outside of partnership. You may feel isolated and lonely, even in the presence of family and relationship and your isolation may take the form of feeling disconnected emotionally. You may even be aware that you are the co-creator of your own loneliness and your own suffering and not know why or how to heal it. There is most likely a self-protective wall that arises out of the terror of allowing yourself to connect. The fear of becoming dependent upon the presence of someone else can cause you to protect yourself by building a wall (this wall exists in consciousness as a perception, an illusion, or it may exist as a vibration and emotional energy). The wall is intended to protect you, in case you got left again and hurt again, on a level that you are unable to integrate. The sad and eternal truth of walls of protection is that they are destructive, not protective and they lead us into, not away from, the thing that we fear most. We cannot experience real intimacy as long as we are hiding behind walls; we will only continue to have a low-grade experience of feeling alone, disconnected, and abandoned. The only way we can be liberated from this suffering is by dismantling the walls, seeing what they are constructed of regarding thought and emotion, then finally transforming them.

BALANCING AND HEALING THE SECOND CHAKRA

The path of the second chakra is also where our sexual trauma and our financial wounds live. If we have ever been raped or even invaded on a physical, psychic, or emotional level in this lifetime or previous lifetimes, then these wounds exist here. If we have been violated and disrespected, we may have all sorts of ways that these wounds will express themselves in the present life. All these injuries can show up in subtle or overt ways. For example, we may literally feel suffocated or trapped by love relationships that invite us into deeper levels of intimacy and vulnerability, making us believe we need to leave or run away, seducing us into thinking that we are being invaded or suffocated to the point where we will die or lose ourselves. The defenses that we unconsciously construct, as a consequence of sexual or emotional trauma, if left unaddressed can create chaos and reap havoc in our lives and in our relationships. This makes us resistant to trusting and works in conflict with the mechanism of surrender and vulnerability, which are required, for us to merge, to experience deep and satisfying intimacy, which can create the experience of deep intimacy and union that we are seeking that can finally heal this wound.

As we dissolve our boundaries, we have the opportunity to enter into union with our partners, with ourselves, and with divine consciousness; inside this experience, we can finally create new perceptions that are balanced and aligned with the truth that we are safe in our connections. This can, at last, provide us with the opportunity to stay present inside emotional intensity and intimacy providing an experience to balance the past wounds and misperceptions so that we can receive the healing that we need.

When it comes to creating intimacy, there are three spiritual laws that are universal and always work, all the time, with everyone. The first law is to communicate the truth, as we know it, in each moment. Being fully present with ourselves and with our partners with a commitment to express the truth of our internal emotional environment. The second law is vulnerability, to allow all of our walls and all of our defenses to melt and disintegrate so that we can be fully exposed, naked with our partners and ourselves. The third law is confession, to talk openly and freely about our fears and our concerns. When we practice these laws and apply them consciously into our relationships, we will see how deeply we can connect with and love others and ourselves entirely. Obviously, it is easier said than done to melt our walls and allow our vulnerability to show, and the processes I have provided share the technologies of how to do this. Firstly applying this technology to the self and then sharing it with others that we are intimately connected with.

"The essence of yoga is balance, and that means not only balance in our bodies or emotions but balance in our relationship with the world" --Alison Gayle

We all want the experience of connection and intimacy. This is a fundamental basic human need that is necessary, for our physical as well as our emotional, mental, and spiritual health and well-being and happiness. There are lots of unspoken energetic obstacles that prevent us from having what we want. Once we remove these barriers and allow ourselves to step out onto the skinny branches, with courage and trust, then the rewards of connection, intimacy, and love, which we reap, far outweigh the pseudo benefits that exist within the walls of self-protection. It is worth stating here that self-protection has a useful function in that it helps us to manage the intensity of our emotion and the amount of energy that we can allow ourselves to integrate and helps us not be emotionally overwhelmed. Our subconscious often determines what we are capable of letting in and digesting, very often we underestimate ourselves and what we have the capacity to integrate. Whatever we affirm ourselves to have the ability for is what we have the capacity to do.

With the expansion of our consciousness and the healing of our emotional wounds, we expand our capacity for integrating intense energetic and emotional experience, so that we can confidently embrace the choice to let go of our emotional armoring. In fact, the whole mechanism of emotional healing is about reaching back into our history, in a way that allows us to reclaim lost energy from traumatic experiences, so that we have it available to us today to use as creative energy and at the same time enhance our capacity to simply be present. When our second chakra is balanced and aligned, we find ourselves experiencing increased level of intimacy, love, and joy in our lives. Our relationships reflect the internal balance we have achieved, and we have a greater opportunity to spend more time expanded in connection and love when we have healed and cleared our karmic wounds around abundance consciousness.

When we raise our vibration and expand our capacity for energy, we find that we can experience greater abundance in our lives. This abundance will be reflected in many various ways, financially, emotionally, energetically, creatively, and the levels of happiness, joy, and opportunity that show up in our lives will be significantly improved.

ABUNDANCE CONSCIOUSNESS

Money is another important aspect of life. It is related to our survival and a source of power in the world and is, therefore, vulnerable to wounds both from the past of your present life and your past-life experiences. If you want a clue into what may have happened in past-lives around your financial history, you simply have to look at what's going on in the present life. You may want to examine your current financial situation and allow that to expose what your belief system is about money. This will reveal everything that exists in your biography, both your history in this life and past lifetimes. As we know, everything that lives in our biography lives in our biology. If you were exposed to and saturated in a consciousness of scarcity, this limited mindset may be running your financial life and creating less than you want and less than you deserve. Your belief in what you deserve may also be dictating what you can have financially. Your attitudes and your beliefs about money, and abundance are within your sphere of influence, remembering that we create from where our energy is most highly charged. We need to align our subconscious beliefs with our conscious intent and desire so that we can create what we want and manifest what we deserve as long as it is consistent with the karmic path we have chosen. In arriving at a place of true abundance, we also need to attend to our energetic blockages that have no language and exist on the level of vibration. Our struggles, the things we have difficulty with in life, provide us with the necessary clues to find where our energy may be blocked.

Janet's journey of walking the second chakra path of arriving at connection. The lone penguin of the second chakra

Very often my introduction to clients is by intuitive readings; this seems to be the most direct way to gain insight and information about where the growing edges of a person's spirit reside. The first impression I got of Janet when I did the reading was that of a penguin sitting on top of an iceberg. This didn't make sense to me, but as always I shared the image with her, and she said that it made perfect sense to her. In my body, I felt like a concrete block weighing down my lower belly. I knew that we were dealing with a second chakra blockage and I could see the energy gathering as if it was backing up into the third chakra. I knew that energy was unable to descend into the lower second chakra.

One of the ways this could manifest itself would be a lack of energy and difficulty in creating the life she desired. I also felt a deep grief and sadness in the heart area, indicating heartbreak, and so it felt like relationships were probably problematic, and the sadness that existed there felt like it arose out of a loneliness that had been there for a very long time. It was likely that she had never really felt the sense of connection that she desired and we all deserve. It was also likely that there was some distance in her childhood relationships with her parents. Another thing that kept repeating over and over again was the phrase "Unrealized potential."

The cards brought these impressions into clearer focus, and my readings almost always have consistency with my intuitive feelings. When they do, the readings flow with grace and ease, and we can connect previously obscure dots and bring them into clarity. When the cards and the impressions do not match, we have a journey together to explore what information is ready to be seen, heard and worked with.

The Tarot reading

On the top line she had: The Empress over the two of cups and two of swords. The Empress represents the creative female power. The card represents the power of the feminine aspect of creativity, which is receptive and magnetic and manifests by attracting the elements necessary to fulfill one's potential and creative expression. This card encourages the development of the downward flow of energy in the form of manifestation. Representing the feminine principle both internally and externally of the self. The symbol of the Empress is the pregnant female and if there is not a physical child to be born there will be a creative one. It represents the mother principle in all its forms and can indicate issues with mother depending on what cards surround it.

In this case, it comes with the two of swords, which does represent confrontation, so this does indicate unresolved mother issues and is worthy of further investigation. This configuration suggests that the universe wants you to realize the full potency of your power and manifest your unique creative contribution and it will reveal whatever is obstructing that. There may be energetic blockages or illusions and misperceptions that need to be revealed and confronted for it to be transformed. The two of cups is the card of soul mates and usually represents karmic contracts that need to be fulfilled. The two of swords represents conflict or necessary confrontation. This has many layers of meaning, but most importantly it tells me that there are unresolved karmic challenges in relationships and will most likely lead to imbalances in the second chakra the sacred home of relationships.

This said that the universe intended for Janet to realize her creative potential. Very often, the way the world supports growth and potential is by firstly revealing where the obstacles are so they can be removed. This told me that Janet would be on a journey towards her own obstacles so that she could see them to recognize and remove them. The next configuration of cards was the five of pentacles with the seven of cups and the seven of swords. The five of pentacles represents financial difficulty or struggle or loss; the seven of cups indicates a choice that needs to be made and a path that needs to be taken. The seven of swords is an invitation to look at your confidence and self-esteem and presents the call for you to evaluate how your mind may be working against you. Financial difficulty or loss would lead to a choice that would require her confronting her relationship with her confidence. This was not as direct and straightforward as it seemed, as people who have abundance can feel and experience financial difficulty without actually having it. Simply by having their flow slow down, they could experience that as loss. Or it could be reflective of an attitude of scarcity rather than it is an actual reality. It felt to me that for her Empress to be fulfilled she needed to confront her family, especially her mother to reorganize and realize her own financial independence so that she could know herself as independently productive. This in and of itself would boost her self-esteem and confidence so that she could find her own real power.

The second line had Temperance with the three of swords, the eight of swords and the eight of cups, then Strength with the Hierophant and the six of swords. Temperance is about flow, the flow and exchange of information between the head and the heart, between the conscious and unconscious mind between your heart and the heart of another.

This card talks about intimacy and refers to how clear and clean that channel is. The three of swords represents heartbreak, and the eight of swords speaks of the mind being filled with worry fear and doubt, which can lead to a consistent experience of indecision and a mind trap of discomfort. The eight of cups is the card of feeling alone, even when in the company of others or in a relationship. From this, I saw that Janet would benefit from clearing out her mental patterns in relationship to intimacy and love and heartbreak. Whatever the fears and resistances were in this area were ready to be confronted and cleared. Once this had been earnestly handled, she would escape that consistent experience of feeling isolated and alone and be free from the feeling of being a lone penguin.

The next line contained The Devil with the ten of cups and The Sun. The devil can represent the ego, the shadow aspect of consciousness. It is a trickster and manipulative energy, and it can also express sexuality in both its positive and negative aspects. The ten of cups is the card that reflects the feeling and experience of the beloved and the ultimate in partnership and relationship and represents the romantic ideal relationship. The Sun is fulfillment, satisfaction, and happiness; it also talks about marriage. The devil at the beginning of this configuration makes prediction difficult, as it talks about expecting the unexpected and the curve ball, around the whole question of future partnership and marriage. With the Sun at the end of the line, this card talks about a mechanism that is put in place that conspires to support you in arriving at your fulfillment and satisfaction, and it also refers to the possibility of marriage. This mechanism is designed to, first of all, remove whatever obstacles are in place that prevents the possibility of these experiences happening then invite you into that experience. This is a really a powerful configuration because it supports deep transformative work and is a great indicator of success.

Janet's story

When Janet came to me, she was desperately lonely and afraid that she would be alone forever. She felt disconnected, isolated, and adrift, an almost outcast. (This was not something that someone was doing to her; it was rather something she was doing to herself as a consequence of her own thinking and unconscious behavior patterns.) She described herself as feeling like the lone penguin, which explains why my intuitive impression made sense to her. She did not like her life, her work, her home, and her living circumstances. There was nothing about her life, the way that it was, that she liked or felt that she had actually chosen. She felt like she was living a life that had been given to her, rather than a life that she created. This contributed to her feelings of disconnection and isolation. She felt disconnected from her own creative capacity and isolated from her inspiration and the manifestation of that in her everyday environment. From outward appearances, it seemed that she lived a very privileged and idyllic life, a fact that she was perfectly able to see. This reality made her struggle even more challenging because she knew that she should feel more grateful, for the abundance and the gifts that had been bestowed upon her, but in all honesty, the benefits that she received were not the benefits she wanted.

She lived in a beautiful mansion in the best neighborhood, with her three children whom she loved and she enjoyed the role of mother, the nurturer, but still, she felt terribly, terribly lonely. In reality, she was not alone; she was serving what society accepts as a significant role of mother and what she thought was important by participating in a career. None of this was feeding her soul or providing her with that essential sense of connection. She had grown frustrated with the conventional wisdom espoused by her therapist, who encouraged her to recognize all the ways in which she was not alone and in fact deeply involved with her family. She felt that all of those years of therapy now appeared to be of no avail, as she could no longer deny the truth of her emotional interior, she felt alone. Her ex-had moved on to a new relationship, a fact that added fuel to the fire of self-doubt and the conviction that she was somehow fatally flawed and doomed to live without love and partnership for the rest of her life. In her darkest times and most contracted moments, she convinced herself that there was something wrong with her. She did not like the way she looked; she felt that she was in the wrong body, the wrong ethnicity, that her face was pudgy and unattractive and so she felt that she had the wrong face.

To compensate for this, she took extra special care of her body. She worked out like a maniac, and she felt that her body looked 20 years younger than her face. But this did nothing to quiet the internal voices of criticism and perfectionism. She felt trapped inside this perpetual onslaught of insults that she hurled at herself and longed for some peace, some quiet, and for some freedom. When she arrived at my door, her energy was highly disturbed, filled with anxiety and self-doubt, desperate for some relief, some hope that things may actually improve in her life. As we started our work together, I noticed how she vacillated between really wanting help to be possible and doubting that anything would ever work, that she was, in fact, a hopeless case. Quite often, when working with people, one of the first truths to establish is that help is possible, that people really do change and their lives really do improve. A task that I feel well equipped to perform since I have witnessed many examples of this happening. So once this was established, we spent some time excavating her inner dialogue around this question, so that we could rebalance the mind in knowing that the work we would be doing together would be effective and would create positive change in her life. Without this foundation solidly in place in the consciousness, the doubt would continue to erode progress and keep her trapped in the cycle of doubt and the trap of the illusion of disconnection.

She responded to this possibility so well and moved really quickly with this shift that she flew high and far without the illusions and doubts that help wasn't possible until the doubt cycled through again. It is predictable that when you make an advance on your path of awareness and truth, that the thing that is moving and changing will create an experience of the same lesson, more intensified, to offer you the opportunity to demonstrate your commitment to the shift, and to the growth. For her, she traveled for about a month into a cycle of expansion and illumination that was so bright that she felt completely reborn as if seeing herself and her life as new and fresh, almost for the first time. She was a truth seeker and recognized truth when she was brought to it. I was struck by her courage and her commitment to her growth and her wellness; she was so ready and so willing to do whatever was necessary to find truth and be well. She was also very intelligent and had an innate understanding of the work. So when she bumped up against the doubts again, it didn't take her long to figure out what was happening, although she needed a little help navigating through.

"I've crashed again," she said as she sat in front of me. "I feel like I'm drowning, losing hope again, feeling hopeless and helpless. I feel like my lower self is winning and I'm stuck in this hole with no way out. I heard myself saying that nothing will change, I'll be stuck like this, alone, forever and there is not a damn thing that I or you or anyone can do about it." Please remember that these darkest moments contain the greatest opportunities, they reveal the portals, the doorways that we can walk through to get to the breakthroughs. Another interesting fact that she shared with me was that she felt that she had no control over her subconscious, that it was all powerful and that it would have its way and create the life that it wanted her to have and that she would be denied the opportunity to create the life that she wanted.

Janet came to me not long after her divorce and even though she had no regrets about her decision to divorce, she was still not over her ex. She carried him everywhere she went in the form of anger and disappointment with men. Janet was not conscious of her self-protection mechanism, and the emotional walls that she had constructed, but they were easily read by the men that she met and every time she attempted to date and start a new relationship. She was unclear why she was unable to start anything new. She felt that she was ready to love again but was consistently disappointed by her failures with new men. She was seeking guidance around what she could do about this; she felt that something was off balance but didn't know what, and was at a complete loss about how to fix it. The overriding feeling that she had was loneliness, and she felt like an outcast most of the time. She spoke about feeling like she didn't belong or fit in with her community. She talked about losing her motivation towards romantic relationship and shared that she didn't know that she even wanted to date and risk exposing herself to that same disaster that she had already endured. She has lost her inspiration for romance.

When she spoke of her ex, she became easily enraged and lost her otherwise highly evolved conscious persona and regressed to an unrecognizable bitter divorcee. He was an unapologetic alcoholic and had betrayed her at the end of the marriage. His inability to take responsibility for his behavior and lack of commitment to the marriage and to himself proved fatal for the marriage. The relationship ended, and she thought that she would feel relieved, which proved not to be the case. She was deeply conflicted and confused about the way she felt in the separation, as it had thrust her right into the center of her own abandonment wound. Throughout the relationship, she had been dealing with his second chakra wounding, which had prevented her from finding or having to deal with her own wound, as it couldn't be found under the weight of his dysfunction. Now that he had left, she was alone dealing with herself and her wounds for the first time as an adult. She missed the protective veil of confusion he created that prevented her from confronting her own issues.

She repeatedly told me that she felt like the lone penguin out of the movie and her sense of aloneness and abandonment were overwhelming and debilitating in her life. She was unable to pick up the pieces and move on with her life. She was constantly vacillating between apathy and anger and disconnected from her emotional truth. She had come from a privileged background and was fortunate enough to have been provided with a career running the family business, and there was not a shortage of money, yet she never felt wealthy. She was always very concerned about money and lived very carefully and very conservatively. Although there was money, there was also a consciousness of scarcity. She responded to this challenge in her second chakra with excessive energy, she was always anxious and seeking advice and support from others to manage her household budget, she bought books and attended endless workshops about creating wealth. (This reveals the fact that it is possible to have both an excessive and deficient response within the same chakra.)

The way that I helped her manage this situation was to deal with the issue that was presenting as the most challenging and what showed up in my conversation with the subconscious. As we progressed through our sessions, it became clear that she had a very difficult, complicated relationship with her mother. She described her mother as cold, distant, and uncaring and that very early on, she had been responsible for providing the nurturing in this relationship. The anger and resentment that she held towards her mother carried the same vibration as the anger and resentment that she carried towards her ex. It was evident to me that there was a wound in karma that was seeking to heal through both of these relationships but had not found a resolution, and she was suffering greatly by continuously rubbing up against this very raw wound. Each time we approached this issue in these relationships, she became very defensive and insisted that she was right to be angry and outraged as their behavior had been outrageously unfair and they needed to be punished for it, and this was their work to change it. What she was not seeing was how she was punishing herself by carrying that degree of intense hatred towards these two significant people in her life. She was trapping herself inside her desire for her version of justice. She had vacillated between tactics of avoidance and fixation, keeping herself caught in the karmic wheel of suffering, denying herself the opportunity to find happiness, love, and connection that she so desperately wanted, but was clueless about how to attain it. She also missed the perfection of the situation providing the perfect ingredients that she, in fact, needed for her own healing to be possible.

In the beginning, she felt that it was outrageous that I suggest such a thing, but with time and the development of trust, she started to open up and soften to the point of expanding her vision enough to hold that spiritual lens and see the possible karmic contracts that may have existed in their union. I suggested that perhaps his contract with her was to show up exactly as he did to fully expose and live out her fear that she would be abandoned and betrayed. That way the wound could be exposed and could be seen and the work of healing it would become possible.

Intimacy and love are the things that we all need and seek the most, but there exists such vast pain and misunderstanding about it, that it can seem impossible ever truly to find it. There are three spiritual laws about intimacy that work all the time, with everyone, that really help simplify this vastly confusing topic. They are: (as represented by the Temperance card) 1.)Truth. Speak the truth of your internal emotional reality in each of your moments. 2.)Vulnerability. Let your defenses and your walls melt, allowing you to have an open-hearted connection. 3.) Confession. Talk about your fears, your concerns and your resistances to love and connection as they arise.

When you allow everything to be out on the table, being exposed and raw and see the energy and the connection that arises out of those circumstances you understand that the discomfort of revealing it is dwarfed by the health and happiness that arises out of truly connecting. As simple, straightforward and attainable as this may sound, it is in fact, challenging to practice, keeping the heart open when everything in you is telling you must protect, is very difficult indeed. When I shared this information with Janet, she had the typical questions. Isn't it sometimes necessary and wise to protect yourself against someone who is chaotic, alcoholic and making such unwise choices in their life? You don't know him, he is an impossible case, and nothing would have worked to save this relationship. It is much healthier for me to separate from him. What if I'd stayed in that situation I would have become his doormat? I understand this dilemma and know that many people struggle with this issue of drawing the line between where one can grow and learn more about acceptance and unconditional love and where one needs to love the self more and not enable dysfunctional ego based behavior.

The question of how to strike this balance gets more complicated when we consider karmic contracts and the importance of us demonstrating wise moral choices, which contributes to our liberation from the karmic wheel. I talk more about this in the chapter about choosing love in the guiding principles. Suffice it to say that, when ending a relationship it is healthier to leave the situation with an open and loving heart, than inside the contraction of self-protection, because that would simply thrust you into a continued experience of your wound, the very thing that the situation was designed to liberate you from. When you relax and trust that this situation is not intended to make you stay in a relationship that is dysfunctional nor is it designed to enable someone else's poor choices, it is designed to liberate you from the karmic wheel of suffering by repeating a karmic wound. Simple wisdom usually works best inside complex situations, so it is important to love yourself unconditionally first. When I say designed, I mean brilliantly co-created by your higher self and the highest power of the universe.

When we started to work on Janet's internal dialogue, it was evident to me that we needed to get more energy to that second chakra, that she would probably be quiet numb and disconnected in this area because she was dealing with a deficiency in this chakra. I felt that I already had a good understanding of what the subconscious dialogue would be. There had been many clues left in her communication about her beliefs and her thoughts, and, as always I felt that it was better to get it from the horse's mouth as this leaves her in no doubt about from where and what she is creating her reality. It is a valuable practice to listen carefully to people talking about their challenges, as they will reveal themselves quite consistently.in their communication, the thoughts, and ideas that are running them and what they actually believe.

Very often when I start talking to the subconscious, we open a portal, a doorway, into the emotional body and we get presented with an excellent opportunity to clear through a blockage. That blockage may have been sitting there for many lifetimes, just waiting to be met, digested, and integrated by using presence, breath, and love. I entered into the process, as I always did, with a commitment from her that she would answer the questions as quickly as possible, that she would not say I don't know and that she would maintain her focus inward and notice what was happening in her body inside her chakra system as we progressed.

"The thing that isn't working in my life is

Me.

I don't have what I want.

I cannot create it.

I don't know how.

Nobody taught me.

Nobody was there for me."

At this point I encouraged Janet to bring her awareness and scan through her body, focusing on her torso where the chakras reside and let me know what's happening inside. She took a moment and reported that she felt nothing. This did not surprise me as I suspected that her second chakra had a deficiency of pranic flow, a lack of energy. So I guided her into the 4/2 breathing technique to support the flow of energy in the second chakra. We breathed together a deep enthusiastic inhale for a count of 4, and a soft surrendered exhale for a count of 2. Once she found her rhythm, I shared some affirmations to start to chip away her karmic lump that resided here.

"You have the right and the ability to create the life that you choose." The truth is you are always connected and supported in having what you want. "You are the creative force in your life." After a few minutes, I asked her to scan her awareness through her body and let me know how she feels. "Lighter," she said. "More peaceful." I then continued with the questions.

The reason nobody was there for you is?

My relationships are weak

I don't have any control over what happens

I didn't get the outcome I wanted

My husband left me

Because things didn't work out

I suppose I am meant to be alone

We arrived at the core cry of the second chakra, a fear of being alone. The reason I went through the breathing process with Janet was to bring more energy and more awareness to her second chakra and allow her body to create a memory or a remembering of how to support her second chakra in coming back to balance. I then encouraged her to do this practice every morning for the next month. I encouraged her to use the affirmations I shared with her and to include the affirmation "You are always connected to the highest power in the universe, to your higher power and to all those you are in relationship with."

I encouraged Janet to take a moment every morning to remember a time (or if you can't remember a time just imagine a time) that you felt connected to someone that you loved. Recollect that feeling in your body now so that you can re-experience it, if it is easier to recall a feeling of being connected to yourself, then feel that, and feel how that feels. Allow all your cells to be bathed and soaked in that energetic vibration. Allow your body to become very familiar with how that feels so that you can bring that feeling back into your conscious awareness any time that you choose to.

This practice allowed her to have the experience, the feeling, and the opportunity for her cells to soak inside the energetic vibration of feeing connected. To feel what it actually feels like in the body, to be connected to yourself, to know yourself in a way that is truly intimate and connected, to be interested in what is going on inside yourself. I knew that I needed to give Janet lots of encouragement to stay present and connected to herself as I felt that this was truly the gift that would set her free. The greatest disconnection that she felt was her disconnection from herself, so her solution lay in reconnecting on this level, so that she could know the truth of who she truly was, and the capacity that she had. She was skilled and attuned in noticing the moment the contraction started to diffuse and in that moment she visualized something that she loved and felt that feeling. She invited that vibration of love to emanate from the center of her chest and move in circles like ripples on a pond, bathing and soaking all her cells in this healing frequency.

The tone of my sessions with her was rooted in this encouragement. We must fully feel all our emotions, or the alternative is to remain unconscious and disinterested in understanding yourself and your own demons. You can blame others, lose interest, disconnect, put work first, and have varying degrees of sleep walking as ways to escape. These are all great tools to keep yourself trapped in the misery of your own self - destructive patterns, that of course were originally created to help you survive, but the outdated machine of survival is now the very thing that creates your destruction. It becomes the thing that works against your possibility of being fully alive, of fully feeling, fully loving, fully being loved and of realizing your own potential. Nourishing the subconscious mind with these emotional vibrations provides the necessary support, by allowing the consciousness to find its way back to the truth in the darkest moments. It doesn't mean there will be no more difficulty, no more challenges, no more doubts. It only means there is a choice, a chance, to waste less time in this territory, an option to recognize what you are in, a choice to put your mental energy in a different direction that supports you in remembering the truth of your essential nature. Reinforcing the truth of your capacity and your power of choice, to know that you are not helpless, you are in fact, powerful, that it is not hopeless, that hope is everywhere when you choose to trust and have that faith.

For Janet, this follows up script started with.

"You are the master of your life; you choose the thoughts that create the reality that you want. You are powerful and capable of navigating through anything. You see all your challenges as opportunities to demonstrate your strength, your clarity. Your light is always victorious, always available, always with you. Your higher self stays connected to the light and consistently brings you to the truth of your ability and your capacity."

This is just a brief example of how to deal with doubt and allow for the possibility of help and change and growth. For Janet, it was necessary to clear this before we went into the territory of the abandonment wound. After working on this for a while, she started to enjoy witnessing this mechanism play out in her life really, each time she experienced periods of illumination and clarity they were followed by seductions back into the doubt. The universe seemed to consistently up the ante. Something would happen like her son got caught smoking marijuana at school, and she would watch her mind unravel into the familiar, old contortions of how wrong she had been in raising him, how she never got anything right and how stupid she was to think everything was going to be okay. Everything was not okay, her son was a drug addict, and he'd probably end up in jail, and she had raised a criminal. Her internalized disapproving mother would raise her ugly head and rant on about her short - comings, just as she had in childhood. (We helped Janet release from her mother's projections once she understood the root of her mother's pain and unhappiness, which helped Janet feel empathy for her and realize that her mother's opinion was not accurate or true but a distorted projection.) She was useless, he was useless, it was all just hopeless, and what was the point of it all anyway, bad things happen then worse things happen, then you die alone with nothing."

The benefit of noticing the workings and the patterns of her mind allowed her some space; a gap, a moment to question is this all-true? Is my mind helping me deal with my life right now? The most powerful question we can ask ourselves is whether or not our behavior, our thoughts, our actions are serving our higher intentions and purposes for ourselves. What can I think and do that will help me realize that? I could put on my mp3 that will help remind me of truth. Also, that was enough to start the whole turnaround in her life. So doubt about things improving and help to be possible was what stood between Janet and her path truly opening up for her.

Her personal script proceeded like this

Janet's script

"You are exactly where you need to be, you are in the right body, with the beautiful right face, and in the right family for you to have the life that

you have. Everything is in divine right order. You are loved, valued, and cherished for exactly who you are. The truth is you are always connected to your higher self, the highest power of the universe and everyone that you are in relationship with. You can continue to create connections with the people that you choose and those connections will endure beyond this body and this life." You are a powerful creator, and you deserve to have the life that you want, now. You are now creating the life that you want. You have the knowledge, the tools, and the ability to create your life the way that you want it, now. You are always connected to all the things, opportunities, and people that you want and need to support you in having the life that you want. You now choose to focus on that and be grateful for all the blessings in your life. You are now able to recognize all the times you were supported, and helped by the people who were there for you. Individuals who support you, love you and are committed to staying with you now surround you. Your relationships are strong with healthy agreements that are kept. You choose to do all the things necessary to keep your relationships healthy. You are in charge of all the creations in your life, you are in the driver seat of your life, and you easily and effortlessly navigate your life towards the outcome that you want. You understand the mechanism of manifestation and the benefit of surrendering after you have firmly cast your vote in the direction of what you want. You allow there to be space for the universe to have its vote if there is something better than you can imagine while you confidently stand in you desire. You are now connected with everything and everyone around you. You trust in the abundance of the universe. You are blessed with a never-ending supply of everything that you need. You honor everyone in your life and trust that their presence is in your highest good. You now choose to bless everyone in your life. All of your relationships are loving and harmonious filled with love, respect, and honor. You are the creative power in your world. You now celebrate your own creative ideas and express your unique gifts and contribution. You allow all of your desires and appetites to be perfectly balanced and aligned."

Janet has had fibroid cysts in her uterus, and one had grown the size of a grapefruit, which caused her to have painful periods and pain during sex. This, along with her pattern, made her unconsciously reject men and their interest in her. The irony of this is obvious—her greatest fear is being alone, and here she is a physical condition that supports her choice to reject the thing she wants the most. Connection, love, and intimacy have the highest value to her (the thing that we all want the most, yet seem to have the most difficulty finding). Janet has now taken ownership of her wound and gained the clarity to free herself from her cycles and the patterns they create in her life.

Most notably she has stopped rejecting and finding fault with the men that wanted to love her. This shift came with its challenges because her wound kept her inside the question of whether or not the person, who was loving her, was the right person for her. When she was able to recognize this as an aspect of the pseudo protective pattern, she developed over time, the ability to discern the difference between the voices that arose from her intuitive communications and her fear-based rantings. The key to this resides in attending to and developing a clear communication with the body. Fear has the tone of negativity and limitation and is soaked in what is not possible and what can't be done. Intuitive communication contains openings, possibility, and optimism. She clearly sees how she has the power to liberate herself from her stinking thinking. Now when the shadows descend, and her thoughts get seduced down into their old trenches, she is awake enough to recognize it and take the action steps to pull herself out of it. With the help and support of her meditations and her yoga practice, she is armed with the tools to support her continued success. It is a continuous, ongoing work in consciousness, to stay clear and awake enough to overcome those shadows but with the awareness and the tools, it is possible to overcome the fear and transform it.

This wound of disconnection is often the prime reason why we participate in addictions. The yogis believe that the reason that we all crave sugar is that of the first experience of connection we remember. Feeding at the breast of the mother and receiving the sweet taste of the milk creates an unconscious association with a sweetness of taste and the experience of closeness. Janet had a secret sugar addiction that had caused her many challenges with maintaining her great body. She was currently winning her battle with the bulge, but her diet was high in sugar. She had a habit when she was stressed to indulge in unconscious eating, usually reaching for the sugar. Addictions give you something to focus on and connect to, rather than dealing with all the problems and difficulties of your life; they keep you from having your heart broken by heart breaking events. We attempt to protect ourselves by running away into numbness into addictions and sugar comas. For us to begin to deal with and heal our addictive patterns, the running has to stop; it needs to be recognized for what it is, a destructive choice. The running, if we are successful, will slowly disconnect us from ourselves and eventually everyone else. It will give us permission not to confront and look at what we are most afraid of. It will keep us locked into the numbness of pseudo comfort, pseudo security, and safety, long enough for us to miss out on actually living our lives and having our relationships, our friends, our families, and our greatest experiences, even ourselves.

The things we are avoiding are the very things that actually support us in living a full, beautiful and authentic life. Avoiding vulnerability, avoiding the risk required to care for someone, to embrace the possibility of loss, allows us the opportunity to have what we value most, intimacy, love, connection, ourselves. Just imagine for a moment what your life would be like if you allowed for or even fully participated in the experience of heartbreak. These are the questions I raised and the invitations I presented to Janet, and she slowly gathered the courage to look at the areas I was inviting her to explore. Of course, it took time, and we moved in gradient steps to get there, but when you do, you discover the truth of your capacity. I realize that it's asking a lot to go against conventional wisdom, which steers us towards pleasure and instead move you towards the gifts that reside in sitting in right relationship with your pain. But when we do, we learn that we are strong, we really can abide with anything, and we really can endure suffering, pain, loss and broken hearts, and actually, grow and improve our character through the experience. It opens the space for us to be loving and close and connected, first of all with ourselves and then with others. When we know this without any doubt, and we choose to face our demons, we actually are given access to peace and to happiness.

Asking you not to escape, to stop running away and break free of the comforts you have so carefully constructed, seems insane and it seems even more crazy to ask you to actually invite discomfort, confrontation, heartbreak, to cultivate an attitude of gratitude towards the very thing we want less of. But this is the very portal, the doorway through which you can walk to actually liberate from the inevitable limitations that arise out of a life lived in the avoidance of experiencing pain and arrive at the fully matured experience of fulfillment and connection. The truth is that you can gather strength in thickening your skin. You have already survived the greatest loss and heartache and pain of your life. The truth is your future is easier than your past, and as you cultivate the courage and fortify yourself so that you can endure and navigate through anything, you will discover how it feels to be free, to be alive, to love. We can even be unconscious of the fact that we are avoiding pain, we may try to convince ourselves and others that our addictions do not prevent us from feeling anything. We may convince even ourselves that when we participate in our substances, whatever it is, we are feeling everything. We try to convince ourselves that we are not altered enough to escape the reality of any emotion, that we become more creative, that we are supported in connecting even more deeply with our spirit. I've heard this idea many times, but when it's honestly examined, and we explore why we are participating in this choice, we discover that at its original root it was about wanting to feel something different from the feeling state we were experiencing. We may be wanting to connect more deeply with our spirit and to take this substance may give us a similar enough experience of spiritual connection for us to confuse it. Genuine spiritual connection requires a high level of mental awareness that any mind-altering substance would work against not enhance. The resistance to pain can be subtle and hidden, creating confusion around our motivation towards choosing a substance. Clients have innocently expressed an association with a substance that reveals the subconscious urge towards it. I've heard people say things like, at least I know that glass of wine or hit of pot or slice of chocolate cake will always be there for me, my constant companion, confirming that everything is okay; I am not alone.

Overcoming the illusion that a painful event or experience can destroy you, by remembering that this concern may be hidden in the depths of the unconscious mind, allows you to learn that moving towards and embracing your pain can only support you. In strengthening the truth of your capacity to endure, you are starting the journey back to yourself and your power, your own potential. If we really look at life these things are obvious. There are clues everywhere, written in every spiritual text, hidden in proverbs and popular sayings, sprinkled into traditional wisdom. One of my favorite poets Jennifer Wellwood invites us in one of her poems to really look at what is right in front of us that we may be pretending not to notice, but still we pretend not to notice, we pretend not to see what is right in front of our eyes. She goes on to say, so let's stop pretending not to notice what is obvious and acting like life has betrayed some secret promise when we suffer loss and heartbreak. Impermanence is life's only promise, let's choose to wake up to the truth that everything that can be lost will be lost. Let's look at it, let's confront it head on and accept the true nature of things. You will lose everything. You will get old; you will become sick. You will die! Everything that can be lost will be lost; this is the natural cycle of birth, life, and death. This circle of life once fully accepted by us can bring us peace and freedom.

We don't have a choice about this, but we do have a choice about how we deal with it. We do get to choose how we manage and respond to our losses. Some people die slow, excruciating deaths losing a little of themselves every day to their past, to their pain, to their fear, to their self-protection; don't let that happen to you! Let's look at it, let's get used to it, let's actually embrace it and see the exquisite beauty that resides in the center of it. The gift at the heart of this harsh and painful reality is awe. The awe that arises out of knowing that each of our moments is precious and fleeting, that each moment is unique and alive and ripe with possibility. It is because they are fleeting and unrepeatable that they have such high value. What would your life be like if you could say yes to this truth of impermanence and live inside that conscious container at all times, how would you show up, how would you treat others? So we need to choose to fully participate with all of whom we are to live this wild, beautiful life with abandon, without walls and protection and fear and resistance. Let's stand in our great big yes to life, by meeting life on its own terms.

Don't die before you die. Don't leave love before it leaves you because you want the outcome to be different, something else, something that it cannot be. Stop trying to negotiate a safe passage for yourself; there isn't any such thing, there is no avoiding it. We could choose to enjoy it and embrace it anyway. I invite you to consider what your life would be like if you lived it that way? I encourage you to embrace your life, to see yourself in your own magnificence and love with all your heart, to go for it, your life is waiting. Very often it is the fear of the intensity of our own (and others) emotions that keep us trapped. It may be time, and it may be wise to consider the alternatives to avoidance, since the cost of avoidance is a little too high, since it leads to aloneness. The truth about feelings is that they are straightforward and understandable, they want to be felt, understood and given the opportunity to tell their story. When we choose to relate to our feelings, we do not need to relate from them. All any feeling wants is to be met with tenderness, an attitude of compassion and kindness so that it can be given permission to dissolve. The presence practice guides you through this understanding and allows you to elevate the idea of loving the self into an act, a practice.

When you don't leave yourself, you discover that actually feeling pain is far less painful than avoiding it. Participating in your broken heart becomes a fascinating journey of discovery. Growing on the spiritual path requires actually choosing to do things differently. It requires deciding that you, not your mind, not your emotions, not your body, but you, the you of you, call it the soul or the spirit or the witness, the you of you is in charge and driving this ship. Choosing to do things differently, wanting to play a new game, choosing to be free. It requires a commitment to being curious about the never-ending discovery of you. When you free yourself from your habitual ways of being, your patterns, you discover that anything is possible even surviving heartbreak, cancer, the loss of a loved one, and yes even the experience of being alone.

Intimacy is such a huge aspect of second chakra wounding and for Janet intimacy had always been a great container for her spiritual growth. She was conscious enough to understand the importance of participating with an open heart but was frustrated by her limited capacity for this. An aspect of this difficulty resides in the issue of responsibility, choosing to take full responsibility for your own happiness is a place of freedom. It is a common habit to avoid responsibility in life, and this habit causes endless problems in relationships. We tend to project the responsibility for our happiness onto our partners rather than working with the exposed disappointments as an opportunity for growth. During our time working together Janet became aware enough to know that for her to get the spiritual growth that was possible in a relationship, certain ingredients were necessary to create the correct cauldron for growth. She knew that the heart needed to be engaged enough for the outcome to be important; there needed to be a vulnerability and a willingness to be forthright with excellent communication and intelligence and vision to spot the patterns. By seeing the shadows, naming and exposing them so that each partner could support the other in understanding how to be free from that place of pain and confinement.

Helping free your partner from their demons can become dangerous territory because a pervasive issue in relationships is the guilt game. Unconscious habitual ways that we make each other wrong or guilty is a game that limits both people to reacting out of their lower selves and remaining inside their walls. Very often the communication can happen silently; we can subtly blame the other person for our own unhappiness and absolve ourselves from having to look at ourselves and take responsibility for what we are bringing into the dynamic. The only way to avoid being a victim of this guilt is to stop doing it to yourself, to become so awake and clear about the many ways that you participate in this habit, will actually provide the space for you to be free. The challenge here resides in the fact that most of this communication is non-verbal and subtle. It is felt and understood to be destructive, but for it to become constructive it requires exposure through precise identification that is articulated. If your relationship is to blossom, you must be vigilant for these destructive communications and work together, supporting each other in eliminating them. The thing to look out for here is the subtle blame that is projected onto the other for your unhappiness. As I mentioned, the solution lies in raising your awareness around how you do this to others, by you undefensively exploring and accepting your own problematic behaviors. Recognizing that doubt, uncertainty, and cowardice invite you to the limited reactions of withdrawal or aggressiveness, will free you from the confusion of self-assertion and aggression and navigate you towards clarifying the distinction between healthy compromise and unhealthy submission.

Sharpening these skills will determine the levels of love and closeness you can enjoy in your relationships. Confronting and resolving the problems of human interaction hold the key to the levels of connectedness you can experience in your relationships. Working with the relationship as a mirror allows you the opportunity to continually choose to bring it home, bring the hurt, the resentment, the blame, home to look at yourself, with honesty. I recommend you be accountable and responsible for what you are doing, what you are causing the other to experience and make the corrections there, rather than think about what the other is doing wrong or causing you to experience. Eventually, Janet arrived at a healthy enough place to engage her partner's support in helping her confront her issues.

I felt strongly that the first obstacle we needed to overcome was the ways in which Janet was abandoning herself. She was vacating her body energetically each time she met the stress of feeling alone. As a consequence of repeatedly using a well-worn coping mechanism of avoidance of stress or trauma, in the fight/flight response, Janet had evolved the habit of energetically abandoning herself, which ironically became a self-fulfilling prophecy of the thing she feared the most, and the thing she was attracting to herself. The experience of feeling abandoned. She unconsciously contributed to the problem mentally, by disempowering herself by telling herself that she has no power over her subconscious and that she was unable to create the life that she wanted. That is why the first affirmation that I gave her to work with was "You have the right and the ability to create the life that you choose." It was important to get her grounded in this truth and grove this into her nervous system, her brain, and her second chakra. It was necessary to support the downward flow of her energy so that she could manifest the life that she wanted rather than repeatedly manifesting the thing that she was most afraid of. She has made the greatest progress in recognizing her patterns in how she rejects others. She thought that she was being wise by having high standards for herself and her potential partners. She never saw how destructive she was being by rejecting every possible mate by focusing on their inevitable flaws, their humanness and making that occupy her thinking. She is now happily engaged to a wonderful man who loves and accepts her for who she is.

Janet has solidified her growth with a yoga practice that I designed for her to overcome the core cry of the second chakra "I am alone." The subconscious mind responds best to commands that are specific and directly addressing the opposite positive ideas and beliefs of the patterns. There are generic meditations available to you through this program or I can work with you directly, or you can use the instructions in the earlier chapters to transform your specific trenches in your brain and resolve your habitual patterns.

Janet is now in a happy, close, connected relationship. She is not yet remarried, but it could happen any day. She has since left her parents' company and with the help and encouragement of her fiancé, is building her own property development company and starting to write children's books. It is common after working through emotional blockages to express the reclaimed energy through a creative project, as life force lies trapped inside those emotionally frozen places, this life force then becomes available to be used as literal energy and expressed in creative projects and in the enjoyment of life's pleasures.

The breath work practices are key to reclaiming this life force and converting this trapped energy into creative potential. When we breathe adequately, we support our nervous system to function optimally. The brain and the spinal cord (which is an extension of the brain) and the nerves themselves are allowed to be their most efficient and effective instruments for generating the nerve currents when the blood is oxygenated by sufficient breath. Oxygen is the essential ingredient in the production of cellular chemical energy. It is through the oxygenation and charging of the nerve currents that we receive life force, chi, energy. When you include these yoga practices, you accelerate your healing and rebalance the second chakra. I recommend that you read the yoga and affirmation instruction into a tape recorder and listen to them as you relax into the pose. If you prefer to be guided through the practices, you can work with the videos that are available to you via my website www.thehabitofhappiness.org

Relationships and abundance

These two areas are such hot topics that consume so much of my practice that they each deserve their own separate handling and toolkits. They are both equally charged with so much wounding, so much hurt and devastation on their own and most often together. I have discovered that both experiences often come together in an avalanche of difficulty and are often linked both in cause and consequence. I will handle them separately here with a full awareness of their frequent connection and influence upon each other.

Relationships

What I know for sure, is that the way you think about relationships and about your ability to have a great one creates the experience you have in relationships. They are the greatest containers for spiritual growth and are, therefore, highly charged with energy that can be experienced either positively or negatively. The number one need that we all share is the need for connection. More than we need money we need intimacy, to be seen for who we really are, to be understood and accepted and embraced with all of our flaws exposed. The drive for a relationship is hardwired in us, yet sharing our lives can be difficult, challenging and messy, yet the drive to merge ourselves with another doesn't diminish in the face of rejection, heartbreak, and betrayal, we still gravitate to others for love, support and acceptance. In its greatest simplicity, there are three spiritual laws of intimacy, which when followed always work, all the time, with everyone no matter what the circumstances are. These laws are worth repeating as they are so essential to our experience of well-being and happiness in our lives.

1)   Speak your truth, be willing to express your emotional truth in each moment.

2)   Vulnerability, allow your walls of protection around your heart to melt, so there is a clear open space between your heart and someone else's heart.

3)   Confession, have a willingness to share your worries, fears, and doubts with those you are intimate with.

The thing that most often keeps us out of deep intimate connection with others is a deep - seated fear that we are unworthy of it. Falling deeply in love with the self is a great place to start understanding how to fall deeply in love with another, and at its root, that is what my Presence Practice is about. Showing you how to actually raise your emotional vibration to love or above, so that you know that you can create it any time that you choose, which is the key to generating progress along the path of establishing a deep connection with others. When you expand into the certainty that what makes you vulnerable makes you beautiful, you will find yourself interested in connecting in a deeply vulnerable and exposed way with others.

Top ten techniques for the Orange path.

1.)   State of relaxed wakefulness, (PRESENCE PRACTICE MP3) A.) Notice for yourself, with curious investigation, all your physical sensations B.) Feel all of your feelings, emotions, energy in motion, C.) Notice the monkey mind, let go of thinking so that you can connect to the witness aspect of consciousness

2.)   Breath

3.)   Awareness

4.)   Compassion

5.)   Visualizations

6.)   Positive memory

7.)   Raised emotional frequency

8.)   Skillful questions

9.)   Affirmations

10.) Behavior changes after nourishment and practice

2.) *BREATHING FOR 2ND* INHALE THE BREATH THROUGH THE OPEN MOUTH Suspend the breath with the glottis open inviting the breath down the central channel until it arrives in the belly gently squeezing the muscles of the abdomen and inviting the prana, the energy to arrive in the sacrum. As you exhale you release the contraction of the abdomen and you invite the breath to rise up the central channel of the body and rest in the area of the heart.

5.) **VISUALIZATION** Visualizing here a beautiful orange wheel of light moving like a fan in a clock wise direction this light allows all illusion and all misperception to be illuminated and brought up to consciousness.

6.) POSITIVE MEMORY AND 7.) RAISED EMOTIONAL FREQUENCY As you recall now a memory of a time when you felt connected to all things when you felt your creativity flowing, and you were easily expressing yourself.

The second chakra yoga practice is available in a pdf file you get via email at lifeguides@att.net You can also see the yoga practice on the You Tube video, or it is included in the 2nd chakra toolkit.

THIRD CHAKRA

The yellow path of activating
self-love and Power.

Alchemizing anxiety into peace

Third Chakra

Affirmations to support the transformation of consciousness
(self-esteem, personal power, personal will.)

1.) You are perfectly loved and lovable just as you are right here and right now. You now choose to extend compassion and kindness to yourself. Always choosing self-forgiveness, self-assurance, and self-support.

2.) You graciously accept and activate the full potency of your power, which has pure motivation to love and to serve.

3.) You are now willing to see your own magnificence; you are unique and valuable and important. You have the power to express your own uniqueness and value through all of your thoughts and all of your actions.

4.) You deserve to be loved. You now choose to love and approve of yourself by demonstrating perfect mastery in your life. You are powerful, valuable, and loved.

5.) You trust your inner voice. You are strong, wise and powerful. You now honor yourself with all of your thoughts and all your actions. You are kind and compassionate with yourself with all your thoughts and attitudes about yourself

Emotionally alchemizing anxiety and self - loathing.
Into equanimity and self - love.

Transforming the vulnerabilities of the
3ʳᵈ chakra into your strengths

Physically associated with Abdomen and stomach, upper intestines, liver, gall bladder, pancreas, adrenal glands, spleen, middle spine, solar plexus

Vulnerability. Arthritis, acute indigestion, gastric or duodenal ulcer, upper colon problems, pancreatitis, diabetes, anorexia, bulimia, hepatitis, adrenal dysfunction.

Mental vulnerability, When stressed or challenged the inner dialogue tone is "I am not worthy" "I am not enough" "I am not good enough" "I am powerless/helpless. I can't change or control anything anyway" "It's useless/hopeless."

Strengthens into the opposite positive form of "You are enough as you are, right here, right now" "You are perfectly loved and lovable just as you are."

"You are powerful and strong and capable of creating whatever you want in your life." **Emotional Vulnerability,** When stressed or challenged the tendency of the mood level is anxiety, over excitability, stress.

Strengthens, when met with awareness, breath, and compassion.. into

Internal peace, and equanimity.

Feeling balanced.

Calmness, feeling at ease

Relaxed

Spiritually this path invites you to walk through the disturbed states of anxiety and over excitement, by using all the tools provided here, so that it can transform into an inner reality that is calm, peaceful and relaxed. By being introduced to experiences that can seduce you into believing your own powerlessness, so that you can discover the truth of your own power and expand into your true balanced expression of positive power, that is creative, strong and potent.

Location and function

The third chakra is located in the solar plexus area, approximately three or four inches above the navel. It rules the stomach and digestion. The liver, the pancreas, and the gall bladder also reside in the territory of the third chakra. Energy, metabolism, and strength are related to this chakra when imbalanced here we become vulnerable to physical disturbances such as indigestion, hypoglycemia, diabetes, liver problems, and energy problems. It is essential to understand the flow of our energy, knowing what feeds and what depletes us and what empowers us with the ability to make conscious choices that literally empower us. We are empowered physically by the regeneration of our energy, choosing the thoughts, emotions, and behaviors that give us juice (actual physical energy.)

What depletes us is negativity and lower emotional states. The impact that these imbalances (in the third chakra) have on us, psychologically range from being either overly controlling, on one extreme or too passive, on the other.

When imbalanced here we may be stubborn or lack confidence, we may be overly ambitious or lack ambition entirely. Anxiety and panic disorders are associated with imbalances in this area. Now that your body is grounded in its foundation of the earth in the first chakra, and moved by the water element of emotions in the second chakra the energy is invited to move up the body into the third chakra. Here the element of fire allows fuel and energy to be created with the potential to become the power that can recharge your energetic batteries and truly rejuvenate your body and mind to leave you feeling inspired, refreshed, centered, and peaceful. The crux of the third chakra is will, that elusive quality that transforms random events into the desired outcome. It is important to know and understand what people, choices, events, and circumstances contribute to and enhance our energy and, therefore our power source, and what depletes it. On the emotional level, we have the opportunity to transmute the frequency of anxiety and self-loathing into equanimity and self-love. Understanding how to navigate this journey is the rebalancing and mastery of this chakra.

Power vs. Force

The ego is related to the third chakra. We need a healthy ego identity so that we can discern which of our intentions are to be given energy to be made manifest. It is important to have a healthy ego, meaning a strong sense of identity and self-worth, so that we can define our goals and stick to them. It is also important that we value ourselves enough to allow ourselves to be the first priority. When we first get exposed to the idea that we need to make ourselves the number one priority in our lives we may feel selfish, self- indulgent or even self-absorbed, but in fact, it supports everyone around us for us to have this focus on ourselves so that we can expand in our personal responsibility.

Perhaps the greatest invitation and challenge that exists in healing the third chakra lies in our ability and capacity to achieve the balance that is required to maintain a sense of high self-esteem while remaining concerned, connected, loving and compassionate towards others. We hear all the time that we need to love ourselves, but what exactly does that mean and where do we begin to learn how to do that? This skill may not be as complicated as you think it is, and I have broken this down into a practice that I am making available to you free because I believe that mastering this practice is an essential foundation for our future health and well – being and happiness. It is the cornerstone of what invites the body back to balance, and it is the access point to working with the subtle energy body. All you need to do is go to my website at www.thehabitofhappiness.org, and you can download the Presence practice, for free. The Presence practice is the first and most essential step to transforming your life, and from here anything is possible for you. As I have mentioned my mission is to provide you with the experience of transformation by providing you with the tools and practices that facilitate this

We all want love in our lives, to fully love and be loved and accepted and embraced by our loved ones. This achievement can become the most significant experience in the world to us. The path of the third chakra is all about understanding our own true worth and allowing ourselves to fully love and accept who we are and not look for that outside of ourselves. Very often we seek power and approval from an external source. An unfortunate consequence to this can be to become dependent upon the love and approval of others for our feeling of self-worth, which leaves us vulnerable to our sense of worthiness emanating from a source that is truly outside of our sphere of influence. Often people spend their entire lifetime attempting to gain the approval of their partner, mother, father, sibling, friend, who may unintentionally or intentionally withhold it, (perhaps to maintain some pseudo sense of power.) This withholding could, if we allow it, leave us feeling disappointed, rejected and hurt, potentially exhausting us in a never ending extension of effort that may never be adequately reciprocated or rewarded, which can eventually deplete us of our own energy and our own power. So, how then, do we liberate ourselves from such a destructive cycle, how do we begin to heal our third chakra wounds?

We go through the three steps to transforming consciousness. We connect to our courage so that we can heal our emotional obstacles and blockages. We do this by fully feeling our feelings on the level of physical sensation until there is nothing left to feel. We bring our awareness our breath and our compassion to our hurt and wounded emotions. The truth is we are already perfect, whole and complete and we are already worthy. We may not know this and be waiting for someone to grant us that sense of worthiness, however only we, ourselves, can truly make this choice, therefore, let's utilize the spiritual technology that is capable of granting that to ourselves now.

Wounds of third chakra and the karmic past

The language of a wounded third chakra sounds like:

I always felt that I'm just not good enough.

Or I don't deserve to have….

Or I'm obviously not worthy of you,

or in its loudest voice, I'm insignificant and worthless.

Also, language of powerlessness arises from the wounds of the third chakra. "I can't do anything about this." Or "you're just going to do whatever you want to do so; therefore, my effort is worthless." Forgetting about or diminishing any influence that we may have on our circumstances and any positive influences towards others. One of the gifts of the third chakra is regaining your creative potential, your ability to assert your will in relationship with the universe, to be a co- creative participant in life. Remember that our current life reflects our wounds in our history. A past life wound of the third chakra could arise from an experience or a perception of being powerless, frozen and unable to take any action to resolve the issues or the challenges we face. A common experience, given the fact that fear and emotional overwhelm freezes us.

We may have been in situations that range in severity from actually being confronted with a force truly larger than ourselves, and being literally overpowered by that force. We could have been in war situations in which we were horribly outnumbered. Or overpowered by more sophisticated weapons which caused us to lose our lives. This experience is an obvious way that could create a wound around feeling powerless. It could be something more subtle and seemingly benign, where we may have been bullied or intimidated by a person, a group or an organization. This bullying could have been a consistent, chronic experience that traumatized us over some years. It is easy to see how this could create a wound in our psyche, in our third chakra that convinces us that we don't deserve to have anything good happen to us. We may have simply been overshadowed by a sibling who matched our parent's image of what a good child was. This experience could wound our third chakra and create misperceptions around our sense of worthiness. One situation is no more damaging than the other on the level of potential third chakra wounding, as the consequence of the experience is dependent on the perceptions we create. What determines the extent of the wound is how we interpret those events through the filter of our perception. Another demon of the third chakra is self- sacrifice, martyrdom and pseudo-sainthood, these are actually acts of self- loathing, (the demon of the third chakra). If we keep ourselves inside the trap of feeling worthless, we rob ourselves and others, of the opportunity of our light, our love, and our essence. When we take responsibility for loving ourselves, we free ourselves to be able to offer our love and light to those we love.

It is valuable for you to evaluate for yourself if this is part of your pattern and notice the effects of this demon on your peace and your relationships, as they inevitably lead to resentment, disappointment, and anger. The truth is everyone benefits when we fully love and embrace ourselves, and our own value. Self-love is the cornerstone of healing if we are ever going to be able to fulfill our potential and raise up to our highest self, it is the act of practicing of self-love. We allow ourselves to be less than we are as a way to hide out and not show up fully for all of who we are. Perhaps we are unwilling to take responsibility for ourselves, or perhaps we refuse to step-up and become all of whom we can be fully. The demon of laziness could be an aspect of this, and false modesty that got confused with humility is another face to this. The truth is that we don't serve the world by playing small and being less than our full potential, and choosing to love ourselves fully instead of being an act of selfishness, may actually be the greatest act of generosity that we can offer to the world.

The physical sensations (the emotions, the energy in motion).

The emotion, (the energy in motion) of a wounded third chakra can feel like nausea, anxiety, upset stomach, butterflies, indigestion, gas, or even excitement. The third chakra rules the digestive system, and if you have vulnerabilities in this area, then this is a clue to there being some wounding around these experiences in your past, either the past of this present life or past life experiences. As we re-enter our bodies and inhabit them in a way that enables us to be connected to the messages our bodies are always attempting to communicate to us, we can begin the journey of healing. Ultimately, we need to learn how to fully feel all of these sensations enough to fully digest and integrate them until there is nothing left to feel. Then we arrive at a neutral state where there is no longer any charge around negative emotions.

The right to act

The basic right of the third chakra is the right to act. Action is the way we channel our energy into creativity and behavior that then transforms the world around us. Remembering that if you ever feel you're too insignificant to make a difference, what an impact a mosquito can make in your bed. We aspire for the impact that we make to be a positive one. The most powerful, creative actions arise from a balanced third chakra that has an awareness of its worthiness and self-love and positive confidence. When this chakra is deficient, there is a tendency to be passive, lacking energy and drive, having a weak will with poor self- discipline. When excessive we can be controlling and domineering, arrogant and highly competitive; we can also be stubborn, hyperactive, and ambitious. The solution resides in healing and rebalancing this chakra.

Healing the wounds of the third chakra

As always, the first step is consciousness, being aware of our own cycles and patterns and vulnerabilities. What are our default patterns of thinking, where does our subconscious take us when we feel we are not approved of or accepted unconditionally for whom we are? What does our stinking thinking do when we feel we are criticized, judged, or condemned? How much of those projections do we believe and allow in? These experiences hold within them the golden opportunity of healing. Healing can happen as long as we can stay present and connected to ourselves, in the center of something difficult or someone else's onslaught, and at the same time allow ourselves to feel our own bodies fully. And be connected and developed enough in our subtle senses to hear our own thinking, then we have the opportunity to transform these deeply rooted wounds. When our third chakra is balanced and aligned, we find ourselves able to fully feel and experience our own power, to such a degree that we find we can maintain our own center, even when we are challenged by others and invited to believe the lies that we are anything other than divine. We will be able to make mistakes without falling into cycles of self-doubt and self-criticism.

The demon of the third chakra is shame, a negative self-judgment. The way we can release from the vibration of shame is by focusing on our own intrinsic goodness, our innocence and our essence, our own positive intent and finally let go of needing the good opinion of others, to have ownership of this part of ourselves. Then we will be able to be mature in our relating to those that we love, with the truth of that love, in the center of our consciousness at all times. Then we may be able to fully surrender into being loving and compassionate and kind with ourselves and with others. We become skilled in knowing the truth of who we are even when we are in the grips of fear we finally mature into a place where we can take ownership for that experience and work through it without pulling those around us into our shadow. This knowing and practice are how we grow our souls and evolve into the higher aspects of ourselves. When we nourish our subconscious with the affirmations that reflect the truth that rebalances this chakra, we are supported in making these choices. When we take full ownership of our shadow and full responsibility for healing it, we are liberated into fully realizing our potential. The healing of the third chakra provides the confidence, the courage, the power, the energy and the self-esteem that is necessary to stand in the world proud of who we are in our own unique expression of ourselves, to stay centered and grounded enough to remain independent of the good opinion of others. This skill transfers the authority back into our own hands and allows us, finally, to be responsible for holding our own standards for the integrity that we need to embody and demonstrate so that we can be truly free. Feeling truly powerful and centered has nothing to do with the ego; there is no arrogance or hubris present, just authentic remembering of our own innocence and our truth and our love to the point where our light emanates from us.

"The secret of attraction is to love yourself." Deepak Chopra

Right action and achievement translates into self-esteem

The mechanism of the third chakra is about transmuting the energy of the digestive fire into will power so that we can take action in the world. This action then translates into accomplishment and success, which in turn builds self-esteem. As we move into the world exerting more of our will power, we are practicing our magic, our capacity to create our lives, as we want them. Through this experience, we start to feel who we really are, as powerful autonomous and creative spirits, and no experience is stronger than this in creating self-esteem. The more we step into our magic, exerting our will power, the more we understand about our significance and our importance, the more we learn to trust ourselves, and our confidence expands, the more energy we can convert in the third chakra into willpower. It is by breaking free of our pseudo-safe comfort zones, by taking risks, that we ignite our fire and expand our power in the world. By stepping outside of our comfort zone by fully embracing risks, we are finally able to heal our third chakra.

> *"Help me to embrace all of the beauty in my life and within myself and to let go of all of the fears and the negativity, so I can be the person I was born to be." Jennifer Gayle*

The following quote by Marianne Williamson truly encapsulates the essence of the third chakra.

> *"Our deepest fear is not that we are inadequate. Our deepest fear is that we are powerful beyond measure. It is our light, not our darkness that most frightens us. We ask ourselves, who am I to be brilliant, gorgeous, talented, fabulous? Actually, who are you not to be? You are a*

child of God. Your playing small does not serve the world. There is nothing enlightened about shrinking so that other people won't feel insecure around you. We are all meant to shine, as children do. We were born to make manifest the glory of God that is within us. It's not just in some of us; it's for everyone. And as we let our own light shine, we unconsciously give other people permission to do the same. As we are liberated from our own fear, our presence automatically liberates others." Marianne Williamson

<u>Integrity and honor</u>

For our third chakra to realize its highest potential, it is necessary to do the right thing, to honor others and ourselves, to choose consistently from the highest aspect of us and come from high integrity in all of our choices. We can engage in an infinite amount of chakra balancing and healing activities, but nothing will create balance and healing in the third chakra as powerfully as choosing to do the right thing. This integrity brings to mind Mother Theresa's profound realization that it's not between you and them, it's really between you and God anyway.

"People are often unreasonable, irrational, and self-centered. Forgive them anyway. If you are kind, people may accuse you of selfish, ulterior motives. Be kind anyway. If you are successful, you will win some unfaithful friends and some genuine enemies. Succeed anyway. If you are honest and sincere people may deceive you. Be honest and sincere anyway. What you spend years creating, others could destroy overnight. Create anyway, If you find serenity and happiness, some may be jealous. Be happy anyway. The good you do today will often be forgotten. Do good anyway. Give the best you have, and it will never be enough. Give your best anyway. In the final analysis, it is between you and God. It was never between you and them anyway."
Mother Theresa

When we have fully integrated this truth, we will understand that it is not enough to be on our best behavior when we know we are being watched, when we are in public, or fully seen. Being our best for the approval of others can easily and quickly fall flat on its face. When we are choosing to always be on our best behavior, because we know it's really the only choice we can make if we want to be healthy, happy, and have peace, then we are creating balance and health in the third chakra. We always know what the right thing to do is in any situation, but we don't always choose it. If we sit long enough to connect to our bodies and our energy, we will find the truth of what is right; we may not like it, and our ego may seduce us into believing we don't have to do it. No one may ever know or find out if we make a low-level choice, but the truth is our soul, and our bodies know, and they reflect it in our health. Balancing the subtle energy body facilitates the awakening of, the connection with, and the expansion of the intuition and its communication and allows us to find balance in this sensitive chakra.

While I was working helping clients with weight loss, a client confessed about a "sneaky bitch syndrome" she was running, which perfectly illustrates the truth that the third chakra can teach us. She described how serious she was about losing weight and having a healthy diet. So she cleaned out her cupboards, dumped all the junk food, and went out and bought only organic, nutritious foods. She was proud of how clean the food was in her kitchen. She was a nurse, so she was constantly tempted by chocolate that was lying around and brought in for the patients. Every day she would succumb to the temptation, but she would make sure that nobody saw her sneak the chocolate. Finally, she realized that she was fooling no one, that she was hiding nothing.

"The truth is, we wear our integrity on our body she said, and all my choices are there in plain sight for everyone to see." The truth is everyone would see the chocolate she was sneaking in the cupboard by the weight she continued to carry. This idea and this truth extend further when we understand that everyone is actually brilliant and capable of reading the truth of who we are and they can clearly see the level of integrity we are currently choosing. All the thoughts we are thinking and all the feeling we are occupying are always communicating out into the world, in our vibes, to others what we believe, and then the Universe helps us co-create that thing. There is such a thing as telepathic communication that we are all participating in all the time; we often pick up a vibe we don't like or have silent fights with our partner. The further we evolve down our spiritual path, the more sophisticated we become in this nonverbal communication, which motivates us to clean up our own act and purify our own negativity of thought and emotion.

> *"This war you fight is a war with yourself. It begins when you wake up in the morning and the bad thoughts that creep in. It starts with the first act of self-abuse in negative thinking. The first shot is fired when you send negative prayers towards another. This shot comes right back to poison you. Listen up people stop your negativity. This endless cycle will fester, bruise, and create illness. This re-evolution of love begins with you." Xango Shola*

The third chakra is fully healed and balanced when we accept that true power arises when we are at last willing to be responsible, accountable, and committed to ourselves first, then to others, then to the Universe. Real power comes from our ability to be able to complete a task, to be responsible (to have the capacity to respond) and to have integrity. Once we have successfully overcome our many impulses to pursue what is desirable and choose what is right, honest, and productive, we have truly mastered our power. These words have the potential to evoke fear and trigger our ego to run in the opposite direction in search of fun and freedom. The truth is, there is no joy and freedom until we are evolved enough to invite and surrender to the challenges that embracing these deeper qualities brings. How can we feel powerful if we function in the lower aspect of ourselves that allows us to escape or avoid responsibility, for here we remain trapped as children in dependency and powerlessness. How can we reap the benefits and freedoms of adulthood without embracing these qualities within ourselves?

When we finally step up to the plate that the Universe continuously invites us to step into, then finally we can be autonomous, then we can practice our magic and create our lives, as we want them. Now finally, we can understand the personal power, self-esteem, and happiness that arise from being a mature, free, responsible adult. The foundation of the journey back to balance resides in establishing a balanced third chakra, and we support ourselves in arriving there by mastering the thoughts and emotions that arise from a wounded third chakra. If this information is resonating with you, I invite you to further explore your third chakra by working with the tools I have created for the path of healing and rebalancing the third chakra.

> *"Offer to the world what it is you want to attract. If you want love then offer love to everyone you meet. Become what it is that you feel is missing in your life." Serena Dyer*

The journey of the third chakra can teach us that it is essential that we like ourselves: that we feel proud of who we are and what we choose to do. Our personal power is a direct result of our integrity, of our consistent demonstration of choosing the right thing. Our self-esteem expands as we step up to the plate and embrace greater and greater responsibilities, as we become accountable primarily to our higher selves and then to those we have relationships with and fully embrace the opportunity to treat those in our inner circle with love, respect, and compassion. The more we do it, the more the Universe invites us to do it, until it is easy and effortless for us to consistently demonstrate ever expanding levels of integrity, truth, and honor. Our personal power grows, and we become able to practice more, and more of our creative potential, our magic, our sense of autonomy expands and we can play inside our own creation. This magic is the gift of adulthood: that we get to feel our power and finally understand what Frank Sinatra was talking about when he sang, "I did it my way." Until then, we are vulnerable to playing out this issue in our personal relationships by attempting to exert power and control over others and be confined within the of trap of, doing it my way or the highway. Personal power is also associated with the mastery of our emotions, our energy in motion through the chakra system. Once we fully understand how to participate with energy in productive ways, to bring about the desired outcome, and we consistently practice that, then we are fully empowered.

Human beings create themselves through their moral choices, by freely and repeatedly choosing certain sorts of things we create our character, and through the character, the future. When we make moral choices, we hold ourselves in our hands and determine our own path, our own destiny, for good or ill.

> *"Watch your thoughts; they become words Watch your words; they become actions. Watch your actions; they become habits. Watch your habits; they become character. Watch your character; it becomes your destiny."* ~Lao-Tze

Particular patterns of behavior lead to certain results. Sow an act and reap a habit, sow a habit reap a character, sow a character reap a destiny. We are free to resist or overcome certain patterns and evolve our way to making new choices. Good intentions must find expression in right actions.

Rosanna's journey to self-love and power

Rosanna came to me as she was entering into a new relationship that held a lot of promise for her. She believed that if she was able to get out of her own way and not repeat the patterns from her history, she might actually be able to experience loving and being loved just the way she wanted. She had enough awareness to know that the real issue that had created problems for her was rooted in her inability to love herself truly. She had been told, by previous boyfriends "you need to learn to love yourself, " and although it sounded true and she really, really wanted to, she didn't know how to do that at all.

"I don't even know what that means," she complained. "I think I'm good to myself; I buy nice things for myself and treat myself to chocolate and cakes when I'm feeling down. I know how to cry and really get it out when I'm sad, I can stand up for myself and tell people to leave me alone when I'm angry. I think I understand about boundaries and talk about what I need, so what am I missing? What am I doing wrong! I also know that when I am alone I usually just feel bad, not exactly sad, just unhappy. Yes, that's it underneath it all, I'm unhappy, dissatisfied with myself, with my life. I guess I'm just not successful enough, I have a decent job, I did everything that was expected of me, and I'm living the life that was supposed to bring me happiness but do I have happiness? No, not really, not really," she said as if the realization was just sinking in for the first time. "I think that if I were more successful, I'd be happier."

The man she had met was exceptional in his capacity for intimacy and his ability to express love, something she had never experienced before. This capacity had motivated her to invest the time in herself to clean up her own act so that perhaps she could be that loving too. She shared with me that just before meeting this guy, she had gone on a yoga retreat, which had been a very weird experience for her. She felt that the exercise and the diet and space pushed her into a different feeling that was unfamiliar to her, not comfortable but somehow she knew it was good for her. Rosanna worked for a startup that demanded everything from her, and she ran from the moment she woke up until the time she went to bed, she felt exhausted most of the time and had a long history of anxiety. Her doctor had told her that she was suffering from adrenal exhaustion. She shared that she always felt like she had to run to catch up with everything and everyone. She had dated a lot but never felt like she had a boyfriend. She had people in her life that had disappointed her and let her down because she felt that she was invisible to them. The way she felt invisible to her friends was that whenever she expressed her needs, they seemed to either turn on her and accused her of being emotionally needy or simply ignore her and exit from her life, either quietly or with drama and blame.

She felt invisible everywhere, in her family, in her work, in her relationships. She was beyond frustrated and seeking spiritually to find herself, although it was not easy or natural for her to see her challenges and her life through a spiritual lens. She was open to the possibility that everything that was happening was happening for a reason. With my support, she was starting to see that everything that was being presented to her was perfect, and exactly on time, as it contained the correct ingredients for her growth, not for her comfort, but for her growth. She proceeded to cultivate this perspective of purposefulness and practiced every opportunity she got, and she found that she had plenty of opportunities.

Rosanna had displayed in her working life a certain level of responsibility and maturity, and her integrity was high, about her work ethics. Her personal life seemed to function under a different law, in her friendships and her romantic relationships she seemed to collapse and expect others to extend the greater effort and carry the burden of responsibility. She just seemed to hide out and want to give as little as possible, yet had high expectations for how others should show up. She expressed concern and a lack of pride in how she participated with those she loved and wondered why she simply did not exert a high level of effort in her relationships; she complained of feeling almost paralyzed.

This choice, she recognized, made her dislike herself and kept her in the trap of repression and self-loathing, which is one expression of the wounded third chakra. It can also express itself in the opposite direction of over giving and setting up a pattern of doing everything, feeling resentful and dominating the other for being lazy and taking advantage of them. I noticed, in her communication, a very subtle negativity beneath a very caring, friendly, kind veneer. This negativity was a thin thread that exposed the way that she actually related to herself inside the confines of her own mind. Being much more critical and demanding of herself than she was of anyone else as if she was saving up all her loathing for herself. I asked her just to speak out her thoughts, at that moment she came out with:

"I hate myself. I am mean, lazy and ugly and disgusting. I can't do anything right. I just don't know what it is; there is something wrong with me, there must be, no one wants to love me. Something bad, something fundamentally is wrong with me." After this conversation, there was little need, but much interest, in talking to the subconscious to see if that conversation matched this one. I know that by now it's fairly obvious that if this is the internal conversation, the external reality would need to reflect it. Which, of course, it was, fortunately, Rosanna had come to me while her relationship was still young, in its period of grace, (that we are all granted), before the patterns start to impact us that can destroy the energy and chemistry that brought us together in the first place. This timing made me optimistic about the future possibilities for this relationship.

As we started with the next session, we went straight into the conversation with the subconscious.

"The thing that isn't working in my life is.

Relationships …. The reason is ….

There's something wrong with me I'm a failure

Can't get anyone to love me

There's something wrong with me

I don't know I'm just not good enough

I'm not beautiful; I'm not interesting It's hopeless, it'll never work

I'm just not good enough; I hate myself...."

This story really reveals the intimate connection between the chakras. For this book and in the interests of clarity, I have separated the chakras, in reality, this separation is much more blurred. Very often, chakras will work together and the third and fourth chakra, often act together, both when they are wounded and when they are healthy. Also, a third chakra wounding although always rooted in a feeling of unworthiness can play itself out in its opposite pole of being overly critical and picky, perfectionism, finding others to be not good enough, or the pseudo puffed-up self- aggrandizing that can happen, but is rarely believed by the self or others. Illustrating the ego's way of finding a way to protect itself from discovering and exposing its own deeply rooted vulnerability. With Rosanna, things were pretty straightforward from this point on; we created a mp3 with all the opposite positive affirmations, the breath work, and the music to raise the emotional frequency. The emphasis for Rosanna was really in the yoga practice, mainly because of the practical application of the principles learned in the Presence practice, as that practice elevates the idea of loving the self to an act, a practice. Because of the enthusiastic inclusion of the physical body in her transformation, Rosanna moved rapidly into her transformation.

She participated in the third chakra practice for two months because she enjoyed the first month so much. She was ready to rise from the limitations of these old beliefs and really allow herself to have the love that was standing in front of her, and the love that was rising from within her. The last time I saw Rosanna, she was basking in the glow of cupid's arrow striking her heart. She commented that the work we had done together enabled her to notice the first moment that her mind attempted to seduce her into her old thinking patterns. The yoga practice had helped her be awake enough to stop the cycle, with her will power, and redirect her mind towards visualizing what she wanted rather than dwelling inside the worry and the fear. This shift was enough to radically change her reality and her experience of love. She found herself worthy to receive it by shifting her negative judgments of herself, which were rooted in her negative inner dialogue, which once fully illuminated with awareness lost their power and their influence over her life. This shift allowed her to show up inside her relationship and participate fully, representing herself for all she is.

This shifted her out of the repressive cycle of being less than she is and freed her to show up with full emotional maturity, taking responsibility for being the best Rosanna that she can be, which magically allowed her to accumulate energy and strength gathered from the experience of doing her best. This new vital force supported her in rebalancing her adrenal exhaustion so that she could come back to her health.

"Wow," she said. "I really do see how powerful thoughts are; they create your life." I don't think anything is more powerful than changing your thoughts. Except perhaps, living with love, self-love first, then loving others. Rosanna and I created a script that she worked with in the third month of our time together; this is how that script went. It was a surprise to her that she had been so consistently negative with herself, and that she spent so much time worrying about herself, her life, her future.

The script that we created together and with her agreement we started with the third chakra affirmations to get her grounded in the correct energy and the correct affirmation for this chakra.

You are perfectly loved and lovable just as you are right here and right now. You now choose to extend compassion and kindness to yourself. Always choosing self- forgiveness, self-assurance, and self-support.

You graciously accept and activate the full potency of your power, which has pure motivation to love and to serve.

You are now willing to see your own magnificence; you are unique and valuable and important.

You have the power to express your own uniqueness and value through all of your thoughts and all of your actions.

You deserve to be loved. You now choose to love and approve of yourself by demonstrating perfect mastery in your life.

You are powerful, valuable, and loved.

You trust your inner voice.

You are strong, wise, and powerful.

You now honor yourself with all of your thoughts and all your actions.

You are kind and compassionate with yourself with all your thoughts and attitudes about yourself.

You now sustain a strong connection to the truth of your own perfection and your own divinity.

The truth is you are already perfect; you allow yourself to feel the truth of your own perfection any time that you choose, whenever you are feeling something different from that you choose to reconnect with this truth.

You are a successful woman; you have had many successes in your life, and you now expand into the confidence that arises from remembering your successes.

Recall now the memory of how that felt and allow all of your cells to be bathed and soaked inside that healing vibration so that your body can recreate that feeling in your present and your future. Trust that we have set that intention and your body is now responding to this invitation. Many people have loved you in your life, and many more people will recognize your light and naturally love you, the truth is you are beautiful and interesting and charismatic, and you are enough, as you are already perfect whole and complete.

Rosanna continued to work with the third chakra toolkit, nourishing her subconscious with positive thoughts and vibrations until she felt the release from her own inner dialogue. Finally, she fully understood that actually loving herself required a positive nurturing consciousness, a liberation from negativity, and a choice to inhabit high emotional vibrations. It required taking responsibility to navigate back to positive thoughts and feelings, each time she noticed she was slipping into old habits that created disconnection and unhappiness.

Do you recognize anything of yourself in Rosanna? If so make sure that you identify your negative cycle of thought so that you can feel sure you have the whole thing. The chakra clearing mp3 is an excellent tool for this discovery. You can also set intentions for your dreams to reveal to you everything that you need to know, so that this cycle can be illuminated, into your conscious awareness when you are awake. If you need my help getting this information and you want my personal assistance with this, you can call me for 30% off the regular rate to bring clarity to this.

> *"The bottom line is whatever you say to yourself when you are feeling really confident is what you need to say more of."* Me

Top ten techniques for the path.

1.) State of relaxed wakefulness, (PRESENCE PRACTICE MP3) A.) Notice for yourself, with curious investigation, all your physical sensations. B.) Feel all of your feelings, emotions, energy in motion, C.) Notice the monkey mind, let go of thinking so that you can connect to the witness aspect of consciousness.

2.) Breath

3.) Awareness

4.) Compassion

5.) Visualizations

6.) Positive memory

7.) Raised emotional frequency

8.) Skillful questions

9.) Affirmations

10.) Behavior changes after nourishment and practice

2.) **BREATHING 3RD CHAKRA** Inhale the breath through the crown of the head repeating the word ___*han*___ *silently to yourself.* Bring breath into solar plexus at the top of the abdomen gently squeezing the muscles at the solar plexus lifting the abdomen in and slightly up

Suspending the breath keeping the throat open inviting the prana to come directly to the back of the third chakra in the spine.

As you exhale you release the muscles and the breath inviting the breath to come into the heart repeating the word silently to yourself *sah.*

What's important about the third chakra is that we are marrying the breath that descends from the conciseness.

Shiva energy on the inhale and the exhale that rises up from the perineum the shakti energy with the han sah.

5.) Visualization

Now see a beautiful bright yellow wheel of light shining like the sun moving like a fan in a clockwise direction.

6.) And 7.) Recall now a memory of a time when you felt very connected to your personal power when you felt proud of who you are. Take a moment now to remember how that feels and start to feel that feeling rise from your solar plexus and soak all of you cells now so that your whole body is vibrating inside that beautiful emotion.

This light allows all illusion and all misperception to be illuminated and brought up to consciousness.

Emotionally

Opening Sphinx with or without a bolster.

Meridian affected kidney, stomach, bladder

Emotionally anxiety to equanimity

Mental Affirmation "you are perfectly loved and loveable as you are.

Core cry "I am not worthy."

THIRD CHAKRA COBRA

1.) Come to lie on the belly and rising up into the sphinx pose with the elbows directly beneath the shoulders.

2.) Slumping so that everything is completely passive so that gravity can have you.

3.) Let go of all the muscles in the legs.

4.) Inviting all the energy that you have gathered in your 2nd chakra to rise up into the area of your solar plexus 2 or 3 inches above the navel.

QUESTIONS FOR 3RD CHAKRA

1.) **Recall now any and all memories about how respected and honored you felt in your past by your family. Or was there something different from that?**

2.) **Did you feel seen for who you are? Did you feel that you were successful in school? Did you feel that you were liked and popular? Were your relationships filled with ease and joy and fun or was there something different from that?**

3.) **Did you feel like you had enough of whatever you wanted or was that limited? Was there conflict or chaos around you? What were the consequences to that regarding how you feel and think about yourself?**

What perceptions did you create about yourself as a result of these experiences?

4.) Do you feel worthy of goodness? Do you feel that you deserve to be loved? Do you feel you deserve to have whatever it is that you want, whether that be love or acceptance or power? Allow yourself to be aware of how you think and feel about these areas of your life that you are now ready to be conscious of.

5.) Do you feel like you are proud of who you are today? Do you feel good about where you are right now in your life, about your path, your choices your achievements and your accomplishments?

6.) Do you believe that you are a successful and worthy person? Are you kind and loving towards yourself?

7.) Do you feel that you are powerful in your life and able to create what you want?

SLEEPING SWAN CHAKRA 3

1. Come onto your hands and knees into table pose.

2. Bring your right knee forward and to the right of the right hip (leg bent 90 degrees) while you bring the right foot in front of the left hip.

3. Make sure the hips are square to the front of the mat.

4. Slide the left leg back, straight behind the left hip. Extend the spine and chest up and then come forward onto the elbows.

5. Stay high with the arms straight either on the ground or raised up onto the bolster, so we invite the stimulation to come more toward the back, behind the solar plexus.

6. Breathe with the sensations in the right hip-buttock. Stay 3 minutes before changing sides.

AFFIRMATIONS

3RD CHAKRA AFFIRMATIONS

1.) You are perfectly loved and lovable just as you are right here right now. You now choose to extend compassion and kindness to yourself. Always choosing self-forgiveness, self- assurance, self- support.

2.) You graciously accept and activate the full potency of your power, which has pure motivation to love and to serve.

3.) You are now willing to see your own magnificence. You are unique and valuable and important. You have the power to express your uniqueness and your value through your thoughts and actions.

4.) You deserve to be loved. You now choose to love and approve of yourself by demonstrating perfect mastery in your life. You are powerful, valuable, important and loved.

5.) You trust your inner voice. You are strong, wise and powerful. You now honor yourself with all of your thoughts, all of your actions. You are kind and compassionate with yourself, with all of your thoughts and all of your attitudes about yourself.

6.) *You now allow all of these truths to settle into your third chakra that you have cleared and healed and transformed so that you are connected to the truth of your being.*

3ᴿᴰ *CHAKRA SADDLE POSE*

SADDLE POSE (Opens feet, knees and thighs, re-establishes curve of lower back)

1. Sitting on your feet with your big toes together and your knees a little wider than hip width, allow your legs to relax and slowly walk your hands back behind you.

2. As you release down, you can support yourself on your bolster by placing it under the upper back or along the length of the spine. If the bolster feels too low, try propping it up with a block or simply resting back on your hands (or elbows instead). If the ankles are inflexible place a folded blanket (or two) under the shins with the ankles hanging off the edge.

3. Once you find your position allow the body to let go and open your awareness to the sensations.

4. When coming out of the pose engage the abdominal muscles and use the arms and hands to support the body as it lifts back up to sitting.

Record this and listen while you are in this pose.

As you transform the obstacles in consciousness and emotion, you will be able to witness changes in your behavior, as you liberate from habitual patterns. You may start to see your energy becoming more confident finding yourself to be more magnetic as you act from a place of deep, grounded confidence. You will see yourself standing tall and proud of whom you are. Acting in a balanced and powerful way, with a strong sense of self - love, self -acceptance, and self- assurance. You will now find that you have more faith in your own power and more confidence in your ability to exert your power in a balanced and an appropriate way, you see how you can exert your influence. You now fully trust yourself, which enables you to relax enough to step into your power fully. You know your own worth and your own value, and you understand how to love yourself fully in a balanced and harmonious way by choosing to fully feel all of your feelings by choosing to be fully present to any and all energy that exists in your own body. You have connected to the truth of your own divine nature, as you fully accept and embrace the divine in you, which allows you to treat yourself well, with dignity, with respect and with honor. You find yourself feeling more peaceful and more relaxed with who you are. You have a greater awareness of the effects of your actions on others, your ability to choose your actions now enhances. You have more choices so that you can create a win/ win for everyone involved. You have a greater sense of mastery in your life; you will even notice yourself having leadership skills as well as being more practical. Cultivating these attitudes is beneficial to you and all those around you, and you nurture these attitudes by listening to this meditation and choosing only the thoughts that reflect the attitudes that you want to have. You find yourself to be more able to be fully in the present moment, so that you can participate fully in life, showing up fully for all of who you are. You find yourself feeling more alive than ever, with all of your energy available to you. Your life is richer and more exciting than ever before.

FORTH CHAKRA

The green path of activating self – love and Personal power.

Alchemizing hatred and jealousy to unconditional love

Fourth Chakra

(Anahata, unstruck, unhurt)
Love, appreciation, gratitude, jealousy, envy, heartbreak.

1.) You now surrender to love and trust in yourself and in others. You now fully allow yourself to give and receive love.

2.) You feel your heart opening to allow love flow throughout your life, throughout your body and into all of your relationships.

3.) Your loving potential is limitless, and you now commit to realize your potential. It is safe for you to love with all the love that is in your heart.

4.) It is safe for you to receive love in all its various forms. You surrender to receiving all the love in the universe. You are worth loving.

5.) You have a kind and compassionate heart that is safe for you to share with the world.

*Transmuting not feeling loved to knowing that you
are loved and capable of unconditional love.*

Transforming the vulnerabilities of the 4ᵗʰ chakra into your strengths

Physically associated with Heart center, circulatory system, lungs, shoulders, arms, and hands. Ribs and breasts, Diaphragm.

Vulnerability. Upper back and shoulder pain. Breast cancer. Congestive heart failure, heart attack.

Mental vulnerability, When stressed or challenged the inner dialogue tone is "I am not loved" "I am not lovable" "Others get more love than me." "I am so jealous of..." **Strengthens into the opposite positive form of** "You now are free to give and receive love fully." "You are free to fully give and receive love now."

Emotional Vulnerability, When stressed or challenged the tendency of the mood level is Heartbroken, grief, sadness, depression.

Strengthens, when met with awareness, breath, and compassion.. into Unconditional love for self and others. Empathy, Kindness, compassion, a sense of generosity and appreciation.

Spiritually this path invites you to walk through the intensity of heartbreak without collapsing into a feeling of being overwhelmed and offers the opportunity to expand into unconditional love independently of all arising conditions. This invitation allows you to rise into an attitude of gratitude by holding a positive perspective around all the potentially heartbreaking experiences that arrive into your reality. You can meet betrayals, separations, and abandonments with your presence, your breath, and your compassion.

Location and Function

The fourth chakra, located in the area of the heart, is the central integrator of the chakra system.

<u>*Wounds of the fourth chakra*</u>

We tend to disintegrate when the heart is hurt. The hurt that arises from heartbreak can potentially kill us. It is, therefore, not surprising we would be willing to go to any length to protect against that possibility. What we may not realize is that the protection that we put in place could potentially kill us too, and sometimes be more damaging than the heartache that arises from the experience of betrayal or rejection. Very often, the fear of being out of control or emotionally overwhelmed is driving most of our behaviors and choices emanating from this energetic center. The truth is we have all, at some point, probably early in life, had the terrifying experience of being emotionally overwhelmed. We discovered, very quickly, that we did not enjoy that experience, so we decided to protect ourselves against the possibility of that ever happening again. We learned how to build our walls and participate in defense strategies that are intended to keep us out of harm's way and prevent other people's chaos invading us. In fact, these "self-protective" choices lead to patterns that should actually be renamed "self-destructive" choices and patterns of behavior because they literally destroy the opportunity for the love and intimacy that we need, and desire deeply to be available to us.

<u>*Karmic wounds of the fourth chakra*</u>

It is not hard to predict what may have happened in past-life experiences to understand how wounding may have occurred around the heart. There may have been betrayals and humiliations that transpired in love relationships—triangles, lies, and secrets, that hurt so deeply, we may have made decisions about never allowing ourselves to feel the vulnerability that arises when we love. We may have created the illusion that loving is a poor choice that leads to disappointment and hurt and nothing good could come from that choice. We may have loved a dream or had a goal that we wanted to manifest that failed so that we become disillusioned and bitter. Losing ourselves to the energetic vortex of disappointment, we could spend all our time and all our energy lost inside this experience, yet still insist that this choice is wiser than risking our hearts being broken and becoming emotionally overwhelmed.

The truth is when we decide to overcome this fear of being emotionally overwhelmed and reconnect to the truth of own power and our capacity to navigate successfully through emotional intensity; then we are liberated enough to allow ourselves to fully give and receive love, which is after all, what we all want.

Liberating the heart

This liberation lies, firstly, in allowing ourselves to liberate from whatever subconscious illusions are causing us to believe we need to build walls around our heart to protect us. These illusions arise from trauma and seduce us into believing we are vulnerable to the intensity of our own energy. As long as we believe we are not the masters of our energy and our emotions, then we are making a choice and casting a vote for our own disempowerment, and our separation, our loneliness, and our heartbreak. We are choosing to remain broken hearted and isolated. Many illusions can potentially feed this isolation and heartbreak. We can believe it is dangerous to open up our hearts and give our love away; we can believe that others can't be trusted with our hearts. We can make a strong case for deciding that we need not to allow anyone close to our heart. All these choices and beliefs may sound logical and rational enough, but in fact, they are deadly. They shut down the natural flow of love energy out from our hearts and disturb our health and our happiness on every level. Therefore, far from being a choice that is protective, it is a choice that is self-destructive.

Healing the wounds

The way out of this dilemma is, first of all, to examine and bring the light of consciousness to each of the beliefs that cast a vote for protection. Then create an antidote for each of those beliefs and install that antidote into the subconscious. This practice liberates our consciousness enough to allow us the freedom to address the essential emotional healing of this chakra. An essential antidote to allow this process of emotional healing is the grounding in the truth "you are the master of your emotions." When we allow ourselves to know this truth, it makes it possible to be present with our own emotional intensity so that we can embark on the journey of healing our emotions.

Being present with our energy intensity and by bringing the breath to that intensity, we can create some space that enables us to have a greater range of choices. No one ever wakes up in the morning and says, "let me confront the emotionally intense experience of being emotionally overwhelmed so I can heal it." That does not mean it's not a good idea to do it. When we do make a choice to be present with our emotions, our energy in motion, as it runs through the chakra system in the body, then we have the opportunity to heal it. When we witness our energy as it flows into the heart, we may feel a clear constriction and contraction when we choose to fully abide with that constriction with our presence and our kindness; then we invite the opportunity for real healing to happen.

When we fully feel our energy and our physical sensations until there is nothing left to feel, then we have the opportunity to balance and heal this chakra. As we are fully present with this energy, we then bring the breath to it. The breath is essential in healing this chakra. Start with the pant and then progress into the deep enthusiastic inhale for a count of four and the soft, surrendered exhale for a count of two. When we practice this to the point of energetic liberation, then we can acquire through experience the knowledge that we are the masters of our emotion and resolve once and for all the fear of being emotionally overwhelmed. This resolution then allows us to progress to transform the illusion with the truth.

Love's healing power

Love holds the power to heal and unite us. To open the heart and love means to honor and respect others. The degree of which we treat them with respect and kindness causing no harm or hurt reflects the extent to which we are allowing ourselves to enter into the healing love vibration. This healing arises and happens naturally when we come from "Namaste" which means the love in me or the God in me honors the love, God in you. Opening your heart allows you to feel compassion and empathy for others. The heart seeks to find balance and the peace that arises from that balance. An open heart can ultimately fall in love with divine spirit and the divine spirit that resides within all of us.

To open this chakra dissolves the walls of protection and defenses melting the illusion of separateness and the self-protective needs of the unhealthy ego. As you open to an attitude of loving your own body, mind, and emotions, remembering the truth of your spiritual nature you will find yourself taking greater care of yourself, of your diet, exercise, and leisure time. You don't have to wait for things to be perfect to love them. The heart is at its greatest place of strength when giving it to someone else. But it is important not to give yourself away by giving more than you can afford. Learning the lesson of the third chakra of truly loving and accepting the self first, having the discernment and the ability to actually put the self first is the key to opening and balancing the heart. You have to be anchored and grounded in your own essence, by being anchored in your cleared and balanced lower chakras first, to progress to the territory of the heart. It is tempting when others hurt or offend us to withdraw our love as punishment for a behavior that we don't like. After all, it would be unhealthy to reward them with our continued, consistent, unwavering love, right? In fact, this is when we have an opportunity to expand ourselves further into being more compassionate and loving. At this time love is best advised and most needed, to invite that person to come from the highest aspect of themselves and become more loving and more authentic.

Our authentic self is naturally more loving, compassionate, and kind and the heart holds the invitation to heal the false self or the persona that we present to others. It is almost instinctive to protect when we get hurt. But if we are interested in the growth of our soul, if we truly want to evolve into the highest aspect of ourselves then we need to liberate ourselves from all cultural ideas and beliefs that state that we should be safe and comfortable inside our "healthy" relationships. The truth is that soul work and healing is messy and challenging it takes you right to the edges of your comfort zone and your capacity; it is supposed to. Life begins at the edge of your comfort zone. Anything difficult that is conquered and mastered, empowers, heals, and contributes to our growth. It is not helpful to assume or imagine that because our relationships challenge us that we need to leave that person. If we can trust the brilliance of the universe bringing us to exactly who we need to work with, then we can be liberated to do the work of the soul and heal our misperceptions in consciousness and melt our energetic, emotional wounds. What would the world be like if we accepted the laws of karma as real and trusted that everything is perfectly as it needs to be? We already have the perfect container for our healing, with the relationships and the people that already exist in our lives. In fact, because it's difficult and challenging, is a good indicator that we are doing the growth work we are intended, or perhaps, contracted to do.

Ego surrender

We develop our persona or personality as a way of attaining the love and approval that we needed in childhood. As we evolve, we are invited to give up the illusions of what is required of us to be loved and accepted and remember the truth, that "we are already loved and lovable as we are." As we allow ourselves to ground in that truth fully, we are liberated to surrender and let go of all the subtle and overt manipulations of the ego, so that we can become free to be who we really are and express who we want to be. We are allowed to fully express the highest aspect of our being, our light, our love, and our joy without concern of what we get back. We have the opportunity to finally let go of all the effort that we believe we have to make, and relax into the truth of our divinity, our essential nature and trust our own authenticity to be enough, to be acceptable.

> *"Love is happy when it is able to give something. The ego is happy when it is able to take something." Osho*

Our ego will absolutely not want to let go of its defenses and manipulations. An internal battle and conflict is entirely predictable. It is useful to identify the different aspects of the self, the sub personalities and give them each an identity, and a voice so they can be honored and heard and ultimately overruled by the greater authority within you. Your love arises from your essence. If we actually want love and peace in our hearts and in our lives, we simply must surrender the ego, and its need for dominance, punishment, and control. If our ego manages to convince us that we are not safe and we need to protect ourselves, then we will only be able to create disconnection and separation. The ego manages to seduce us inside the voices of cleverness, convincing us that we need to be savvy enough to outwit the next man. To be better, smarter, stronger, more switched on, in a never ending, exhausting, outdoing of the next guy or girl or partner or parent.

"My dear ego, I want to tell you something..... I will win"
Unknown

The importance of gratitude and forgiveness

To maintain a healthy balance in the fourth chakra, it is important to practice the positive qualities of that chakra. Gratitude and appreciation invite the heart to open. Start every day before you get out of bed energizing the things you are grateful for. Think about them, visualize them talk about them, and open up a dialogue with your loved ones about what you are thankful for. Spend time enjoying exchanging this energy, so that it can expand in your body and in your life.

We are told over and over about the need to forgive, yet we resist this, sometimes because we believe it gives others permission to do bad things. If we think of forgiveness in terms of energy only, we are more able to see if we give others back the energy that they gave us we can be liberated into finding forgiveness. Allowing the poor behavior and choices of others to infiltrate and permeate into our hearts, hurts us. No one can determine the degree to which we get hurt by others actions, more than ourselves; this is truly a choice within our sphere of influence.

If we imagine another person's choice to lie and cheat, or just generally behave badly, as a toxic, painful energy that we allow into our heart, we can see that it would be a wise choice to allow that energy to return to its source. The karma can be played out at its source, and something productive can be achieved out of the negativity.

> *"Forgiveness is not about forgetting, it is about releasing from our memory the emotional charge that tortures our soul so we can let go of the injustice and move on." Feddrick Zappone*

Forgiveness is an essential practice of the heart; it liberates us to move freely forward into our future. Holding a spiritual context around everything that happens to us, supports us in allowing in the lessons and accepting the universes' way of helping us grow. Once we remember the truth of the ultimate benevolence of the Universe, we can accept our lessons, whatever way the Universe decides we need them, forgiveness flows easily when we surrender all resentment, anger, and punishment.

> *"To forgive is to set a prisoner free and discover that the prisoner was you." Lewis Smedes*

Rebalancing and aligning the heart.

By participating in the practices of gratitude and forgiveness, we create the opportunity for us to rebalance and align this chakra. When the energy in the fourth chakra is excessive, we tend to be codependent and have poor boundaries. We may suffer from jealousy and tend to be a martyr or a pleaser. When the energy is deficient, we can be antisocial and withdrawn, leading us to feel lonely and isolated, as we are, in fact, isolating ourselves. This isolating may arise out of a fear of intimacy and rob us of the opportunity of having the love and connection that we truly want. I have consistently seen people with deficient energy in the fourth chakra struggle to allow themselves to have the goodness that they have in their lives. This struggle becomes a having-ness issue that can expand, just beyond the issue of love and include things like, joy, money, sex. So it is essential that we create balance here cultivating the qualities of compassion, empathy, acceptance, equanimity, and contentment. By using the practices provided here, these qualities will be naturally awakened, supported and naturally achieved.

> *"Forgiveness is not forgetting the injustice done; it is the understanding that allows us to set aside the emotional impact of that injustice about ourselves. When we no longer hold those emotions and have understanding for the person, we have forgiven them." Moon singer*

Amara's journey along the fourth chakra green path of opening to love

Amara is a beautiful, dynamic, deep, spiritual woman who comes from a wealthy family that is privileged and highly politically connected. She is highly spiritual and connected to the principles of Yoga, Vedanta, Buddhism, Hinduism and various other Eastern religions and philosophies. She has a rich understanding of karma, astrology, karmic patterns, shamanism, and nature. She had experienced many deep spiritual journeys and processes that had revealed insight into her past lives. She found me through my Awakening Intuition online e-course, which she also found to be very helpful in illuminating her access to past life information. She shared with me one of the more significant journeys she had experienced, in which, she was able to see herself in the distant past, as a trusted advisor to the authority, where she was attempting to get them to understand about a trap that was being laid for the town. Her town was exceptional, in that it had prospered highly during three centuries of peace. The people enjoyed an idyllic lifestyle of abundance and stability and peace. She had been the advisor to the ruler for many decades and brought her unique gifts to the ears of the powerful. She had been warned that fear would cause the downfall of the town and had been hyper-vigilant each time this demon raised its ugly head.

Her psychic visions had allowed her to gain insight into the bigger picture of what was happening. There had been fear of invasion in a neighboring town that needed the extra protection of her townsmen, this fear caused those in power to make poor choices about their own well-being, (which is something that fear consistently does) and they allowed their men (and the town's protection) to go elsewhere. This departure, of course, left her towns women and children vulnerable and their own town open to invasion. She knew that others viewed her in her community as a problem, because she was so powerful, and she had been targeted as a witch. She had a reputation for being powerful in her capacity for compassion and unconditional love and had advised the authority with this power for a long time, which had contributed to the great success of the town. It had been rumored that she had the much coveted and highly elusive two hearts (the second heart being just to the right of the first and possessing the quality of unconditional love, which is a reality on an energetic level, the heart chakra has two orbs, two energetic locations). Myth had propagated the idea that if you steal that extra heart, you too could embody its qualities.

She had the foresight to know what was coming as the men marched away and her warnings went unheeded. This time the fear was too great, greater than the capacity for wisdom of the community to prevail, and poor choices were made. Fear had won its battle with the light and she and the town were left vulnerable to attack. The following day they came in their thousands, and it didn't take long for three of them to chase her down, pin her the ground, rip open her side, pull apart her ribs reach inside her and rip out her heart. Amara actually recalled how this felt and re-lived this entire experience in a regression session. As difficult as that was to re-experience she actually felt a reclamation of vital energy after the process. It was as if this remembering actually liberated her from the wound itself and allowed her to heal and rebalance her energy. Which, of course, is exactly what these processes do. She also shared with me that her astrological chart had revealed to her that this lifetime was about her coming into her power, and that journey, for her, was intimately connected to her romantic relationships and the integration of her sexual energy, with her fierceness, and her unconditional love.

Some years ago she had been strongly attracted to Crete and could not resist the urge to visit. She arrived at the site of the palace of Knossos and felt an instant recognition, a sense, and feeling of returning home. After completing the tour, so many flashes of recognition had occurred that she felt sure that the past life she had re-experienced was here in Crete. So much of the information that she gathered confirmed this reality, to the point that she was able to see what had caused the downfall of this utopian society. After the tsunami had hit, the people lost their faith, their innocence and their trust in life. This loss led them to fall into a fear-based group consciousness and society, which eroded their strength and left them vulnerable to invasion from Greece, a much less evolved society at the time. Amara felt that the reason she was so compelled to help people overcome their fear was that she witnessed the downfall of her beloved utopian community and was heartbroken to witness exactly how destructive fear was.

Amara seemed to always be in relationships that were aligned with her spiritual growth, by flowing with synchronicity she was able to connect with her erotic soul mates. This supported her into the evolutionary edges of her soul but brought her into somewhat psychologically unhealthy, but spiritually necessary experiences. This time she found someone who was living on the brink of going to prison, for a minor offense alongside a felony past, so it added up to the second strike for him, and to him potentially, having the book thrown at him. Through his last break up he caused some damage to the property that he shared with his partner at the time and managed to navigate himself into a restraining order that forced a premature close on a relationship that had not yet naturally completed.

Amara's edge of growth resides in learning how to respond differently in the center of conflict, instead of reacting with fear and her usual automatic self-protective mechanisms that can only create separation and distance. She needed to learn that she can expand into creating enough space to give her choices. This way, she may be able to respond with the compassion that she can so effortlessly extend to her clients, and has, as yet, been unable to extend to her partners. Her habitual pattern was one of responding with anger whenever her partners entered into their fear based patterns—a teacher of compassion who was unable to extend compassion to the person that she loves the most when they are lost in their wound, in their illusion, and in their fear. Seeing her partner in fear re-stimulated her, and triggered her into a need to fight for clarity, which only resulted in her partners consistently shutting down, which resulted in truth being eluded, polarity and ultimately separation happening. She had also entered the question of whether or not she kept herself small and disconnected from her potential, by connecting with men who would anchor her in survival issues and prevent her from flourishing into her creative projects, which were too numerous to mention. This, of course, is a function of a contracted and fearful mind and heart.

   This particular crisis in relationship had brought her to herself with deeper, more searching questions that forced her to reevaluate everything that she thought she had known about herself. This evaluating is not unusual when we are confronted with the edges of our deepest spiritual growth. She noticed that her creativity actually increased each time she got connected to intensity, instability, and chaos in relationships. She wanted peace, passion, love, and creativity together, and secretly feared that this might not be possible. She wanted an experience of life that was fully alive, yet felt unclear about how to achieve that aliveness and intensity without destruction. She was aware of the Buddhist concept of relaxed wakefulness and wondered if this truly was the path to attaining her full potential. She wondered if this was really available to her without being a devout practitioner. She wanted to learn how to respond differently, with compassion instead of anger, fear, judgment, and disdain each time her partner lost himself inside his own patterns, inside his own fear. A handy excuse for her to be consumed with something, other than dealing with her own pattern, her own illusions, her own fear. It's amazing the lengths we will go to, to avoid confronting the edges of our own internal growth, we will literally create destruction and devastation in our lives and those that we love, over confronting ourselves, our fear of going inside is so great.

   We fear the same experience of overwhelm we have had in our history, sweeping us up in a tornado of emotion, that we assume we cannot successfully navigate, let alone eventually master. This fear, this assumption, is the cause of most addictions, and self - protective mechanism that create distance and separation, pain and heartbreak even death. She came to me to ensure that she had nowhere to hide this time, and she truly wanted to be liberated from this trap, which created nothing but unhappiness and separation from love, her love for herself and her lover and her life. As we moved towards examining her mental patterns, many clues lay in the information uncovered in the past life regressions.

The time spent in Crete had left such a huge imprint on her soul, the idea that she had to eradicate all fear, whenever she encountered it in others, she had pinpoint clarity in identifying it, revealing it and supporting in transforming it. This mechanism served her well in her work, but in her personal relationships it took on a different form, that was much more problematic and disruptive. For her, this mechanism took on a very, self-critical and judgmental edge. Whenever fear arose in herself and her partners, instead of being supportive and compassionate, she became frustrated and judgmental. This lack of compassion and empathy indicates a deficiency in the heart chakra.

Because of her deep connection to her wounds, I asked what she thought her negative cycle of thought might be, to see how closely that aligned with her subconscious expression. She was able to identify that she was afraid of losing herself inside the chaos and destruction of her partner and that she felt trapped inside a prison of limitation and loneliness away from the world of possibilities that she could connect with, when not inside this stress. As always with the fourth chakra wounding an essential healing affirmation to ground the energy in truth is, you are the master of your emotions. As with all my clients, after lots of observation, it is easy to recognize the energy that is highly charged, and carrying a strong creative potential. In this case, Amara was so afraid of losing love that the possibility of creating that outcome becomes almost inevitable. Here is how the conversation with Amara's subconscious went:

"The thing I'm most afraid of is having my heart broken

And the reason why is.......

I wouldn't survive it

death,

I will be unloved and alone

because I'm so angry

I have been judged

not lovable

I judge

People get it wrong

I am afraid that I am not loved or lovable."

Amara managed to get right to the root of the pattern quickly; it was so close to the surface, and she was so ready to be free from the pattern as it was also consistent with what she was aware of consciously. We went to the opposite positive along with the fourth chakra affirmations. This is the script we created for her healing journey:

"You are strong, and you really are able to endure any emotional experience with grace and courage. You really can endure any emotional challenge and be better for the experience. You know that when you get hurt, you heal perfectly well and remain whole and become stronger. You now surrender to divine love and trust, and you know that you are perfectly loved and lovable already as you are. You have learned how to respond effectively to emotional challenges so that you are always in charge of your choices. You are free of judgments and free of the good opinion of others. You allow people to be themselves and experience what they need to experience to get to where they are going on their own journey.

You allow your partners to experience the full spectrum of their emotions and you trust they will arrive at the end point that serves them best.

1) You now surrender to love and trust in yourself and in others. You now fully allow yourself to give and receive love.

2) You feel your heart opening to allow love to flow throughout your body, throughout your life and into all of your relationships.

3) Your loving potential is limitless, and you now commit to realize your potential. It is safe for you to love with all the love that is in your heart.

4) It is safe for you to receive love in all its various forms. You surrender to receiving all the love in the universe. You are worth loving.

5) You have a kind and compassionate heart that is safe for you to share with the world."

After about two weeks into her program, Amara was exposed to what it was like to be on the receiving end of her pattern. Very often when we invite change, the universe supports our positive intention and so reveals all the obstacles to change. Her boyfriend supported the final liberation of her pattern through conscious choice; he got mad at her for being in her fear. Witnessing him do this hurt her so much that she vowed never to do that again, never to him or anyone else. This choice allowed her to raise her unconscious pattern into the level of conscious choice, which is ultimately where we all need to arrive for full liberation to happen, it happened beautifully, clearly and directly for Amara. The tools and the practices that I provide in this program support you in being armed with awareness and fortified with nutritious thinking and feeling patterns so that when confronted with an opportunity in life to make a new choice you are ready and able to do so. If you feel that you want the mp3's and the yoga videos that support you in deepening your own forth chakra alignment, they are all available to you at a discounted rate; you can proceed to the end now to see these offers if you want.

As you progress down the path of rebalancing this chakra you support yourself in reclaiming any lost inspiration towards love and intimacy. This energy will naturally emerge as you confront and integrate all the injuries from your past that caused you to build the walls of self-protection. You will find yourself feeling motivated and interested in moving towards romantic opportunities. The courage that is necessary to this take leaps of faith will emerge, and you will be strengthened and energized inside the vulnerability of falling in love.

Top ten techniques for the path.

1.) State of relaxed wakefulness, (PRESENCE PRACTICE) A.) Notice for yourself, with curious investigation, all your physical sensations B.) Feel all of your feelings, emotions, energy in motion, C.) Notice the monkey mind, let go of thinking so that you can connect to the witness aspect of consciousness.

2.) Breath

3.) Awareness

4.) Compassion

5.) Visualizations

6.) Positive memory

7.) Raised emotional frequency

8.) Skillful questions

9.) Affirmations

10.) Behavior changes after nourishment and practice

Breathing for the 4ᵗʰ chakra

The banda that we use for the heart center is the constriction in the back of the throat with the ujai breath. Inhaling and exhaling, making the sound of the ocean in the face. Inhaling shiva consciousness from the crown of the head descending through the central channel arriving in the heart to meet and merge with the shakti consciousness that arises from the perineum and arrives into the heart center.

Repeating the word han on the inhale and sah on the exhale

5.) <u>Visualization</u> as you visualize a beautiful green wheel of light circulating like a fan in a clockwise direction and as it moves it heals, and it clears removing all obstacles and blockages allowing you to create space so that you can remember the truth of who you are as a spirit and as a soul

6.) Positive memory and 7.) Raised frequency

Recall now a memory of a time when you felt completely loved when you felt love for yourself or for someone in your life. Recall all the wonderful details around that special experience and feel that feeling of love emanate from your heart center and feel it move in circles like ripples on a pond allowing that emotion to touch every cell in your body. Feel all your cells vibrating inside that energy of love as you choose to release and let go of all protections around the heart. Now allow yourself to remember the truth of who you are as a spirit and as a soul.

Inhaling shiva consciousness from the crown of the head descending through the central channel, arriving in the heart to meet and merge with the shakti consciousness that arises from the perineum and arrives into the heart center.

Questions for 4th chakra

CHAKRA FOUR YOGA POSE Triple Facing Diamond

1.) Lying on the back bring the arms over the top of the head with the thumbs and the index fingers touching making the shape of a diamond. (Stimulating the heart chakra as the heart meridian runs the length of the arms to the fingertips and raising the arms helps to stimulate this meridian.)

2.) Bring the soles of the feet together, and let the knees fall apart.

Allow these questions to pass through the conscious mind and arrive deeply into the subconscious.

1.) How safe do you feel it is to give and receive love fully? Are you able to do that? If not, what prevents you?

2.) Do you feel you can love with all the love in your heart?

3.) How do you feel about your family and parents and their ability to love? Allow any and all memories to surface into your conscious mind so that you can write in your journal all of your perceptions and misperceptions around this whole experience in your past.

4.) How powerful do you feel in your romantic relationships around the whole question of feeling loved and lovable? How does feeling vulnerable affect your thoughts and your behavior.

5.) *How powerful do you feel about your own emotions? Do you feel in control? Do you feel the master of your emotions?*

6.) *Did you feel emotionally supported in childhood? Did you feel loved?*

7.) *Were you shown how to love?*

8.) *Do you believe that you deserve to be loved?*

9.) *Do you feel that you are perfectly loved and lovable just as you are?*

10.) *Do you feel comfortable inside the experience of intimacy?*

Suptabadakanasana

4ᵀᴴ CHAKRA YOGA POSE SUBAKAN PHOTO 9

It is wise for us to take our time to get into the position that is correct for us. Take your bolster and align it with the spine making sure that the edge of the bolster is touching your bottom. (For the most intense position leave an inch gap at lower back and bolster edge, any lower back issues bring bolster right to the edge of the back)

Now bring the soles of the feet together and open the knees wide. You can straighten the legs if it's too intense to put the soles of the feet together.

Gently lie back onto the bolster, which lifts and opens the chest.

Bring your awareness back into the breath using the ujai breath

Affirmations

1.) You now surrender to love and trust in yourself and in others.

2.) You now fully allow yourself to give and receive love. You feel your heart opening to allow love to flow throughout your body, throughout your life, and into your relationships.

3.) Your loving potential is limitless, and you now commit to realizing your full potential. It is safe for you to receive love in all its various forms. You surrender to receiving all the love that is in your heart.

4.) It is safe for you to receive love in all its various forms. You surrender to receiving all the love in the Universe. You are worth loving.

5.) You have a kind and compassionate heart that is safe for you to share with the world.

If you feel that you want to relax deeply into this position, you can stay here and simply deepen into this pose, or if you want more of a challenge and an opportunity to get deeper into some places of stored energy around the heart, you can change into this new shape. When you feel ready to move into a new pose you can very gently roll over onto your right side and give yourself a hug, then as you feel ready to push down with the left hand and rise to sitting.

__Puppy Pose__

4TH CHAKRA PUPPY POSE

1.) Come into tabletop on hands and knees.

2.) Come onto your elbows, walk the elbows out and rest the head on the ground behind the wrist bending the right elbow and straighten the left arm, allow the space between the shoulders

3.) Release the chest and allow it to melt towards the ground.

Relax: To make it easier, lower the hips toward the ground as you are releasing the chest towards the ground. Take some time to find your place in the pose so that you can breathe without straining. Hold as still as you can resisting the urge to fidget but staying attuned to your body so that you are honoring yourself, coming out when you need to.

This stimulates the heart meridian in the hands and the arms

Making sure you can still breathe fluidly and keep the muscles in the face relaxed

Behavior changes

1.) You have heightened your awareness around all of the subtle and obvious ways your ego creates separation. You now choose to melt these walls and defenses so that you can move towards connection so that your heart is open and flowing. This melting allows you the opportunity to move towards love instead of away from it.

2.) You know the truth that any protection that inhibits the flow of love is destructive and not protective. You are now more aware of all the subtle and obvious ways in which you attempt to protect yourself.

3.) You allow yourself to surrender pride and any behavior that creates distance and separation. You are now committed to allowing yourself to be vulnerable, seeing the benefit of that choice and how it enables you to be closer to those around you,

4.) Feeling more connected, more intimate and more loving than ever before. Trusting that it is safe for you to move towards an open and vulnerable, connected intimacy in your relationships. Holding truth in the center of your consciousness, knowing it is a wiser and healthier choice to surrender the ego and connect in an open-hearted way with compassion, kindness, understanding, and forgiveness towards yourself and others.

5.) You now choose to see the strength that resides within your vulnerability. This allows your defenses to simply melt away giving you the freedom to create a closer bond and deeper intimacy both with yourself and your loved ones.

6.) The benefits from this choice are tremendous, facilitating greater love and intimacy in your life and a stronger and healthier heart. With a deep and profound connectedness and intimacy.

7.) You will more easily recognize the harmony in everything, in nature, and in all of your relationships. You more readily and more easily have the opportunity to see God in all things and choose unconditional love for all.

8.) Your heart can now realize it's optimum functioning and greatest health as it is liberated from the confines of protection.

9.) You reclaim your capacity to trust the continued presence of love in your body and in your life so that you can broaden your range of choices allowing you to come from gentleness, kindness, and love.

10.) As you choose to extend more love and compassion towards yourself and others, you find there is a never ending supply of love available to you.

11.) A continuously, replenishing supply of love energy that you are creating through your wise choices and wise behaviors. As you expand to integrate the presence of this healing energy, you notice a greater sense of health, happiness, and vitality in your life.

12.) This new found energy settles into a greater sense of peace and well-being in your life.

13.) As you cultivate these new attitudes, the new behaviors naturally follow. You will find yourself having a greater acceptance for all that is, and seeing that everything is all as it should be. You will see your relationships becoming more harmonious.

FIFTH CHAKRA

The pale blue path of activating expression

Alchemizing fear into love

Fifth Chakra

Visuddha

(Expression, truth, surrender of will, transmutation of fear)

1.) You surrender your will to the will of the highest power of the universe. Trusting the flow of life and allowing it to take you wherever you need to be.

2.) You are free to lovingly and compassionately express your authentic truth.

3.) It is safe for you to speak your truth. Your communication is easy, words flow easily and you represent yourself fully, for all of who you are.

4.) You choose to express only positive thoughts and ideas. Everyone you come into contact with benefits from your authentic communication.

5.) You express yourself freely and joyously. You speak up for yourself with ease. You express your creativity.

Transmuting from the experience of repression and
lies to authentic expression and truth.
From fear to love

Transforming the vulnerabilities of the 5th chakra into your strengths

Physically associated with

Throat, thyroid, trachea, neck, vertebrae, mouth, teeth, gums, jaw, esophagus, parathyroid, hypothalamus.

Vulnerability. Raspy throat, chronic sore throat, mouth ulcers, gum difficulties, TMJ, scoliosis, laryngitis, swollen glands, thyroid problems.

Mental vulnerability, When stressed or challenged the inner dialogue tone is

"I am unable to speak up for myself."

"I feel repressed."

"I hate lies,"

"I need people to tell me the truth."

I feel like I have to force things to go my way."

Strengthens into the opposite positive form of "I am free to express my authentic truth compassionately." "I can speak up for myself and easily express my wants and needs."

Emotional Vulnerability,

When stressed or challenged the tendency of the mood level is repressed, suffocating, trapped, stuck, suppressed."

Strengthens, when met with awareness, breath, and compassion.. **into** Freedom of self-expression, personal empowerment to find authentic self.

Spiritually this path invites you to walk through the discomfort of stagnation, repression, and disconnection from the self. This practice brings you back to your own authenticity, freedom to connect to who you truly are and express that to others. On this journey, you can expect to encounter many forms of challenge to this vulnerability to disconnect from your own truth and align with other's truth, until this experience becomes so uncomfortable that you are invited to decide to express your own truth honestly and compassionately.

The fifth chakra (Vishuda, purification)

Location and function

The fifth chakra is located in the throat in the neck, which is a very important area of the body because it is where fear energy gets transformed and transmuted into love energy. This is a very active and also a very vulnerable part of the body because this process of transmuting energy is a very intense, yet delicate process. The release of sound clears and aligns the physical energy body for entry into higher consciousness. The fifth chakra is the bridge between the lower three world-based chakras and the upper, more spiritually-based centers. It is the place in the body where heaven and earth meet, merge, and marry. It is the center of communication and, therefore is, strongly connected to the truth and expression and communication.

Spiritually, it is related to the surrender of your personal will to the will of the highest power of the Universe. It is the filtering system that protects the mind from being flooded with unnecessary information, supporting the process of expressing the truth. It also filters what descends from the consciousness so that only what is essential is expressed and charged up with energy for verbal communication; it also filters the wisdom of the heart allowing that wisdom to be authentically expressed, integrating body and mind, aligning them into a single vibrating truth. As you open your voice and speak your truth that descends from the intellect and arises from the wisdom of the heart, you will free your authenticity and your creativity. As you express yourself in the world, you expand and connect with others on a deep and authentic level. Surrender is another lesson that the fifth chakra that invites us to participate in letting go, which is the intersection between acceptance and change.

It sounds simple and straightforward to speak the truth and represent yourself authentically, but actually, it's very complex. We often lose the truth to illusions and misperceptions that arose at times of trauma, so it becomes increasingly difficult to express our truth because we may no longer have a clear connection to what that is. The fifth chakra when balanced and aligned affords us the opportunity to balance the human self with the spiritual self. We can be authentically all of who we are and speak our truth, and universal truth can be expressed through us when our fifth chakra is functioning at its highest potential.

Issues and challenges

The fifth chakra is associated with the surrendering of the personal will to the will of the highest power of the Universe. This soul path addresses issues with illusions, deception, self-deception, ego struggles, speaking up for yourself, feeling free to express your authentic truth, and feeling polarized inside this imbalance. The rebalancing of this chakra resides in mastering the art of listening. Knowing and acting on the knowledge that communication goes two ways, involving both speaking and listening. It is not difficult to imagine past- life wounds that reflect the karmic path of the speaker of truth. Those who have possessed wisdom, knowledge, and insight may have been persecuted in the past for sharing information that may have gone against mainstream society. This can obviously be perilous to the health and can lead to a premature passing. When this chakra is out of balance because of excessive energy, there is likely to be too much talking, gossiping, or even speech impediments like stuttering or perhaps excessive loudness. When this chakra is deficient, there may be a fear of speaking or speaking really quietly with a weak voice. There may be shyness, secretiveness, or tone deafness.

Karmic path of the fifth chakra

We can be persecuted, hunted, and tortured for being committed to our truth and wisdom especially when it is not consistent with the current cultural beliefs of the society in which we live. If we struggle with the fifth chakra, it does not mean we go about our lives and function in the world as a liar. It, most often, is more subtle than that, meaning we may simply be struggling with a pseudo self, a mask, a subpersonality perhaps an aspect of the self that was reinforced in childhood as acceptable and supported in expanding and growing. This personality, because it is acceptable to the family, or the peers or society can develop so strongly because of their reinforcement that it comes at the expense of the authentic self. This can lead to a disconnection from the authentic gifts and true expression of the spirit. When this happens, life becomes a lie because the true self is sacrificed to the forces of the ego, the personality. This is how a narcissistic personality disorder gets set up. The Narcissistic tendencies and personality traits of being self-absorbed and self-interested lead to experiences of separation, disconnection, and loneliness of the individual with this kind of imbalance (This personality type often has a fifth chakra vulnerability.) There are misperceptions and illusions around the idea of needing to protect the self from being authentic, feeling unsafe and exposed by letting the true self be born and expressed.

We all come to a place in our lives when we are playing roles that fulfill expectations that others may project onto us. We may develop masks and hide behind the illusions of who we are expected to be at the expense of who we really are. This leads us into the prison of inauthenticity. This experience chokes and confines us until we find the courage to be truthful about who we really are and how we can embrace every aspect of ourselves and share that with the world as our authentic expression of ourselves. This choking would reveal itself in the throat as tightness or constriction. When things feel inauthentic to us, we often express it as something sticking in the throat. That's because that is actually what happens. This inauthenticity manifests itself as energy, which accumulates and stagnates, and can get stuck in the throat.

Raising the vibration

The fifth chakra is about the consciousness inside of us clearly and authentically expressing itself, and therefore influencing and creating the reality around us. Vishuddha means purification, the release of sound purifies and orders the energy body for entry into higher consciousness. The function here is to refine the body's raw energy, for the focus of consciousness. This focus is essential for going into the higher chakras so that our soul's light can shine and our truth can be expressed so that the music that is in us can be expressed outside of us and made manifest in the world. The demon of the fifth chakra is most obviously deception, lies. When lies are present, our vibration is lowered; we cannot live in harmony with our true intrinsic nature. Lies create disturbance in our vibration that affects our health, our peace, and our well-being.

Another demon of the fifth chakra is control, the overexertion of our will. If we are successful at being controlling and getting what we think we need, the result is not happiness, far from it, the result is limitation and fear and constriction and energetic congestion, which leads to discomfort, pain, and disease. Choking can result from others overexertion of their will on us and/or our overexerting our will onto the Universe. Another, more subtle challenge of the fifth chakra, is not listening and over-speaking or speaking over others so that we are not participating in a communication that involves an even exchange of speaking and listening. Listening and cultivating a higher level of skill on that level supports the healthy balance in this chakra.

Physical symptoms

The thyroid gland is located in the fifth chakra, and this gland is responsible for producing important hormones that influence cellular communication in the body. The thyroid also regulates cellular metabolism, temperature, cell function, and growth. When the fifth chakra is out of balance, things like body temperature disturbance, indigestion, sleep disorders, and immune system vulnerability will occur. When any of these symptoms are present, you may want to explore for yourself what may be holding you back from communicating truthfully.

What is the truth, that resides in the center of your heart, that you want or need in your life, to feel authentic? Are you over controlling or are you under assertive? The real reasons for this may or not be fully available for the conscious mind to see. The cause of the obstacles and blockages may be locked in past life experiences, but there will always be clues in present lifetime experiences that can offer the doorway to liberation. There may have been lifetimes of living in oppressed families or communities, whose belief system was different from yours, where it would not be wise or even possible to be truthful or authentic. It's possible that we could be so disconnected from our own authenticity that we do not even know what our truth is, and could not express it even if there were the perfect container to do so.

The fifth chakra is also the chakra of surrendering your will, to the will and the wisdom of the Universe. When the fifth chakra is balanced and aligned, we can manifest in a way that expresses our desire and meets the wisdom of the Universe's determination of what is in our highest good and our best interests. This creates the correct balance of the masculine and feminine energy for manifestation. The best story that I can use to illustrate how this balance is achieved, is if you imagined that you wanted to get your favorite meal from your favorite restaurant what would you do? You would take yourself to the restaurant; you would sit down and order the food that you desired and then you would surrender and trust the chef to prepare that food. You would not go into the kitchen and tell the chef how to prepare it. You would trust, and you would surrender, allowing the chef to do his job perfectly, to fulfill the manifestation of what you want. The same process is required when it comes to manifesting whatever it is that you desire and the Universe is the chef.

Let's imagine that I was an actress and I really wanted a role in *General Hospital*, and I pushed and pushed for that part, and I prayed and prayed for that part; finally, the Universe opened and gave me exactly what I wanted. Yippee, you think you got exactly what you wanted. But what if it was possible to have a leading role in the next

Matt Damon movie and that's what the Universe intended for you, that aligns with your deepest heart felt desire for yourself? You'll never find out if you are too forceful if you are too controlling if you push too hard and exercise the muscle of your own power of manifestation, your own making it happen, exactly as you want it. Manifestation, ideally, is that perfect marriage between the masculine principle (your vote, your I want), and the feminine principles merging in perfect balance and harmony. You'll never receive the brilliance and the wisdom of the universe and its input and wisdom if you don't open up the space to listen, to receive. Surrendering and softening to the wisdom of the Universe allows the space for you to expand in the direction of your highest potential, into your destiny.

So there is great wisdom in surrendering your will to the will of the highest power of the universe and allowing yourself to be informed by the Universe in how it's going to be, instead of telling the Universe how it is. Surrendering does not mean giving up anything or doing nothing, what it means is flowing with the opportunities that present themselves. It is not permission to be passive; it is melting and softening into that which is the highest. Merging and communicating with whatever is showing up, the healed response is to surrender all judgments, efforts to control, and attachment to the outcome to the direct experience of your feeling.

The throat is the bridge between the brilliance of the intellect, the intuition and the wisdom of the heart, so when balanced here our communication is tempered, and we are fully able to marry the brilliance of our balanced mind and the wisdom of our heart. There is a connection between truth and integrity; if we are not honest with ourselves, it becomes difficult, if not impossible to have integrity. Integrity means wholeness when all aspects of ourselves are aligned with truth, authenticity, and the highest intentions we have for ourselves and are expressed and fulfilled in all of our thoughts and all of our actions, then we have integrity.

If you are experiencing difficulty with this chakra, it is essential to excavate and uncover where you may be inauthentic or lack integrity by not telling yourself the whole truth about what's transpiring or what you're thinking or feeling. Look in every corner of your life, every nook, and every cranny until you are clear that everything is revealed and honestly addressed. If symptoms or issues persist, it is because you still need to uncover what's residing beneath the surface. Radical honesty is the best guide on this path. The liberation out of inauthenticity into truth is what supports you in the journey into your upper chakras, and the highest aspect of yourself. This is how you can lighten and enlighten.

Fiona's fifth chakra journey on the light blue path of freedom of expression

Fiona was constantly struggling to find the balance between being overly controlling and being overly surrendered to the point of passivity. She had recently been given the diagnosis of throat polyps, which were precancerous, and she wanted to get to the root of the problem. She had opened up to alternate options since the path of conventional medicine had run her into the dead end of the doctors believing that there was nothing more they could do to help her in understanding how this could be related to her spiritual and emotional health. Her research into the alternative options had led her to my door.

She arrived in a distressed state, dismayed by the possibility that she may actually be causing or contributing to the cause of her problem herself. She had read some books that talked about taking personal responsibility for our health and discovered that there might be some choices she was making, either consciously or unconsciously, that may be contributing to her condition. This information seemed to throw her further off balance and contributed to her plummeting into a contracted, stagnant, fearful state about her future health. I just want to say here that a real benefit of expanding into our personal responsibility for our health, is to be empowered into knowing how to master our mind and emotions.

Fiona is a hardworking, moderately successful, mother of two grown sons, who owns her own retail business. She devotes herself to her work and her family, yet found herself in a marriage that she felt had run its course and lost all its passion and a job that was fulfilling someone else's dream, not her own. She did not know, at this point, what her dream was. She felt like she was living a lie somehow, living someone else's life, someone she was supposed to be, not truly herself, she was feeling alienated and disconnected from herself. She was bored and wanted some excitement in her life. She had met a man she was attracted to, who had visited her store looking for a gift for his girlfriend. She had been thinking about him a lot and discovered he had recently, broken up with his girlfriend and so she started to pursue him. Her commitment to spicing up her life had become the priority, and she was not acting correctly. She had thoroughly justified her behavior by victimizing herself to the degree that she felt she might as well have a good time now since she probably didn't have that much time left anyway. Fiona was on a spiritual path and interested in participating in her practices, but she was not really clearly looking at herself and how she may be doing things, and making choices that led her to this ethical problem, causing her to dislike and disconnect from herself.

We very often find ways to justify our unethical choices to avoid the full responsibility it requires to make right and appropriate decisions, which very often means not having the immediate gratification of the thing we want. We forget the inevitable truth that every choice has a cost and a benefit; if we focus on the benefit in the short term without weighing the cost in the long term, we will set ourselves up for difficulty later. We often fall into a convenient, but unwise and costly slumber, that at some point we need to be awakened from. We also enter into the mysterious territory of self-punishment and find many excessive and diabolical punishments for ourselves that very often outweigh the crime. These punishments very often take the form of self-defeating and sabotaging behaviors that act against the intentions we set for ourselves. Our happiness resides in our ability to make choices and take actions, which are consistent with our values, and anytime we take actions opposed to that, is depleting our potential for happiness.

Fiona had struggled with her relationship with her mother all her life. She had been narcissistic and controlling all her life. This had pushed her to leave her native Norway, at the age of 17. She had never really confronted and resolved the effects of that relationship, nor had she really examined or dismantled the personality structure that she developed to survive her childhood. During her formative years, she had created a false, pleasing, accommodating personality style that her mother approved of, that allowed her to get her needs met at the cost of her connection to her own authenticity. After she had arrived in the United States, she felt liberated from the constriction of her mother constantly getting her own needs met from the relationship. She then bumped up against the opposite equally debilitating possibility of manipulating men into getting her pseudo-needs met—a choice that leads to the feeding of her own false self at the continued expense of her authenticity. After a decade of playing with this new possibility, she married the man that she could most successfully manipulate who fell in love with her inauthentic pleasing ways.

This contributed to her demise, as it further disconnected her from her own authenticity, and pushed her into a state of imbalance that, if left unaddressed, gave little or no possibility of fixing. It also established her polarized response to survival, which was to swing between being overly controlling to overly submissive. Her control expressed itself in submerged manipulation, and her passivity expressed itself in her willingness to give away her power in major life decisions so that she agreed ultimately to a life that she didn't want. This agreement to be silenced in her expression of what she truly wanted and the disconnection from her own authenticity, compounded her imbalance to the point of creating this physical imbalance. The imbalance had most likely existed on an emotional level from childhood and beyond into past lives.

Fiona had expressed through our sessions that she often felt silenced. Either something would arise externally in her circumstances that convinced her it wasn't safe for her to talk freely, or something would rise from within her that convinced her it wasn't safe for her to express herself and talk authentically about what she wanted. She really didn't feel like she even knew who she really was, or what she really wanted, she had spent a lot of her life pleasing others and actually ignoring her own voice. This over giving led her to the place where she didn't even know who she really was and what she really wanted or needed to be herself, to be happy. Talking to her subconscious revealed the following internal dialogue:

"The thing that isn't working......

My health.... ......(silence) umm ...

I can't really say.....

I'm not well I'm not balanced .... Silence ......

I'm not clear I don't even know who I am or what I want... [crying]."

    I invited Fiona to breathe into the spot that was most uncomfortable and put her hand to it. She slowly raised her hand to her throat. I instructed her to gently pant and bring all her awareness into this area so that she could fully feel it. Tears silently fell until there was no more discomfort and no more tears; she felt immense relief as if some great weight had been lifted. I asked her how she felt and she said, "lighter, free somehow." I knew that we weren't yet finished and invited her to continue with the discovery process to find out what else was there. And then I asked her what she was afraid of.

"The thing I'm most afraid of is......

disappearing into nothing ....

I'm not really showing up.....

I'm afraid of doing something wrong, so it's better not to show up at all...

So you're not to blame for messing things up...

Don't want to be set up to fail, so I don't speak ....

Not safe to talk not safe to show up will be blamed…...

Better to say nothing……."

In fully illuminating this inner dialogue, Fiona was able to see the amount of force she was using to push back her own expression of herself. Her spirit wanted her to push forth, her authentic expression of her truth of herself. Her human self, (her personality, the false self that was created to protect her childhood, was now acting destructively) could not and would not and pushed back against her desire to express, thus creating a mass of energy in the throat. We had more sessions to build a deep connection to the voice of Fiona's authentic self, and she found that her real interest lay in illustrating children's books. She had always been interested in art, but her mother felt that her work was not good enough to support her financially. She had pushed back her own expression, her own truth, on every level of her life and it was going to take time to reconnect Fiona to herself, to her gifts and to her ability to express herself. She really felt now that she knew her work and her path and that was enough for her to get re-inspired about her future and her life. She ended her unethical relationship and decided it was time for her to be with herself, for the first time and honor who she really is. She felt that when the time was right, the right man would come along. She continued to work with the fifth chakra toolkit, and her health continues to improve.

As you rebalance this chakra, you naturally reclaim your motivation towards your creative expression. You can expect to feel inspired to create, to write, or draw or sing out whatever is in your heart. The ability to correctly express yourself will naturally be present as you find your voice and feel strong and capable of speaking up for yourself and advocating for your deeper needs.

Top ten techniques for the path.

1.) State of relaxed wakefulness, (PRESENCE PRACTICE) A.) Notice for yourself, with curious investigation, all your physical sensations. B.) Feel all of your feelings, emotions, energy in motion C.) Notice the monkey mind, let go of thinking so that you can connect to the witness aspect of consciousness.

2.) Breath

3.) Awareness

4.) Compassion

5.) Visualizations

6.) Positive memory

7.) Raised emotional frequency

8.) Skillful questions

9.) Affirmations

10.) Behavior changes after nourishment and practice

2.) Breathing for 5th chakra

The breathing for the 5th chakra is the ujai breath inhaling and exhaling into the back of a constricted throat, making the sound of the ocean in the face.

4.) Visualization

Now see a beautiful light blue wheel of light moving like a fan in a clockwise direction. This light allows all illusion and all misperception to be illuminated and brought up to consciousness

Allow any and all information that is stored in your 5th chakra to surface to your conscious mind. Integrating any unfinished emotional experience integrating into your body and integrating into your mind everything that you are willing and ready to complete.

Now as you are breathing invite your subconscious mind to release to your consciousness everything that you are ready and able to see.

Your information may come in the form of pictures or symbols, or it may come in the form of language whatever form it wants to take allow it to come into your conscious awareness now. Simply trust that you now have access to whatever you are ready to be consciously aware of. Staying with the breath the deep enthusiastic inhale and the surrendered exhale. Know that you are completely safe and entirely supported right here and right now breathing, feeling connected to any and all physical sensations as they move through your body now. All of the information that surfaces will be easily and effortlessly available to you to recall as you write in your journal when you are awake and out of this process you have created the intention and the invitation for all fears illusions and misperceptions to be available to your conscious mind. As you visualize a beautiful pale blue wheel of light circulating like a fan in a clockwise direction and as it moves it heals, and it clears removing all obstacles and blockages allowing you to create space so that you can remember the truth of who you are as a spirit and as a soul. As you recall now a feeling in your body of clear, honest and authentic communication and remember how that feels recall that feeling in every cell of your body and allow that feeling to reenergize all of your cells and feel the pale blue light as it warms and heals and clears this area now.

<u>Visualization for letting go of ego</u> Allow yourself to see in your mind's eye an image of what your ego may look like and allow this image to take whatever form it needs to. The ego contains that part of you that exerts your will and makes things happen exactly the way you want it to. The positive aspects of the ego, allows you to manifest in the world. And you love and welcome this part of yourself. The negative side of your will seduces you into forcing too strongly into the way you want things to happen and may obstruct the Universe from exerting its will.

The fifth

Now visualize this part of yourself, you may see it as a muscle or an organ, or it shows up in another form.

Whatever form it wants to take allows it to show up and reveal itself to you now.

Now watch as this aspect of your ego grows smaller and smaller and you release and let it go, and you watch as it fades, fades, fades and you let it go. You now completely surrender this part of your ego. And you are completely free to allow the divine guidance and support of the universe to enter your consciousness now. You are free to connect to the truth of your essence now.

The fifth chakra yoga practice is available in a digital download you get via email at thehabitofhappiness.org. You can also see the yoga practice on you tube video, or it is included in the 5th chakra toolkit.

SIXTH CHAKRA

The deep blue path of activating intuition

Alchemizing confusion into clarity

Sixth Chakra

Ajna (to perceive and command)
Truth, sight, clarity, knowledge.

1.) Your higher power is clear and honest in all its guidance. You surrender to trusting the guidance that is continuously available to you.

2.) You trust the intelligence within you. Your mind is a powerful tool that you use to create the reality that you choose.

3.) Your mind helps you to consciously create a belief system that is honest, supportive, compassionate and kind, creating a reality that is peaceful, balanced, empowered and healthy.

4.) You now make correct and appropriate choices and decisions that truly reflect your internal strength and power.

5.) You use your mind to fearlessly breakthrough illusion and see only truth. You now create positive mental patterns that create love, joy, and happiness in your life.

Alchemizing confusion into clarity

Transforming the vulnerabilities of the 6th chakra into your strengths

Physically associated with, seeing the opportunity in the challenge.

Brain, nervous system, eyes, ears, nose, sinus, pineal gland.

Vulnerability. Brain tumor, hemorrhage, stroke, neurological disturbances, blindness and deafness, spinal difficulties, seizures.

Mental vulnerability, When stressed or challenged the inner dialogue tone is "I'm confused, I can't decide." "I don't know what's right, what to do, anything" "I can't see, I can't visualize" "I already know everything, I don't have anything left to learn."

Strengthens into the opposite positive form of "I know what to do." "I trust my intuition." "I am clear and confident."

Emotional Vulnerability, When stressed or challenged the tendency of the mood level is doubt, uncertainty, indecision, passivity, or the opposite of arrogance, ignorance, and a know it all tendency.

Strengthens, when met with awareness, breath, and compassion.. into

Balance between intellect and intuition, clarity, certainty, vision, clairvoyance

Spiritually this path invites you to walk through the challenge of confusion, indecision, and disconnection from your own innate knowingness. On this path, it is easy to be seduced into a false sense of knowingness that puffs up into arrogance or an incorrect idea of unknowingness that spirals down into confusion. As you gather strength on this path, your spirit will co-create with the Universe the experience of being thrust into experiences that cause greater and greater confusion, until you meet and transform whatever obstructs you from expanding into the truth of your own clarity.

Michelle Bradshaw Kanti

Location and function

The sixth chakra located in the center of the forehead is the home of your higher power and your intuition. It is also the storehouse of all of your illusions and misperceptions. We can easily fall into patterns of confusion if we are not clear about truth. The truth is the remembering of our true authentic nature, a reconnecting to knowing who we truly are as spirits and souls. All of our wounded ideas and thoughts of who we are residing here in our third eye and can potentially block us from our true intuitive, clear sight. This can create confusion, insecurity, and stagnation. The sixth chakra like the fourth—has two energetic centers one in the center of the forehead and other at the base of the skull; this second energetic center covers the area that the yogis call the mouth of God as it was traditionally believed that this is where we connected to Universal truth.

Issues and challenges

Every time that we got hurt or traumatized, and we created perceptions that were not reflective of our innocence and our divinity, we created illusions that energetically connected to our sixth chakra. Our negative mental patterns, our illusions, our misperceptions created trenches in our brain that reinforce our confusion and doubt, and if left unresolved they can continuously seduce us into believing our own stories. All this keeps us hypnotized by our illusions and disconnected from our clear, intuitive vision.

Balanced and aligned

When this chakra is cleared and balanced and aligned we then begin to have the opportunity to have access to our higher selves, to our intuitive knowing, our divinity, and truth. The misperceptions that we have about ourselves have the potential to create complete chaos in our lives and seduce us into sub consciously believing the illusion of our guilt, shame, jealousy, all our inadequacy, and imperfection. The

328

journey to remembering the truth is critical to our realizing our full potential and our spiritual and human evolution.

The mental evaluation process that we are all invited to participate in requires us to thoroughly examine our thoughts and beliefs so that we can be discerning about the thoughts we are choosing to energize up with our thinking. Whatever we put our mental energy into will be created in our reality and reflected back to us. We constantly receive clues about our mental choices, by what's playing out in our reality, our experience of life. If we don't like what we are experiencing, then the best decision we can make is to examine our thoughts, so that we can change our thinking to reflect what we want to experience in our reality.

> *"Intuition is really a sudden immersion of the soul into the Universal current of life, where the histories of all people are connected, and we can know everything because it is all written there." Paul Coelho*

When we realize how powerful our thinking is, then we can harness the power of our sixth chakra and use our mind as a tool to help us create the life that we choose. As we heal and dissolve our mental obstacles, then we can find our true wisdom, use the magic of our imagination and find our clarity and our light within. The sixth chakra is the center of our illumination the home of our visions, our dreams and our intuitive guidance and wisdom. As you clear the obstacles of illusion and misperception, you can begin to perceive the true nature of reality Do you think of confusion as a thought or a feeling? As we work in the upper chakras, we are invited to create a new relationship with our subtle energy body, so it's less about sensation and more about awareness of vibration and frequency.

Power of manifestation

Ajna means, to perceive and to command, so it is necessary to remove all obstacle of illusion so that you can manifest your clear visions. Imagination is more important than knowledge, as Einstein said. We all know how important the technique of visualization is. It is important, even if we don't believe our wishes or our aspirations are possible that we hold the vision of the outcome we wish for because by literally seeing things right (the way we want them to play out) we can help make it so. We can use our sixth chakra to create our map of our future. Ignite the power of your imagination and start breathing life into the visions of the things you want in your life and if you can't see it, create it, draw it, do something to put it there. Create a vision board from magazines that contain ideal or similar images of the things that you want! This is the chakra of sight, by focusing our consciousness in a particular direction we illuminate and reveal our illusions for the truth of what they are. By bringing the light of consciousness to these illusions, we dissipate their power straight away. We liberate ourselves into the light where we can exercise our true sight, our insight. Here we have the freedom to choose the thoughts that we want to energize with our mental energy. This is how we begin the process of manifesting what we want, rather than blindly attracting what we fear.

Disadvantage of using intellect

We tend in today's society to overvalue thinking. As a result, we overuse and have become over dependent on our intellect and our rationale. There is no doubt that the mind can be a brilliant servant when we use it as a tool to help us to evaluate information, and acquire knowledge, and create what we really desire, fulfilling the visions of our dreams. It is a useless master. If we continue to overuse or be over dependent on the intellect and value thinking, over knowing, which emanates from the higher self, the intuition, then our connection to our own brilliance is compromised and possibly lost. If we don't use it, we lose it. I have never met anyone who doesn't want to improve their connection to their higher self, their intuition, but I've met many people who don't know where to start with the journey of reconnecting to this power that naturally exists within all of us.

"Do not follow the ideas of others, but learn to listen to the voice within yourself." Zen Master Dogen

The place to start this journey is by removing the obstacles of the mind, the intellect, that compromise our connection to our own truth and intuitive knowing, and interestingly, both aspects reside in the sixth chakra. The language of intuition is the language of body. Learning to receive, relate to, and correctly interpret the messages, that continuously rise from the body is essential to activate our intuitive capacity. For this to work accurately, we need to reconnect to our own physical sensations, overcoming the numbness we have accumulated through the choice to escape our feelings? Once we have learned to do this, we need to cultivate the habit of acting upon the information we gather on this level. We can do this in very practical and simple ways, by attending to our bodily signals, our feelings, and our sensations, we can instantly know if we are better, stronger, happier and to say yes to and move forward, towards and into that situation or choice or not. Just by noticing how we feel when confronted with a situation, a person, or a choice and honestly responding to that, we can authentically respond to our own guidance by moving towards the things that generate positive vibes for us, and away from the things that create negative vibes.

Awakening the third eye

The sixth chakra is the chakra of sight; it is about seeing, both internally and externally. The pineal gland is located in the sixth chakra and is often referred to as the third eye because its function is to act as a light meter for the body. (Meaning it translates variations in light into hormonal messages to the body.) The pineal gland also produces serotonin and melatonin essential hormones related to happiness and sleep. Exposure to light is key to healthy pineal gland functioning.

The sixth chakra is where we can envision our future, and this is also where we reflect the pictures that we hold from the past. If we are trying to repress pictures from our past because they are too difficult or painful for us to see, this can be an obstacle to the awakening of the sixth chakra. As we awaken the intuitive ability of the sixth chakra, we can surface both positive and negative pictures from the past, and this can be frightening and potentially lead to a disconnection from the sixth chakra. An effective tool in supporting the continued awakening of the sixth chakra is when we see images of the past that are difficult or disturbing to view, to see those images as if they were a movie. You hold the remote control in your hand, and you can fast forward, pause and rewind these images.

When any associated emotions come up with these images, make sure that you are committed to fully feeling and integrating your feelings. Remembering that fully feeling your feelings means connecting with the physical sensations that are arising and stay present with those sensations with kindness and acceptance. Then allow the breath to come to those sensations and this way you integrate those emotions. By breathing fully, feeling fully, and allowing the energy to dissipate and dissolve, we actually digest our emotions. This way you remove the energetic and emotional obstacles of the past. Also, often we are not really encouraged to develop these psychic gifts, so we haven't allowed ourselves, or been encouraged by others to focus on this area. So entering into altered states of consciousness and using visualization techniques and working with our dreams all support the awakening of the intuitive center.

Keep your journal by your bed this month and set intentions for your dreams to reveal everything that you are ready and able to see and record what you recall in your journal. The highest truth of how we creatively manifest is to focus on what you want to create, rather than what you believe is true. Our illusions, our wounds, and our misperceptions seduce us into believing in our limitations and our past. When balanced and aligned in this chakra, you reconnect with the power of your imagination, your magic and your ability to manifest your life, as you want it. It is so important that we engage our imagination and allow our magic to be unleashed through using our vision, our sight, which actually dictates what we manifest.

When this chakra is excessive there can be hallucinations, obsessions, and nightmares; there can be difficulty concentrating and even fantasizing. Some people who are obstructed here are not able to project into future visualization of what is desired, which is necessary if we are to create our lives as we want them. When it is deficient, you can lack imagination. You may have difficulty visualizing; there may be insensitivity, excessive skepticism, or denial. When balanced you have insight and a strong intuitive ability. There is a great creative imagination with a good memory; the greatest quality is to have the ability to visualize and have a bigger picture perspective of your life. Notice if your energy is excessive or deficient and visualize it coming to a balance point in the middle. It is important to have balance and health and vibrancy here so that you can utilize this essential energetic center to its highest potential.

Past Images

The sixth chakra is not only the home of future visions, but all the images of our past memories are accessed here. Every single impression from our history is connected to the sixth chakra. When re-stimulated either intentionally or not, those pictures spring forward from the past into the present. These unhealed images of the past impact the awakening of this energetic center. The more you can integrate the associated emotions that arise with these images, the more you will be able to rebalance and align this chakra and reclaim the power of your intuition. It is possible that this chakra was never developed in childhood simply through neglect, which can be remedied by practicing focus and visualization. It is important here to know the subtle distinction between hunch, hoax, or truth. The pineal gland is literally a third eye in the early developmental stage of the embryo. It acts as a light meter for the body, changing variations of light to hormonal messages that are relayed to the body through the autonomic nervous system. Over 100 bodily functions have daily rhythms that are influenced by exposure to light. The final outcome of the sixth chakra is the emergence of your own personal vision of the life that you want to live, moving from the real to the ideal is about shifting the focus away from what is, towards what you want, then infusing that vision with your time and attention and energy.

Michael's journey on the sixth chakra deep blue path of awakening intuition

Michael is an attractive, fun, creative, intelligent, articulate entrepreneur, who came to me with an interesting issue. He was disturbed because his relationship of 18 months with a woman, whom he was in love with, had ended badly and he could not understand why such a great relationship had such a negative ending. He wanted to know what could have happened in their karma that brought him to such a painful and difficult heartbreak. She had betrayed him at the end of the relationship and was currently participating in a new relationship with someone who had all the qualities she had complained about him lacking. This just fanned the flames of anger and grief and pushed deeper into his wound, making him feel that he didn't know anything, that he had been stupid and deluded in his choice to be with her and was incapable of making good decisions for himself. Michael had previously made good choices in his relationship partners and had enjoyed a few long, loving, and loyal connections in his history, so this relationship was different. Looking back, he could see the imbalance and emotional inequity that he had put up with and was really curious about why, why had he chosen this, why had he not seen this coming and why had he not been more prepared and responsive to the red flags that had been there.

These were all essential and valid questions, so we explored them together. Michael noticed and his partner complained about a mouth odor problem, for him it showed up as a bad taste in his mouth. For her, it showed up as bad breath, that she was consistently complaining about and repulsed by. It seemed that nothing helped; it was there even after brushing, flossing and rinsing with mouthwash. Michael was frustrated as he was unable to resolve it, this situation seemed to make the problem worse, but it did not create it, it simply revealed it. Michael had a keen intuition, and when he met Rosa, he felt certain that he was supposed to be with her and that certainly carried them through the initial resistances that she had constructed to him keep him at arm's length. Whenever she suggested that they should be friends, he knew that was not consistent with the feelings he had for her, and he felt the same attraction and chemistry from her.

She was highly involved in a small religious group, which Michael was curious about, and they launched into a fun magical connection that for him contained all of the elements that he had been longing for in a relationship. They became very close and had a very deep, lively, loving, intimacy that opened his heart further to fully loving, embracing and accepting her. Their connection felt magical to him, the type of relationship where you can literally see the sparks fly. Rosa was an attractive, successful designer who had never been married but had several long-term relationships with men from her religious group. She was at a difficult crossroads in her career and had decided she wanted to be exposed to new ideas. Shortly after she set that intention, she met Michael, who was both very attractive and very scary to her as his spiritual depth and experience contained new and different ideas that threatened her status quo. She was functioning within an unresolved second chakra wounding and, therefore, limited to the traps and projections that are inevitable and predictable from that. She ascribed herself the role of the one that was desired and the one that was resistant and rejecting, even though, in reality, her attraction to him was as great as his attraction to her. This propelled her to be rejecting and resistant to the vulnerability that love and intimacy invite, pushing her into the safer role of being the one that is desired.

She did this to give herself permission to play out the love and attraction and inevitably the karma that was there between them, without actually having to become vulnerable to him and commit to him. Her greatest fear is of abandonment, aloneness, betrayal, and rejection and a sure way to protect herself from the devastation of those experiences was to reject him first. At the same time, she wanted the opportunity to connect with those same energies in a manageable way, thus inflicting that experience on her partner, causing him to experience the very thing she herself was unwilling or incapable of integrating. This projection caused Michael to have a consistent low-grade experience of loss or abandonment, which confused him to the point of re-stimulation of his sixth chakra wounding of not knowing. (This happens often and contributes to a secondary third chakra wounding of self-loathing and until this dynamic arrives into the consciousness of the person it will continue to create suffering in the lives of everyone who comes into contact with this person.)

From that perspective, Rosa is a toxic person and a negative choice for Michael. From a spiritual viewpoint, she is perfect, (this is usually the case, as I have pointed out previously, those who appear to be psychologically unhealthy people very often can be our spiritual teachers.) Rosa was Michael's teacher, and vice versa, each of them brought the perfect ingredients to the table to support the other in healing and rebalancing the wounds that they exposed for the other. It is quite common that a second chakra person would connect with a sixth chakra person, as there is a connection between these two chakras. The core cry of the second chakra being "I do not want to be alone" and the core cry of the sixth chakra being "I do not know." An injury to, and disconnection from your innate wisdom, your sense of knowing, can resemble the same low vibrational frequency of fear inspired by loss or abandonment of love of a romantic partner or family member. It is a similar experience of being alone without support or guidance, a terrifying experience of disconnection, in the second chakra indicating a loss of others and the sixth chakra is a loss of self. This vibration draws people with these injuries together.

Rosa had some interest in the Nazis; her perspective was disgust and shock that such a thing could happen, yet there were such an alive curiosity and almost fascination with this chapter in history, and some concern that such a thing could, indeed, happen again if we allowed it. Michael was dealing with a bad taste in his mouth that had caused problems throughout their relationship because it lead to bad breath, which was unpleasant for Rosa and also gave her a tangible reason to pin her resistance.

Michael arrived in my office in a distressed state angry at himself for not taking better care of himself and believing that he didn't know anything anymore. How could he have missed all these red flags and be stuck in a situation that lead him to this confusion and deep distrust of himself and his wisdom? As is often the case, this state of distress gave him access to his negative internal dialogue. As he proclaimed "I am so stupid not to see this coming, and not protect myself." He continued to say that "he was not able to make it work, he couldn't handle it or her" revealing a real lack of confidence in himself in his ability to make his relationship or his life work the way he wanted. This negative inner dialogue was also repeated in his reality, and it arose in the conversation we had with the subconscious mind. We spoke to his subconscious, and this is what came through:

"The thing that isn't working in my life is?

Me.

The reason I am not working is

I can't make my relationships work; I am unable to see what's wrong

I MUST BE STUPID

Things don't work

It's me I can't make it work

I don't listen to myself

It's hard to hear

Truth is not convenient

I don't know.

I don't know what's true, what's right, what's good for me, I don't know anything."

Here we see his core cry of *I don't know* cycling through and repeating itself. We can see how this internal dialogue will inevitably lead him to an experience of not knowing what is going on in his relationships so that the relationship ultimately ends and leaves him with an ongoing experience of this feeling. Michael had been hypnotically regressed and re-experienced his birth and was able to recall the smell and taste of gas from his mother receiving gas and air during his delivery. He was regressed further to his first experience of that smell, and this brought him to a concentration camp. He did not recognize or recall Rosa being his persecutor then, but they both had a vague sense of familiarity and, karmically, it would make sense that you would arrive at a romantic relationship with your persecutor. This set of circumstances, of course, creates a container for many varied and intense emotions to be called forth in their relating that may be difficult to understand or make sense of without that knowledge. Even with this knowledge it can remain elusive to know how to begin to heal this wounding and can often leave one wondering how on earth to start the process of healing and rebalancing these wounds.

Michael consistently bumped up against this problem and was re-stimulated in his sixth chakra wounding of not knowing how to solve the energies within the dynamics of their relationship. He became stuck inside the internal dialogue of I don't know how to fix this; I don't know how to make this work, I don't know what to do. He was aware that he loved her and wanted it to work, but he didn't know how to make it happen, a typical sixth chakra issue.

Michael wanted to jump into his transformative process, so he started with the detox course. Previously, we had worked with the sixth chakra mp3 and yoga practice for a month, by the end of which time Michael felt that he had a strong understanding of what had happened in his relationship with Rosa and why he went through the experience. It had ultimately brought him into a deeper relationship with his wisdom and helped him navigate back to himself. He decided that Rosa was not a good choice for him, that he did not have an interest in being with someone who was resistant to him. He knew that he wanted a partner who could truly love and appreciate him for who he was and was currently in the process of creating a vision board to help him manifest the relationship, which he now knew was possible and had clarity and certainty that he wanted.

He was finally in right relationship with his sixth chakra and able to know himself thoroughly and know about his ability to manifest what he knew he wanted. As time progressed and Michael healed from the loss of his relationship with Rosa, he began to recall dreams and insights that he had during his relationship that he barely remembered and just dismissed during his time with her. Throughout his relationship, he had a recurring dream of being betrayed by Rosa in various ways, most consistently through infidelity. The consistent theme being when confronted, her denial and lies confused Michael into not trusting himself, disconnecting him further from the voices of his intuition. He also concluded that the bad taste in his mouth was his intuition's way of communicating his truth about his feelings about Rosa's lack of integrity and low-level moral choices. He found her distasteful. Very shortly after the breakup, the taste disappeared and so did his bad breath. After a couple of months of working with the toolkit for the sixth chakra, listening to the mp3 every day, and consistently practicing his yoga routine, he was able to recognize his internal dialogue enough to release himself from it. He is now in a happy, healthy relationship with someone who shares his affections and his moral standards. He is with someone who can love and appreciate him for who he is and share a deeply connected intimacy with.

As you rebalance this chakra, you will find a deep reconnection to your intuition, which will naturally provide the inspiration necessary for you to be fully yourself and to connect with your innate wisdom and your ability to make the best possible choices for yourself. This connection opens a profound and active channel of energy that can motivate you towards your gifts and the expression and fulfillment of your purpose.

Top ten techniques for the path.

1.) State of relaxed wakefulness, (PRESENCE PRACTICE) A.) Notice for yourself, with curious investigation, all your physical sensations B.) Feel all of your feelings, emotions, energy in motion, C.) Notice the monkey mind, let go of thinking so that you can connect to the witness aspect of consciousness.

2.) Breath

3.) Awareness

4.) Compassion

5.) Visualizations

6.) Positive memory

7.) Raised emotional frequency

8.) Skillful questions

9.) Affirmations

10.) Behavior changes after nourishment and practice

6th chakra breathing and meditation

Visualize the breath rising from the pelvic floor up through the central channel arriving at the top of the spine to the back of the head suspending the breath with the throat open. Allow the head to bow forward allowing the prana to come to the forehead. Exhale allowing the head to come back repeating to yourself the word Han on the inhale Sah on the exhale. Breathe using the ujai breath here.

5.) Visualization

Visualize that beautiful deep blue wheel of light circulating like a fan in a clockwise direction, and as it moves, it heals, and it clears, removing all obstacles and blockages. You will be healing and integrating all obstacles with the breath. Recall now a feeling in your body of surrendering to the truth of your intuition and your guidance. Remembering how it felt to lose yourself to the power of your guidance and truth, a time when your intuition was guiding you and supporting you, a time when your sight was clear and honest, and your mind was focused, you knew you saw the truth. Remember that experience and think about that time and recall exactly how that felt in your body, allow your whole body to remember how that felt.

6th chakra questions

Triple facing diamond

6th Chakra yoga pose

1.) Come to lie on the back with hands above the head thumbs and index fingers touching making a diamond shape.

2.) The arms raised behind the head to support the heart meridian opening, so don't worry if you get pins and needles here.

3.) Place the soles of the feet together knees splayed apart.

Allow these questions to pass through your conscious mind and arrive deeply into your subconscious.

1.) How confident do you feel about your intelligence, about the brilliance and the clarity of your mind? What is your ability to think clearly and use your mind efficiently in a balanced way, that respects the brilliance of your intelligence and the truth of your guidance and intuition?

2.) How effective do you believe yourself to be at mastering your mind and working with it in evaluating your beliefs?

3.) Can you use your mind as a tool to support you in creating your reality?

In fulfilling your purpose?

In manifesting your destiny? Allow that to surface and be revealed.

4.) What negative mental patterns do you know that you are ready to release and let go?

5.) What do your voices of self-doubt and fear say? What are you believing? What attitudes are you holding that do not serve you?

6.) How do you feel about your intuitive abilities?

Were they respected and supported in your past?

Do you believe you have the ability and the right to be an intuitive being?

6ᵗʰ Chakra yoga pose

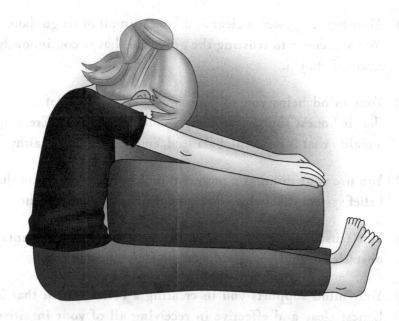

Forward Fold

1. Sit up on a folded blanket. Straighten the legs in front of you.

2. Lengthen the spine up and then extend forward from the low back into the chest.

3. Drape the spine down, allowing the back to round.

4. Support your forehead with a bolster, either under or over your knees (like this illustration). 5. Enjoy a few soft breaths and then turn your awareness towards the sensations in your body.

6h Chakra Affirmations

1.) Your higher power is clear and honest in all of its guidance. You surrender to trusting the guidance that is continuously available to you.

2.) Your mind helps you to consciously create a belief system that is honest supportive compassionate and kind. Creating a reality that is peaceful, balanced, empowered and healthy.

3.) You use your mind as a powerful tool to help you create the belief system that helps you create the reality that you choose

4.) You trust the intelligence within you to clear all mental obstacles so that your guidance can flow through you.

5.) Your mind supports you in creating a belief system that is honest clear and effective in receiving all of your intuitive information.

6.) You now create positive mental patterns that reflect the truth of your intuitive gift and the essence of who you are as a powerful being.

7.) You now fully embrace your intuitive power, and you trust that you are supported in sharing your gift with the world.

Behavior changes

6th Chakra Dragonfly pose

1. Sit up on a folded blanket. Straighten the legs in front of you as wide as you comfortably can.

2. Lengthen the spine up and then extend left arm straight up, lean towards the right opening the side ribs on the left side.

3. Enjoy a few soft breaths and then turn your awareness towards the sensations in your body.

4. Repeat on other side.

1.) As you have now balanced and aligned this chakra, you have created the foundation for you to cultivate new attitudes that lead to new behaviors of trusting and listening to your guidance and intuition.

2.) You find yourself having greater clarity as your mind is less confused and cluttered with thoughts. You can more readily and easily see the truth,

3.) You can know from your intuition exactly the right thing to do, and the right choices to make for yourself.

4.) It is easy for you now to recognize your fearful thoughts and choose to put energy only into the thoughts that create the reality that you choose, the thoughts that support you in manifesting what you want to create.

5.) You find yourself to be more able to be fully in the present moment so that you can participate fully in life, more able to flow with the opportunities and challenges as they present themselves to you. Showing up fully for all of who you are.

Inhale rise up and come to the other side.

6.) You find yourself feeling more alive than ever with all of your energy available to you. Your life is richer and more exciting than ever before.

7.) These new thoughts lead to new behaviors of fully trusting your intuitive hunches and insights, and you now choose to respond to these messages that rise from your knowing.

8.) You now commit to living life in that flow, in a way that is directly responsive to your intuition and your guidance. You trust that you already know all that you need to provide you with all the guidance that you need to respond effectively to all challenges and opportunities that may arise in your life.

9.) You now step into and optimize all opportunities. You trust your capacity to make good and wise choices. Trusting yourself always to know the right thing to do and the right thing to choose that leads you to your highest good. Knowing that you are always exactly where you need to be, doing what you need to be doing.

10.) You now know how to master your mind and use it as a tool that supports you in choosing the thoughts that reflect what you want in your life, which helps you in creating the life that you want. You put energy only into the thoughts that are reflective of the reality you want to create.

SEVENTH CHAKRA

The violet path of granting trust

Alchemizing skepticism into faith

Seventh Chakra

Realization
God, spirituality, living in the present

1.) You now surrender to divine wisdom and guidance and allow it to fully enter your consciousness. You love and welcome this guidance to seek your higher wisdom in all situations.

2.) You trust the process of your spiritual evolution as you gain new and deeper levels of consciousness. You are supported and guided by the highest power of the Universe.

3.) Your spiritual growth comes in ways you don't expect or fully understand. You trust the synchronicities in your life. You are always exactly where you need to be.

4.) You are pure spirit. You are aware of your spiritual nature, and you surrender to trusting your ever-evolving consciousness.

5.) The truth is that everything that exists in your life is perfectly as it should be. You accept the support and guidance of a benevolent and abundant intelligence. You now choose to live fully in your present moment.

From disconnection and alienation to knowing
your divinity and connection to all things.

"We are here to awaken from the illusion of our separateness"
Thick Nhat Hanh

Transforming the vulnerabilities of the 7ᵗʰ chakra into your strengths

Physically associated with the Muscular system, energetic system disorders, skeletal system, skin, connective tissue, nadis.

Vulnerability. Spiritual depression, sensitivity to light, sound and other environmental factors.

Mental vulnerability, When stressed or challenged the inner dialogue tone is "I can't trust others" "I don't have any faith in or belief in anything" "I can't see the bigger picture" "I don't feel inspired "I feel disconnected" "I have lost all hope."

Strengthens into the opposite positive form of

"I choose to trust others."

"I surrender all judgments, and have faith that everything to."

"I feel my connection to all things."

"I am hopeful that my life will go well."

Emotional Vulnerability, A feeling of isolation, disconnection and isolation, hopelessness and a loss of inspiration, feeling lethargic and disinterested.

Strengthens, when met with awareness, breath, and compassion.. into

Hope, inspiration and a strong sense of connection, to all things, at all times.

Spiritually: This path invites you to walk through the challenge of not trusting yourself, others and the Universe. Your opportunity lies in navigating from not trusting that goodness is possible, or a lack of belief in the benevolence of the universe, towards the choice that you reside in a friendly universe that is always conspiring to support you in your growth, wellness and evolution. As you travel along this path, it is predictable that you will be brought into circumstances that can, if you allow them, indicate that others are not to be trusted. You can arrive at the choice that you will grant trust to others and not wait for them to demonstrate trustworthy behavior but you can choose to take a leap of faith and witness what happens.

Location and function

The seventh chakra is located at the crown of the head. It is where we connect with the highest power of the universe, with God or source, however you perceive that. Many people believe that we have a silver cord that descends from the Universe to the crown of your head and connects us to that highest power. This cord is the channel through which we are connected to source and to the information that comes from source. Two different aspects make us who we are. There is our personality, our ego that is a whole collection of defense patterns that we have learned throughout our childhood to ensure our survival, and there is our essence.

Our soul or spirit is that divine aspect of our nature that remembers the truth of our being; our soul invites us to enhance and improve our loving, compassionate, creative, forgiving, joyful, and free part of us. Our journey through life is about shedding the ego, the wounds, the illusions, the misperceptions, the fears, and the anxieties so that we can reconnect to the authentic spiritual truth of who we actually are. On a physical level, the seventh chakra is associated with the pituitary gland and the hypothalamus at the crown of the head. The hypothalamus joins the nervous system and the endocrine system. The hormones secreted by the pituitary gland regulate growth, reproduction, and metabolism and skin pigmentation. The seventh chakra located in the crown of our head is our connection to source, to God, to the Universe, to that eternal aspect of consciousness. It is the point where our individual consciousness meets and merges with that Universal aspect of consciousness. This union is pure yoga, union, and the awareness of this union is realization. When our seventh chakra is balanced and aligned, we have the capacity to be trusting of the benevolent nature of the universe, which in turn supports us in being connected to that part of ourselves. This connection allows us to relax into trusting ourselves and others and the Universe, knowing the earth and your body to be a safe, benevolent place to be. A healed seventh chakra is about understanding the true nature of reality to be about connectedness and oneness to the point of certainty so that it becomes a knowing.

Trust

Trust is an essential lesson of the seventh chakra; we may believe that we become trusting of ourselves and others and the Universe by having others demonstrate trustworthy behaviors to us. However, when it comes to healing seventh chakra wounds of trust, the mechanism that is set up for us to surrender into trusting fully, may not be what you expect. To heal a wound around the lesson of trust, we most often find ourselves in experiences of betrayal.

"Peace comes within the souls of men when they realize their oneness with the Universe when they realize it is really everywhere; it is within each one of us." Black Elk

Our human selves, our instinct, will fall into self-protective patterns of rejecting the person who brought such injustice to our door and we may reject that individual and miss the opportunity to embrace the wisdom of that experience. If we choose to forgive the betrayals we experience in life and use them as the teachers they potentially are; we can trust the experience to forgive the individual. We fondly embrace the growth we acquire when we make the wise choice to surrender into feeling and healing the wound that opens up each time we encounter the challenging teacher that encourages us to choose trust.

Manifesting through surrender

Once we finally and fully embrace the truth of this courageous choice, to surrender, the Universe no longer needs to invite us into the lessons of betrayal. Learning to let go and let God is another lesson of this chakra. Surrender means to melt into that which is the highest and is not about giving anything up or away. Learning to trust is often very challenging because we are asked to let go of our attachments. Something that is not easy to do. We may have something we want to manifest, so we go through the steps we know about manifesting. The steps are about doing what it takes to remove our mental and emotional obstacles so that we can be clear in our communication with the Universe about what we want. Then consciously participate in the descending chakra practice of manifestation, the information about this is contained in the journey of manifesting chapter and the mp3 meditation, the You tube video, and in the manifesting toolkit. So it could seem that we are given contradictory messages about how we are supposed to create, on the one hand, we are told to create our reality using the power of our mind, and on the other hand, we are told to let go and let God. So how do we resolve this apparent conflict? The truth lies in the point of balance in the middle marrying both truths. We are responsible for doing our end of things, and when we have done everything that we can, then we can surrender and let go and let God. The expression of our desire, the clarity of knowing what we want and the raising up to that frequency is the masculine aspect of manifesting. The invitation to include the wisdom of the Universe, the allowing space for something better than we could have imagined, is the feminine aspect of manifestation.

For example, if we knew we wanted chicken for this evening we would find our favorite restaurant, sit down, order the chicken, and then let go. We wouldn't go into the kitchen of the restaurant and make the chicken; we would trust that the chef knows how to make the chicken better than we do. We simply apply that same principle to manifesting anything. If we become too attached to how we want things to play out, we run the risk of not allowing the Universe to show us something better than we can imagine and we run the risk of never being surprised or elevated into our highest potential of ourselves.

Those of us who may have control issues may prefer life to be low on surprises but imagine how dry and boring life would be if we never allowed ourselves to be surprised. It is true folly to believe that the Universe may be quite capable of running the whole world but my life is entirely up to me. Manifesting then has both a masculine and feminine aspect to it. The masculine resides in us putting forward our vote in creating what we want, and the feminine power resides in us opening up to receiving input from life, others and the Universe and what it wants. This receptivity does not mean, however, that we should not be committed. Our commitments are made more powerful when we are free from attachment to specific outcomes.

The journey of manifestation

The journey of manifesting through the body originates in the seventh chakra with the spark of a creative inspiration and descends into the sixth where we can visualize its potentiality, as it drops into the fifth we start talking about our ideas. By the time it reaches the fourth, we are starting to love the idea; we nourish it with our heart energy. In the third chakra, we put some of our will behind it and start taking actions and actual steps towards making it happen. In the second chakra we are creating it, and finally, in the first, it has happened, and it finds its roots in the ground. For this journey to be truly successful it is our responsibility to clear and balance our chakras so that they are free from obstacles and blockages. This practice is how we ensure that we are doing our end of things to support our choices, and our reality reflecting what we actually want. Allowing us to fulfill our dreams and manifest our heart's desire and fulfill our purpose and realize our potential.

Accepting synchronicity

The seventh chakra continually invites us to hold that spiritual perspective of purposefulness that encourages us to see the perfection in everything. To see that we are exactly where we need to be, experiencing everything that we need to experience, meeting the right people, doing exactly what we are supposed to be doing. Looking at life through this lens lightens our load straight away, relieving us of a sense of being burdened and weighed down by life's responsibilities; we no longer worry that what is happening is somehow supposed to be different. We finally and gratefully let go of all of the "shoulds." This perspective also offers us the opportunity to release and let go of all regrets. Once we accept that we are exactly where we need to be, we can start to be awed by the brilliance in the universe, that co-created all of our histories perfectly as it needed to be so that we could stand where we are today in the perfection of our current reality. These shifts in perspective and consciousness support us in allowing ourselves to fully be in our present moment. Breaking free of the misperceptions and illusions and fears that inhabit our ego, our subconscious, and our bodies enable us to be free to reclaim our energy for our present moment. When we fully reside here we have a glimpse of heaven, of true peace and the seventh chakra fulfills its potential.

A Benevolent Universe

The Universe wants, needs, us to be creative, and is constantly conspiring to support us in being successful in that endeavor. Surrendering to believing that to be true, is a life changing choice. It offers us a lens to look through our life experiences that are powerfully expansive and supportive of us realizing our full potential. Once we soften into this reality we can connect with our natural talents and aptitudes, so that we can deliver our true creative expression. This expression opens up the opportunity for us to find our vocation, our true life's work. Our purpose opens up magically for us to step up to fulfilling and we connect with our magic in a way that enables us to create the life that we want, and fully deserve to have. Many of us have heard that we must bring our music from within us out into the Universe, because if what's in us isn't brought out of us—what's in us can potentially kill us.

Awakening

There isn't anything that I can say here that will awaken you. There isn't anything that is written that you can read that will awaken you. The best that I or anyone like me can do is inspire you to do the work that is necessary, in whatever form that may take to embark on your own personal journey of transformation. This journey involves entering into altered states of consciousness to enter into the depths of the subconscious so that the mechanisms of transmutation and clearing and balancing can be ignited. The journey and the processes that I have created are not the only path, but they are a path. I am offering you the tools to assist you on a journey, inviting you on a voyage of transformation into awakening to the truth of who you really are. Please visit my website or email me at thehabitofhappiness.org to get all the information that you need to take your next step to have your best life.

The awakening of the seventh chakra starts with questioning, evaluation, inquiry, and self-knowledge and leads us to enter into altered states of consciousness that support our experience of connection to source, which allows us to know the truth of our divinity. The whole process of this Lifeguides transformation program helps you in this task within each of the chakras. Becoming more conscious and aware allows us to understand the effects of our behavior and our choices on ourselves, on those around us in our environment. This awakening is the first step to our cultivating a more reverent attitude. If you start by recognizing and honoring the divinity within you, we can then start to see that divinity in everything and everyone around us. This practice helps us to develop a sense of awe and hold an attitude of reverence and respect and honor towards life, which makes our experience of life awesome. This attitude shifts our whole reality and opens up the possibility of our having a rich, full and awesome experience of life.

Yoga and awakening

Your body is the temple for the divine within you, your essence. Your energy runs all over the body, through what the yogi's call the nadis, the rivers of energy throughout the body that feed into the meridians, which feed into the chakras. It is essential for us to nourish, nurture and care for the connective tissue of the body so that we can support our journey towards enlightenment, the realization our divinity. The Lifeguides transformation yoga is a perfect tool for us to help this process in our energetic, emotional, mental and spiritual body. The practices in the mp3's support this connection to our spiritual nature and clean and balance our pathways through the energetic vortexes of the chakras out to all the meridians and nadis. It is not necessary to be a yoga practitioner to benefit from this program, but if you do have an interest in yoga and are not currently practicing, I would enthusiastically invite you to try and work with my yoga videos. Guided meditation, and entering into altered states is the tool of healing and clearing and balancing the seventh chakra. It clears the mind so that it can receive the Universal guidance.

As we practice letting go of thinking, we open up the space to hear silent wisdom. In the stillness, our bodies speak to inform us of truth. We all know to sit in a comfortable position with a straight spine or lie down on a flat back so that our breath can flow freely and fully. We are aware of finding a quite spot, where noise is kept to a minimum. It is wise not to get concerned or disrupted if the silence is disturbed, only use all such disturbances as an invitation deeper into you own internal stillness. It is wise to include the whole body in this meditative journey honoring each of the chakra and all of the nadis to support them in fulfilling their task of embodying enlightenment. The real skill of meditation is to transfer that inner peace and harmony into our everyday lives so that we can occupy a state of relaxed wakefulness, independently of what is happening in our reality.

Sam's journey on the seventh chakra violet path of granting trust

I met Sam when he was 24 and making a really concerted effort to overcome his old addictive patterns, he was drug- and alcohol-free and cleaning up his eating habits, eliminating sugar and gluten from his diet. Sam was a graduate philosophy student who had always been interested in truth and the nature of the Universe. He had sat with the question of who and what is God for as long as he could remember. He had a natural curiosity about how things worked and seemed to have an interest in pretty much everything. He was willing to raise and confront the question of who he really was and what he was doing here in a way that led him into a search for truth that led him to study religion and spirituality. He had a very quiet, unassuming nature, a sharp intellect and a pleasing personality, meaning he was gentle and kind and wanted to please others, even sometimes, at his own expense.

Sam's curiosity about the reality of spiritual experience led him into a bad habit with acid trips and he got himself hooked on acid trips, searching for that spiritual experience of oneness. He overdid his journey out into the ether and fried his nervous system. He arrived at my door feeling rather anxious, introverted, depressed and generally out of touch with himself. Paradoxically as he reached to find that oneness, he found himself feeling more isolated and alone. This alienation and disconnection from himself and everything led him to lose trust in pretty much everything and his faith were shaken to its core. He felt lost and had no idea about how he could reconnect with himself and others and rediscover his faith and trust. He was feeling really anxious and was concerned that he might never feel right, and back to his normal self ever again. He wasn't sure about his goals and his future anymore, he was still attending his classes but he wasn't sure how to proceed. He didn't even know what he was going to do with his Ph.D. once he obtained it. This uncertainty gave Sam a vulnerability that betrayed his authentic courage and love of adventure, and his willingness to take risks and jump off cliffs. He disliked his loss of trust and his tendency to make safe, rather than exciting choices about his life that lead him into an inertia, a boredom of life that really bothered him. He was not used to feeling this way and had no intention of getting used to it. He started by telling me that he felt isolated and alone, not feeling any real connection with anything:

"I'm not as happy as I know I can be, I feel like I'm just floating around not connected to anything or anyone." When I asked him why he thinks that is he said, "I don't think I like myself, no that's not exactly it, I don't know that I make the best choices, I've found myself in lots of trouble. He went on to say I know I did it to myself; no one else did it I did it, how can I possibly trust myself?"

As we proceeded into the conversation he shared how hopeless he felt. It was clear to me that his thinking was keeping him trapped in a repetitive experience of suffering. As we proceeded further with our conversations with his subconscious, and his internal dialogue surfaced with excellent clarity. Not surprisingly, his sub conscious communication matched his conscious thoughts of himself, sometimes this is a clear alignment and sometimes it is not.

"The thing that isn't working in my life.….

Everything

Broken down

Not connected to myself or anything else

Not myself I feel alone, isolated

Can't trust myself

I make stupid decisions about everything

I don't trust me

I hurt myself

I can't trust me

Feeling like I'm just floating

I have no purpose, no direction.

I feel like I don't even care.

I have no connection or caring,

I want to give up on myself I don't care about anything

Feel like life is against me,

Nothing is fair; everyone is against me,

You just can't trust anyone anyway I don't even trust myself anymore ..."

Interestingly, as so often happens, when Sam brought this inner dialogue up to his conscious awareness, he started to get brighter, feel better and noted "no wonder I'm feeling so bad about myself. No wonder everything feels really difficult for me because as long as I believe that on any level I'm creating my own trap, my own prison of unhappiness. I want out, help me out of this."

I was happy to help. The release from the trap of his internal dialogue started, as always, by raising his awareness. Then shift it to its opposite positive cycle, which translated for him into its opposite positive cycle. It is interesting to note here that when he was just talking to me, he was able to do so without as much self-awareness and ability to witness his own inner dialogue as he was when we went through the subconscious communication. This difference is not unusual; we can be blind to what we are thinking and saying. The next step is to state the subconscious in its opposite positive form and Sam's inner dialogue translates into this:

"You now see yourself as perfect, whole, and complete, choosing to establish a profound, active, fluid connection with yourself that has easy and effortless communication between your higher and lower self. This allows you to stay connected to and trust yourself deeply. You now surrender to trusting your ability to make wise and appropriate choices for yourself, giving you a strong direction that is about developing your spiritual path. You care deeply for yourself, and all those around you, choosing to invest in and care about yourself, your life, and your choices. You now decide to trust in the karmic justice that exists in the

Universe in a way that allows you to know that life is fair and you are free to rest and relax and enjoy your life."

Sam had experienced his disconnection as a state of all over anxiety, which rebalanced into a state of inner equanimity when he worked with the seventh chakra toolkit. A lot of the work that I do with my clients is focused on helping people create "a life by design," which is all about supporting people to understand how to manifest. Manifesting is an automatic descending chakra practice, which, when raised to the level of conscious awareness, empowers us to truly use our magic, to the point of consciously creating the life that we want rather than getting a diluted or disappointing version of an unwanted life. For us to be effective creators, it is wise to work with both the masculine and feminine aspects of each of the chakras. We hear a lot about the importance of vision boards and activating the power of the sixth chakra by visualizing the things that we want to create. Visualization is important, but on its own is missing essential information, and not as effective as utilizing all the chakras for the purpose they were designed.

As you rebalance this chakra you will naturally reclaim your inspirational energy. This is the chakra where inspiration is ignited towards all our dreams, goals, and visions for our lives and our future. This is the portal to your connection to divine consciousness and supports your journey towards your enlightenment. You will be naturally familiar with who you are in your spiritual nature, and feel supported by the experience of living from this awareness.

Top ten techniques for the path of granting trust.

1.) State of relaxed wakefulness, (PRESENCE PRACTICE) A.) Notice for yourself, with curious investigation, all your physical sensations B.) Feel all of your feelings, emotions, energy in motion, C.) Notice the monkey mind, let go of thinking so that you can connect to the witness aspect of consciousness.

2.) Breath

3.) Awareness

4.) Compassion

5.) Visualizations

6.) Positive memory

7.) Raised emotional frequency

8.) Skillful questions

9.) Affirmations

10.) Behavior changes after nourishment and practice

The four pillars of transformation

All of the tools that I have shared with you can be used in numerous ways. I encourage you to make them your own, to adjust them and work with them in a way that works for you and your life. They can be used as curative tools, to help you navigate through moments of anger, anxiety, confusion, or heartbreak. Using the presence practice to support you heightening your awareness, to the point where you can notice the very first moment of a discursive thought or low emotional vibration, giving you the gap, a moment in time in which you can make a choice, and free yourself from the habit of reactivity. From there you can reach into your toolkits and apply whatever practice works best for you in the present situation. You may need to clear some generalized disturbed emotional energy and want to work with the chakra balancing first. Or, you may notice that you are residing in your abandonment wound and want to work with second chakra daily yoga practice, or you may just need a faster solution and do the butterfly pose with affirmations for five minutes. Perhaps you have a lot of anger coming up that is throwing you out of balance and a couple of the first chakra poses, to soothe the liver meridian may be the best choice. You may have decided you want to lose some weight and decide you want to work with detox toolkit. Or the practices can be used as preventative tools that help you to transform your vulnerabilities into strengths in the form of a regular practice that nourishes your subconscious to the degree that it aligns with your conscious choice, allowing you to arrive in the empowered position of being the creator of your life.

The four pillars of the lifeguides transformation program are both the benefits that can be embraced as a consequence of traveling your path, or they can be a pathway themselves, a way to greater peace, balance, and happiness in your life. It is not unusual for clients to approach me with a request for wisdom about detoxifying, awakening intuition, enlightenment or how to manifest and create the life that they are wanting. That is why I wanted to give these four topics a special chapter of their own. The tools and techniques are the same and the information within each subject is slightly different. The awakening the inner-lite pathway toolkit, contains all the information in all the pathways and therefore it is redundant to give it its own chapter as it is simply the sum total of all the chapters. We arrive at enlightenment when we truly know ourselves and have done the work of healing and rebalancing our wounds and have successfully transformed our vulnerabilities into our strengths.

Detoxification and Purification

Thankfully, we have finally arrived at the full wisdom of who we really are; we now know that our health and our weight is as much about what happens between our ears as it is about what happens between our lips. Our thoughts, our consciousness, and our energy shape us and determine our weight at least as much as our diet and our exercise choices do. When we finally add these important factors into the equation then we can really start making progress in utilizing all our faculties in arriving at our perfect weight. No longer are we limited to the ideas of starving ourselves until we pass out or having to run ragged around a million tracks in order to drop a few pounds and arrive at our optimum health or weight. In moving towards our new holistic consciousness and away from the old black/white polarized thinking, we expand into a fresh new perspective about how we can arrive at our healthiest most balanced weight.

This course is designed to bring all these factors together in a complete practice, by utilizing a potent detox breath, the use of affirmations to heal and align the consciousness and inviting the chakras back to balance. The body shapes itself around the chakras so when you are balanced internally you will be externally in shape. Throughout this toolkit and e-course that you can get online, you will be guided back to the truth of who you are as a spiritual being, along with a skillful use of the breath, visualizations, and affirmations. With the cultivation of compassion, (extending loving kindness to the self) as a support in managing stress, by stimulating the relaxation response, you will be shown how to practice actually loving yourself. This will support you in returning to your balance mentally and emotionally.

A shift in consciousness is required for us to start wanting what is healthy. When our thoughts are balanced and in alignment with the truth of whom we are in our essence, in our spiritual nature, we will naturally make choices to be healthy. When we are balanced, we will make choices that keep us balanced. When we are imbalanced, we will make choices that keep us imbalanced. So to attain our best natural weight we need first to arrive at our remembering of the truth of who we are in our essence. Accepting ourselves as we are and knowing what is realistically possible as opposed to what we are supposed to look like, actually, frees us up and allows us to arrive at our best, healthiest body. Loving ourselves is essential to allow ourselves our most beautiful body; this practice teaches how to elevate the idea of loving yourself into an act, a practice.

Detoxing on the physical level with yin yoga practices

The yin yoga applies pressure to specific meridians to flood them with chi, to support them in flushing out any stored toxins in relation to those channels, the liver, the kidney, the spleen, etc. The health of the organs is directly related to the health of the meridians that flow through them. As we support the vitality and flow of chi through the meridians, we also support the health of the organs. As we flood the meridians with chi, we support the detoxification process. Bringing the energy to the center of the body where the chakras reside supports in harmonizing our chi, which brings about a state of coherence. This is a chi enhancement practice that amplifies the quality of energy and the focus of the mind, cultivating the more contemplative aspects of our nature, which allows us a portal, a pathway to remember the truth of our essential nature. The yogi's believe that the root of the chakras relates to our karmic rebalancing, so bringing coherence to these areas enhances our sense of well–being and our sense of happiness significantly.

Obviously, diet and what we eat is an essential piece of this detox program and you are encouraged to lose weight at a sustainable rate of approximately two pounds per week. I have discovered that a key to a strong will-power and sustainable weight loss is about blood sugar stabilization and eating foods low on the glycemic index—foods that elicit a lower and slower blood glucose response. This helps avoid the roller coaster effect, when blood sugar quickly rises, and falls rapidly a short time later, the glycemic index of a food reflects how fast its carbohydrate content hits the bloodstream. Foods with a low GI (50 or below) metabolize slowly. Thus the amount of insulin released is less than eating foods with high G.I. (70 or above), which release glucose more quickly into the bloodstream.

The secret to lifelong health is to keep your insulin level stable all day long by eating a low-GI diet. Blood sugar concentration can also determine how well or unwell one feels. A stable blood sugar level keeps energy up, helps control hunger, and prevents mood swings, while low blood sugar can cause irritability, fatigue, lethargy, excessive hunger, moodiness and cravings for sugar and sweets, factors which can undermine success. Sugar raises insulin levels inhibiting the release of growth hormones, which depresses the immune system. Too much insulin promotes fat storage, which facilitates rapid weight gain and elevated triglyceride levels, both of which are linked to cardiovascular disease. Eating slowly digested low-glycemic carbohydrates helps control the insulin response, and when less insulin is secreted more fat can be burned for energy. The point is to have a sensible structure that makes it easy to lose weight without fatigue or hunger. Eating foods that are fresh, locally grown, and seasonal is your best option. Weight loss experts know that starving yourself or going without food for extended periods of time creates the starvation response, which works against weight loss goals, by slowing down the metabolism and can create more fat cells. As I mentioned earlier, I am happiest with juice plus as it is user-friendly high-quality food.

Awakening Intuition Toolkit

This toolkit is about waking and utilizing the power of your intuition in fresh and exciting ways that enhance your health and well-being. It provides you with the tools necessary to optimize the connections between your mind, your emotions, your spirit, and your body. By learning the skill of listening to the communications that are constantly arising from your body in the language of body, you can enhance your mind-body intelligence and empower yourself to create a healthier and happier life. You will be guided and supported in learning the tools that allow you to master your mind and your emotions. You will be given all the information necessary to rebalance and align each of your chakras and clear your central channel, which naturally awakens your intuitive ability.

Health is largely a function of reclaiming our memories of past trauma in a way that allows us to release the energetic charge that inhabits them, as we go through the journey in our biography, which resides within our biology, we begin to heal our lives and reclaim our natural intuitive capacity. As we release from the repetition of old negative patterns, we free ourselves to be present, to be creative and connected to our authentic selves. Memories of negative emotions stored in our bodies can affect our physical health; our negative emotions must be moved out so that we can move forward. Otherwise, those emotions will accelerate into masses in our bodies, causing cells to make progress towards patterns of disease. The energy of dis-ease can be released by meeting our feelings with awareness, breath, and compassion letting go of negative habitual patterns and establishing new healthy habits.

Intuition is the process of meeting accurate conclusions based on inadequate information. This information arises in ways beyond the normal five senses, in the form of hunches, insights, or gut feelings. The word intuition means to look within; it is an internal language that facilitates insight and understanding. For this function to open fully to us, we have to accept the possibility of information arising from our bodies in a somewhat illogical way. Intuition is simply a sense that is available to all of us, its information is practical and carries the potential to greatly enhance and improve our lives. It is not a magical power, simply a capacity that is available to anybody willing to tune in and listen. It arises quite naturally as a consequence of clearing up your chakras, your energetic system, by meeting and removing all the obstacle that linger in our emotions and our consciousness until we decide to clean it up. This toolkit provides you with the means to do this. Intuitive insights involve emotions and it is associated with empathy, it is an inner sight, intuition is the soul's communication through the body. The real power that the intuitive capacity gives us is the authority to change our destiny.

This toolkit invites you into that state of perceptual aliveness, igniting a journey of direct knowingness, connecting you to that small still voice of certainty. Increasing the incidents of synchronicity, enhancing your creativity and your imagination as well as establishing greater faith and trust in your own instincts. I believe that everyone is intuitive, but not necessarily in the same way, I have been doing intuitive work for 20 years and am just now beginning to understand how my intuition works. I perceive that intuitive abilities have a close relationship to our purpose, which is connected to our skills, talents, and abilities. I am interested in supporting people understand their belief system and I seem to be skilled in uncovering the beliefs that may be running you. I have discovered that when I do readings, I am entering into a conversation with your higher self, so your higher self and my higher self are communicating. I am led to whatever your strongest sense is; meaning if you are a visual person, I will see pictures, if you are more auditory, I will hear things, and if you are kinesthetic, I will feel things. I think it is important to be open enough to respond to whatever shows up for you and follow the signs, the signals, and the communications.

By truly letting go of any and all ideas about how it should be, and allowing it to be what it is, by listening very carefully to everything that shows up and paying attention to and responding to everything, we support our intuitive skills. I find it helpful to talk things out with clients and include them in on the whole process, while primarily trusting what is arising from me. Intuition is an innate gift of the soul and when it flows, it is the juice of life, bringing fluidity, joy and instant answers to profound and important questions. This toolkit will support you in dissolving the obstacles of indecision and doubt and invites you to arrive at a deep and profound certainty, heightened clarity and truth. The more you practice and use your intuitive perceptions the more you will enhance all your perceptions, reclaiming lost abilities and acquiring new ones. Developing intuition is a way to expand your spiritual awareness and a way to get to know the true self. Knowing who you truly are is the most liberating force there is, as it allows us to shed everything that we are not. All the patterns and projections of who we think we should be or who we have to be to be liked to be accepted, are released. This releasing, letting go of habitual ways of being lightens our load and allows us to be ourselves, this gives us a chance to share our gifts with the world and be who we are intended to be, allowing us to make our contribution and fulfill our purpose.

Being present and responding to what is, is an essential intuitive skill. Spend as much time as necessary to master this skill before moving forward to rebalancing and aligning the chakras, as this is the foundation that is needed to choose the vibration and frequency that we want to occupy. Choosing to occupy positive emotional states is important in manifesting and attracting synchronicities, very often perceived as the intuitive communication from the Universe.

Here are the first five steps to expanding your intuitive capacity:

1)   Practice presence.

2)   Participate fully with everything that is present, and move towards the open door.

3)   Pursue positive thoughts and positive emotions.

4)   Choose the vibration and the frequency that you want to occupy.

5)   Be sure that what you are saying yes to is reflecting what you want now.

Gratitude and appreciation are the frequencies that expand your intuitive capacity, always remember that the Universe is simply a big Xerox machine, reflecting back to you what you are putting out regarding thoughts and feelings. Practice makes perfect if you intend to read others start today, now, immediately, practice, practice, practice. There is no way around it. You have to get in the ring with the bull, so start sooner rather than later, even if you are terrified just start where you are, do what you can and get started straight away, work with everything that shows up.

As fear arises, work with the three-step process of transforming that consciousness and transmuting that energy into its opposite positive form. Know that your primary relationship is with the field of infinite possibility, and be sure to inject into the field, the reflection of what you want, not what you are afraid of. Practice makes perfect, so practice everywhere you can. If there isn't anybody available right away then read yourself, read the people on TV. or the people at your cafe, just take that leap in that direction.

Personally, I find it very difficult, if not impossible, to read myself, so I avoid it, but I know that when I was successful at reading myself, then everyone else is easy to read. Letting go of the need to be right and allowing yourself to open up and flow with the information that is arising is the key. Initially, it is not so important if you are right or wrong what is most important is that you are aligned with the creation cycle. This means that you are taking charge of your consciousness and you are breathing life into the thoughts and vibrations that reflect what you want to create, not what you believe is true. Intuition occurs naturally when you are living in the flow. Freeing yourself from worry and fear, letting go of your "shoulds" and freeing yourself to be responding to requirements that are arising in each of your moments, then you are in the flow and you are increasing your intuitive abilities.

Letting go of automated behaviors, to be fully present in your moment, is the key to fully awakening your intuitive capacity. The intuitive and the creative process invite you to pass through three stages:

1) Inspiration, meaning to be in spirit, this is where we formulate concepts and plans.

2) Moving from your mind as motivation this is doing-ness

3) Moving up from your body as completion this is having-ness.

This movement through spirit, mind, body, and back to spirit again, correlates with the three simple actions be, do, have and back to be; creation begins and completes with the spirit. I go into the fine details of the mechanism of manifestation in my manifesting toolkit.

As I have mentioned several times intuition speaks in the language of body and it is important to heighten the sensitivity of the body so that you can hear more and more of the subtleties of that communication. Noticing the very first moment a sensation or a communication arises allows you to be in right relationship with that energy, and that communication at the moment, so that you can respond accurately in the moment. These signals start as instinctual urges or resonances or vibrations. You may just get a hit or a sense that you need to call someone or someone may just cross your mind, and it's important that you pay attention and respond by showing up and reaching out and communicating with that person. If you do not, you may get stronger communications from your body that feel less pleasant like chills or butterflies or goose bumps, like your hair standing on end, here the communications have a more anxious or nervous quality.

If we are not fully present and paying special attention here, then we might suppress those voices and indulge ourselves in our addictive patterns that numb out this delicate and essential information system. Suppression and avoidance are never a good idea, no matter how it is attained, this is one of the reasons why medication for these symptoms of nervousness, anxiety, grief, may not be a good idea. It is important that we are in harmonious relationship with our environment and our bodies for intuitive opening to happen. Remember that your ego is invested in maintaining the status quo, and it does not want any change or improvement or anything to be different from the way things are now. It will set up seductions for you to indulge in the lower vibrations of emotions and consciousness.

Intuition is a feminine aspect of mind— the cooler, softer side of our nature—the fluid, accepting, magnetic, and adaptable part of who we are. This is where we can choose to strengthen, nourish, and ultimately reside, if we want to reach our intuitive potential. Occupying this state is a choice and when we make it, we invite a deeper connection to this intuitive part of whom we are. The yin yoga included in my toolkits provides access to this aspect, practicing presence allows us access to this potent state. Noticing what you notice is a valuable practice here, increasing your powers of observation by observing everything, notice more and more fine details around everything. Expand and include everything in your awareness.

Look for beauty; choose to be grateful and appreciate everything that happens without resistance or judgments. This is where the perspective of purposefulness is useful, as it supports you in choosing to be grateful. Express gratitude for everything especially the things you want more of. Get clear and focused on achieving your goal of awakening your intuitive ability and know that, that reality will follow. Also holding an attitude of appreciation for our challenges and our barriers helps us navigate them with greater grace and ease. Barriers are necessary; they assist in strengthening us and allow us to connect to the skills required to overcome them, which in turn helps enhance our self-esteem. A smooth sea never made a skilled sailor. Accepting that we live in a benevolent Universe that loves us enough to send us barriers to strengthen us, which supports our allowing that to become our reality. So bless the barriers, embrace the obstacles, and apply your intelligence and skills and be sure of your ability to overcome them. This is how you embrace the perspective of purposefulness.

Rebalancing and aligning your chakras, activating them with positive consciousness allows you to come home to the truth of yourself, your authentic nature and gives you access to your own insights, that small clear voice that is consistently communicating with you. All intuition begins with a physical vibration either externally in the world as an event, or internally in the mind as an insight. There is a subtle pressure caused by the flow of awareness from one level of your awareness to the next. My goal is to support the smooth flow of communication through all aspects of your consciousness. This is why it is essential that we work with all aspects of consciousness on our journey of awakening and we allow for the communication to be full and complete; working with the audio and video tools that engage our physical as well as our mental and emotional bodies is optimum for the awakening of the intuitive mechanism.

Working with each of the chakras and the consciousness and the emotional vibration embodied there is the pathway to your full intuitive and creative potential. Improving your intuition is supported by going out of your mind and into your senses, by dropping beneath the words and arriving into your feelings, your physical sensations. Arriving at a place of comfort in relationship with your feelings supports the expansion of your intuitive capacity, verbalizing the feelings completes the circuit in the brain to expanding knowingness on all levels. Using the presence practice to develop your ability to be a curious investigator supports the communications becoming complete in your intellectual and intuitive understanding. This is the rebalancing of the third eye and the sixth chakra.

We know that imagination is more important than knowledge, the development and expansion of our capacity to imagine are essential on the path to awakening our intuition. I often encourage my clients to set intentions in their dreams to support them in the things they are seeking to create change around, to manifest or to awaken. In this case, your dreams can support your intuitive awakening simply by putting forth that request. You can invite your guides, spirit supporters, or angels to come forth and communicate to you through your dreams, your body or simply through an open and receptive channel. I don't work with guides; I work through my higher self, communicating with my client's higher self. Everyone has different preferences and different abilities and what is most important is that you attune to yourself, and create an invitation along with the space to connect to your intuitive capacity to come forth and let you know what form it wants to take.

Truth speaking is one of the oldest and highest forms of intuitive communication, you are your own best expert and the journey always begins within. Prophecy is one of the most precarious of all professions, and even though it may be precarious to one's life to speak the truth, it is also possible that it becomes the thing that saves your life. By attuning to yourself, to your sensations, your gut, your hunches and fleshing those communications with language and awareness opens the space for direct knowing and truth speaking to happen. You can use your intuition in a real practical way; it is a means to solve problems, heal imbalances and create the future of your dreams.

In its purest form, intuition is an ability to interpret energy information accurately, to support you in making wise choices in each moment. Intuitive information flows into you; you never have to leave yourself to know more. Your accuracy is related to your clarity, to how clean your energy system is, how detoxified you are on every level, mentally, emotionally, and physically. The Detox toolkit provides you with everything you need to assure this cleanliness. Working with the tools and techniques provided in this book is a great starting place. Avoidance, denial, addiction, drama, illusions, karmic wounds, and negativity are all obstacles to your intuitive flow, clarity and purity are very helpful in opening the intuitive channel and detoxing are very beneficial before awakening. I recommend using the detox toolkit to begin all awakenings, creations and manifesting. For the intuitive flow to be optimal, you benefit from having a simple yet solid code of ethics.

It could be as simple as following the golden rule, never causing anyone to experience something that you would not want to experience yourself. It could be, being clear that you are not creating any further negative karma by your choices and your behavior. Following the guiding principles would be optimal. Always check your own intentions and motivations and be sure they are arising from the highest and cleanest possible place. Be true to yourself and walk your own path, always honor and respect others by seeing them in their greatest possibility and bowing to the light in them, yet still know that you walk your path and they walk theirs.

If you are looking into someone else's life, ask their permission and only reveal what is ready to be seen and able to be integrated and in the highest good for everyone involved, seeing only what is ready to be seen. Balance is necessary; never give too much or too little to a situation, a thing, or a relationship. The Universe seeks balance in all things, so be sure to accurately measure how much you are giving and how much you are receiving in a situation. Pay close attention, make sure as much as possible that there is an even exchange of energy. Pay close attention to your signals of comfort and truth to confirm your accuracy; if you feel like you are overextending or over-giving in a situation you probably are, and it is in your best interest to pull back and find equanimity.

This balance is your responsibility to find. It is important to watch your words; right speech enhances accuracy, radical honesty with yourself supports you in raising your awareness around your own negative tendencies. Remember love is always the answer no matter what the question is. Whenever you run into obstacles and roadblocks, practice consistently asking yourself, what would love do. Self is infinitely lonely; love is infinitely inclusive. By following the guiding principle, you have a roadmap that can keep you on the right track to awakening your intuitive capacity.

The Mechanism of Manifestation

A lot of the work that I do with my clients is focused on helping people create "a life by design," which is all about supporting people understand how to manifest. Manifesting is an automatic descending chakra practice, which, when raised to the level of conscious awareness, empowers us to truly use our magic, to the point of consciously creating the life that we want, rather than getting a diluted or disappointing version. For us to be effective creators, it is wise to work with both the masculine and feminine aspects of each of the chakras.

Each chakra holds an obstacle and an opportunity and through the practices presented here we can navigate away from the obstacles that exist in lower emotional vibrations and frequencies and lower thinking patterns and arrive into occupying their opposite positive vibration. We hear a lot about the importance of vision boards and activating the power of the sixth chakra by using visualizations of the things that we want to create. Which is important, but on its own is missing essential information and not as effective as utilizing all the chakras for the purpose they were designed, to support us in becoming human magnets and manifesting our heart's desire and creating the life that we want.

Manifesting starts at the crown with the seventh chakra, the home of ideas and inspiration. The masculine aspect of the seventh chakra is about ideas, getting clear about the idea of what it is that you want to create. The feminine aspect of the seventh chakra is about inspiration, opening up to receiving information from the Universe about what you could create. This is about what could be possible, that you have not yet thought of or could conceive. Energy starts to gather here as we open up to these possibilities of our creative potential. I usually advise my client to set intentions in their dreams to receive inspiration and ideas, here we have clear blue sky possibilities, no need to restrict with practicality at this point, just pure possibility and potentiality. For the Universe to support us in achieving our goals, we are first presented with everything that is an obstacle to it. Every thought, every emotion, every vibration that is not in alignment with the achievement of that goal is surfaced for us to confront and overcome. Each chakra contains its own flavor of specific obstacles and the seventh chakra is about overcoming and transmuting mistrust and lack of faith, into surrendering into trust and residing in the affirmation that you now surrender to trusting yourself and others.

Once this is achieved the energy gathers and naturally descends into the sixth chakra at the center of the forehead, this is where we can activate the masculine energy. By making vision boards and visualizing ourselves in the center of the pictures of the things we want to create, seeing ourselves having or doing or being the thing that we want. We can activate the feminine aspect of this chakra by receiving the impressions that arise out of our dreams or our imagination, by allowing ourselves to be informed by the Universe, about what else might be possible through dreams or visions or any other way. The obstacle of the sixth chakra is confusion and a seduction into the idea of not knowing, and the opportunity resides in opening up to your own certainty about the thing that you want to manifest. The energy we gather here naturally descends into the fifth chakra, where we start to talk about our ideas and our visions, letting others into the loop of this creative possibility. The feminine aspect of this chakra is activated by listening, by opening ourselves up to gather more information, in conversations of possibility, from the Universe and others. The obstacle is believing lies, and the opportunity resides in expanding into trusting truth.

The energy then increases and descends into the fourth chakra where we are invited to start to really love our creation, activating the masculine principle by becoming emotionally invested in our own ideas, daring to love them towards their next step of existence. The feminine aspects allow for the possibility of receiving love for the creation, by inviting it into existence. The obstacle of this chakra resides in not feeling lovable and the opportunity resides in knowing and affirming our own lovability. As we gather energy here, we move down into the third chakra the home of action and activity.

Here we benefit from being practical and realistic so that we can start to take the action steps that are necessary to bring our creative potential into reality. We can start by doing the things in the world that are needed to realize our dream. This is a much more masculine oriented chakra as it is about doing. The feminine aspect here is about receiving support and practical help from others. The obstacle of this chakra resides in believing we are not good enough, and the opportunity resides in knowing the truth of our own worthiness, supporting us in establishing our own intrinsic knowing of our worthiness.

By gathering energy, we invite the movement of our creative energy into the second chakra that is all about creation; here we are creating our vision into reality, it's when you actually move into the dream home, write that book, or make that boat you always wanted. The feminine aspect is about the surrendering of the how to, so that you can be open and be receptive to attracting the things, the people and the energy necessary to create the vision. The obstacle resides in feeling that we are all alone and the opportunity is met when we remember the truth of our inter relatedness, and our connections. By the time the energy descends into the first chakra, the vision is here in physical reality.

Through the mp3's, yoga practices, and workshops that I teach, I literally guide you step by step, and teach you how to skillfully navigate through each of the chakras, clear the mental and emotional blockages, and expand into the consciousness and emotional vibration that brings you to the manifestation of the life that you choose to design for yourself. The online practices are as potent and as effective as the live workshops and they allow you to grow in the comfort of your own home.

Awakening Inspiration

Inspiration is the upward flow of awakening spiritual energy that has both a masculine and feminine aspect an obstacle and an opportunity. When the journey of awakening your inspiration is intentionally participated in you holistically support and strengthen yourself in igniting the power of your awakened inspirational energy that holds power to support you in fulfilling your purpose. I know that purpose is most often viewed as the work we do in the world yet our purpose really answers the question of what we are doing here in a body and applies to every area of our lives.

It starts in the first chakra by creating a stable foundation by engaging the masculine principle by choosing to reside in the positive mental antidotes that affirm your safety security and stability. Occupying the feminine aspect by raising the emotional vibration from anger to compassion cultivating the courage necessary to ignite a solid sense of grounded manifestation. This removes the obstacle of insecurity and transforms it into the opportunity of strong, stable connection to the earth that supports the experience of materialization.

This energy then gathers strength as it rises into the second chakra by engaging the masculine principle of choosing to reside in the positive mental antidotes that affirms deep connection to yourself and all those you are close to. Occupying the feminine aspect by raising the emotional vibration from fear to wisdom, cultivating the clarity necessary, to ignite a solid sense of connection. This removes the obstacle of disconnection and transforms it into the opportunity of creative expression.

As this energy center then gathers strength and invites the energy to rise and rest in the third chakra, it ignites the masculine principle by choosing to reside in the positive mental antidotes that affirm your worthiness and your value. Occupying the feminine aspect by raising the emotional vibration from anxiety to equanimity cultivating the inner peace necessary to ignite a solid sense of confidence and power that awakens the willpower to take the actions necessary to support your awakening. This removes the obstacle of self-loathing and transforms it into the opportunity of connecting to and asserting one's will.

The energy then gathers and rises to the heart, the fourth chakra energy center, by engaging the masculine principle by choosing to reside in the positive mental antidotes that affirm your choice to freely give and receive love. Occupying the feminine aspect by raising the emotional vibration from hatred to love, which cultivates the loving frequency necessary to ignite an open, loving heart. This removes the obstacles of ingratitude and jealousy and transforms it into the opportunity of appreciation, gratitude, and love. This supports the upward flow by freeing your trapped spiritual energy that got stuck inside the experience of heartbreak and lost love and reclaims it back as a creative motivational force towards your reclamation of your inspiration and the fulfillment of your purpose.

As the energy gathers and rises into the throat, the fifth chakra, by engaging the masculine principle by choosing to reside inside the positive mental antidotes that affirm your freedom to express your authentic truth. Occupying the feminine aspect by raising the emotional vibration from fear to love, cultivating the surrender necessary to ignite free flowing expression. This removes the obstacle of silence and transforms it into the opportunity of communication and the expression of truth.

This energy then gathers and rises to the center of the forehead resting in the sixth chakra, engaging the masculine principle by choosing to reside in the positive mental antidotes that affirm your certainty and clarity. Occupying the feminine aspect by raising the emotional vibration from doubt to clarity, cultivating the intuition necessary to ignite a clear channel of intuitive flow. This removes the obstacle of confusion that comes from negative thoughts and transforms it into the opportunity of certainty and clarity of vision.

This energy then gathers and rises up by engaging the masculine principle by choosing to reside in the positive mental antidotes that affirms your choice to trust that you reside in a friendly Universe. Occupying the feminine aspect by raising the emotional vibration from isolation to connectedness, cultivating the faith necessary to ignite an experience of unobstructed trust. This removes the obstacle of distrust and transforms it into the opportunity of faith. This final step fully ignites your spark of divine inspiration for you to begin the descending chakra journey of manifesting your purpose.

Conclusion

In closing, I hope that I have inspired you to take some action to create some positive changes in your habits and in your life. Happiness truly is available to everyone, not just to the fortunate few who are born with the character traits that support a happy experience of life. Cultivating a perspective of purposefulness, reinforced through establishing some guiding principles to help you, lays the foundation for you to develop a more positive and optimistic outlook. Knowing your happiness archetype and understanding your vulnerabilities, from a position of transforming them into your strengths can inspire you to choose optimism and positive thinking as a consistent practice. Knowing the anatomy of inspiration supports you in understanding how to choose the correct, positive and inspirational thinking that strengthens your particular vulnerabilities into positive qualities in your character. The tools and practices provided by the Lifeguides transformation program not only teaches you how to master the mind and the emotions so that you can raise your emotional vibration and reside in positive mental and emotional states but the added toolkits actually guide you through the experience of transformation. This experience improves the quality of your choices and behaviors, which will inevitably magnetize the life of your dreams to you. For those who learn better with the support of guided meditations and yoga practices, the toolkits are perfect for you. These tools take your transformation to the next level because of their ability to engage and access your subconscious mind and energetic system.

I am happy to say that I am an opty-mystic who sees the world through the eyes of possibility and I invite you to join me by feeding your thoughts and emotions positive food. Feeling good and residing in positive vibes attracts the good that you want, and you have learned how to do that here. My intention is to invite you towards a genuine experience of transformation that honors you exactly where you are and encourages you through your experience of humanness to find your divinity, your highest happiest self that can be found right in the center of your difficulties.

The journey in "The habit of happiness" begins with you knowing yourself so intimately, on a deep soul level, that you have a clear understanding of who you are and who you are not. Honestly understanding who and what your unhappy lower self is and what it is constructed of (regarding your negative emotions and your inner dialogue) is the first step of raising your awareness to the level where the transformation to your higher happy self becomes possible. Raising your awareness and your understanding of who your unhappy lower self is empowers you to the point of liberation. Through the transformative practices shared here, you are invited to cultivate the habits that are healthy and reflect the things that you want to create in your future and to live your life by design.

Knowing and mastering the top 10 healthy habits that increase an experience of well-being empowers you to have a happier experience of life. You could start at number 10 and take a month with each of the healthy habits, which can potentially increase your happiness quotient by 10% until finally, you master them all when you establish new healthy habits you will probably significantly increase your happiness. Using the tools and toolkits is indeed practicing the art of creating happiness. Through my work over the last 23 years, I have come to believe that we are spiritual beings within a body suit that we plug into, through our energetic system, bringing with us our karmic history that is seeking its pathway to healing. I have provided for you some tools to support you on your particular path home to yourself.

You are invited to use the archetypes as a way for you to identify both the main path you are walking in this lifetime and the secondary path that your circumstance may be challenging as a way to invite you back to balance. By asking you to attend to a current issue that can be healed, and by attending to it in such a way that it brings you back to balance and wholeness. I feel strongly that our consciousness reincarnates with us, and the work that we do in expanding, healing rebalancing and awakening our consciousness brings significant benefits in this lifetime and beyond. I feel, in fact, that the best insurance that we can have to support our happiness now and in eternity, is to know how to master the mind and master the emotion.

By learning and cultivating healthy habits, we can establish a recognition and understanding of how powerful and expansive we truly are. You may have found it easy to identify yourself and your vulnerabilities, or you may have seen parts of yourself in all the archetypes. You may have a lot more diversity in your challenges and find that your inner dialogue contains more than one chakra's characteristics and perhaps have more randomness. If that is the case, do what works, still work with the archetypes and with the three steps to master the mind and the emotions, and if it is helpful, let go of the specifics of each of the individual archetypes.

The anatomy of inspiration is constructed of 5 affirmations for each chakra, along with positive memory, visualizations, and specific breathing, which alchemizes negative mental and emotional vibrations into its opposite positive possibility. This mechanism allows you to reclaim your natural, inspirational energy. By working with my all -natural, holistic, mood management method expressed in the yoga practices and the meditations, you can shift from negativity to a more positive productive mindset and high emotional frequency, that has the potential to magnetize the experience of life that you most desire. By increasing your awareness of and your relationship to your energetic system, you can positively influence your health, manage your stress, increase your wealth and improve the experience of happiness in your life. You can empower yourself by understanding the difference between an internal disturbance and an external issue that allows you to be able to choose and exert your influence where and when you most effectively can. My work has revealed to me that most physical, mental and emotional disturbances have their roots in a trauma that overwhelmed our system, which can be helped by gently touching and abiding with the energetic impact of that experience. This simple, yet profound method is a worthwhile skill to acquire and practice to establish a new healthy habit.

Just imagine what your life would be like if you were free of fear, anger, anxiety, and negativity, imagine what you would be doing, where you would be living, what your relationships would be like and how all of that would feel. By honoring your life exactly as it is now, invites you to see the gifts in the center of your challenges. By holding this perspective of purposefulness, you are given the road map to happiness that shows you how to navigate through your humanness to arrive at your divinity. A very wise man once said that a person is just about as happy as he decides to be, I invite you to decide to increase your happiness by embracing some healthy habits that lead you to the habit of happiness. Do what works for you, what allows you to have positive forward movement and growth.

We can make whatever choices we want, we live in a container of free will, and it is important that we take full responsibility for those choices, by expanding into knowing what is predictable from the habits and patterns that we participate in, whether consciously or unconsciously. The benefit of understanding our archetypes, our habits, and our patterns, is that we can predict what is going to happen and how our life will unfold. When our thinking is identified, our behaviors follow predictably, and our experiences come as no surprise. This predictability allows us to become more involved in our choices with greater awareness and care. You are invited to purify your thoughts and your emotions as part of your daily routine, learning how to ensure that you are attracting the reality you want to experience so that you can live your life by design rather than by accident.

Let's make no mistake—it is not easy to change your habits. The mechanism of change is straightforward and effective, yet the application is a practice and a skill. The process of change is definitely possible by following the steps that I have outlined here, but the application of the steps, is where the real work and artistic license resides, you truly are the artist of your life. By working with the practices and especially implementing step three (nourishing the mind), you can support yourself to awaken to the best version of yourself. Being positive, cultivating the habit of happiness, is about exercising your power of choice to have a full experience of life that contains the full spectrum of emotions. This journey is not about denial of the painful emotions and thoughts; it's simply about not indulging them or feeding them, and deciding that you can help yourself with the quality of your life and your experiences by exercising your power of choice. By mastering how to practice choosing where you focus your mental energy, you are establishing the healthy habit of mastering the mind.

You may already be familiar with this information, yet still be unfamiliar with knowing how to implement the changes and establishing the healthy habits. With this book, and the supporting tools and practices, you can know, without a doubt, how to create the changes you want in your life. The affirmations that I have shared in the anatomy of inspiration are simply suggestions and if they resonate with you, use them; if they don't, and you have better ones, use them. What is important is that you do something. If you want to get affirmations that are more accurate to your unique inner dialogue and you want support, you can always work with me individually. What is most important is that you do something to create the positive changes that you want to see in your life. Choose the healthy habit that feels accessible to you and commit to that one simple change then move on to the next until making changes and embracing new habits becomes fun. The tools that I have provided are the most potent tools that I have discovered on my path of spiritual growth, both as a practitioner and as a teacher. There are other simpler, gentler tools available if you feel like you would prefer easier, more spacious journey. I recommend studying the yoga traditions and the mindfulness meditation teachers, as a simpler yet perhaps more spacious and slower way to embrace improvement in your life, the tools in the Lifeguides transformation program are really for those who are seeking a profound and accelerated path to change.

The anatomy of inspiration provides the food for the mind and the emotions that support the rebalancing and aligning of the chakras. For the interests of clarity, I have broken the chakras down into separate chapters, yet some people may not be quite so neatly divided. Some of us may have second, third and fourth chakra imbalances that have equally charged edges of growth that need to be attended to. My intention is to support you in identifying your happiness archetype so that you can recognize and heal a wound, a predominant pattern that may be misdirecting your life. The practices and the tools support you in understanding and knowing how to liberate yourself from some automaticity that you may have had your whole life, perhaps even before this lifetime.

This liberation brings you closer to your essence, your authentic self that reflects your spirit, your light, and the truth of who you are. These tools are capable of bringing you into the experience of transformation through deeper knowledge, more profound wisdom and insight into your innate gifts that can help you find and fulfill your purpose. If you were to invest your time and energy into pursuing any new skill wouldn't the skills that lead to the practices that become the habit of happiness, be the most worthwhile. The skills that are shared here as so essential to creating a positive experience of life that I would love them to be taught in school. If they were, our lives would be drastically different, perhaps without the challenges that we are currently facing and the world would be transformed into a drama free, highly creative, deeply loving place.

Identifying your path to happiness through the happiness archetype quiz gives you more insight and information about what your vulnerabilities are. And how to strengthen them to the point of being free of your automaticity, your conditioning, and your unhealthy mental and emotional habits that create your unhappy lower self and contributes to all the difficulties in your life. This program is a simple mechanism that can be quickly learned that carries the power to transform your life by navigating you from your lower unhappy self to your happy higher self. Understanding the simple three steps that allow you to master your mind and the three steps that support you in mastering your emotions gifts you with the opportunity to change your habits and the physiology of your brain freeing you from the traps of negativity, stress, and dissatisfaction.

Knowing yourself and establishing your truest, deepest values and beliefs allows you to consciously create your own guiding principles that can support you in arriving into your most profound experience of well-being. Knowing your default unhappy thinking and it's accompanied emotions helps you in making choices, and participating in practices that liberate you from negativity, and bring you to a positive and inspirational experience of life. We are habitual beings, and we become what we consistently do, learning the habit of happiness is the biggest vote you can make for a happy future. All this helps you gain awareness around your agreements and allows you to be more connected with and involved with the agreements you are currently making with life, with reality, and with all of your relationship. The act of updating and cleaning up these agreements is life changing. We may subconsciously be sabotaging or blocking our happiness potential and would benefit greatly from uncovering and transforming what we are doing on that level.

I have spent the last two decades teaching the skills and practices necessary to empower others to have a greater experience of happiness in their lives. I have discovered how to work with the physical and energetic structure within your bodies to help you harmonize your system so that you can align with your highest happiness potential, aligning you with positive emotional states that range from stability and security to unconditional love and bliss. Whether that happiness arises from shifting to a perspective of purposefulness so that your compass is directed towards true north, or by learning the skills of mental and emotional mastery or from a deeper understanding of yourself through the happiness archetypes, the end result is the same—an increased sense of well-being in life.

I want to support you in understanding how to be the very best version of yourself so that you can realize your highest potential. I am interested in helping you get connected to your authentic self and the reasons you are in your body so that you can find and fulfill your purpose. This book can support you in overcoming the things that can be difficult in your life, fear, anxiety, depression, financial difficulty, addictions to name some of the most common challenges that my clients have faced, that can distract you and disconnect you from fulfilling your purpose. The reality is happiness is a skill that has to be consistently practiced and established as a habit, so that it becomes your default pattern of thinking, feeling, and being. It is a skill well worth investing your time and energy into, as it the most important goal that we can have. I do not want to pretend that this is a quick fix to all of life's challenges; I am still learning and practicing the happiness habit myself, and I know how hard it can be to establish new habits. I am a fellow traveler on the path to greater fulfillment, satisfaction, joy and, dare I say one last time, happiness. I teach this every day, and I am still very much on my path, so I know that it can be hard to change, but I also gather evidence every day that change is possible and worthwhile.

How to Work with the Tools

What follows is a detailed description of tools that you can use to support you in the alchemical process of turning your vulnerabilities into your strengths are. Please check in with your intuition and follow its guidance towards the tools and timing that works best for you. Everyone is different, and in the interests of honoring those differences, I defer to the wisdom of your guidance.

If you are interested in my recommendation, I suggest you work with the tools in the order listed in the list of toolkits I have assembled for you. If you prefer to work with me in person, at your own pace, then please contact me via my website www.thehabitof happiness.org. My intention is to empower you to connect to your inner guru and activate your inner physician so that you can best support your body, mind, and spirit to heal and nourish itself. If you want to go more in depth, I recommend you work with the online courses.

Happiness Tools and Practices

If you feel like you would benefit from gaining additional support on the path please know there are more tools available to assist you. Refer to the roadmap to see when you can best use these tools. I designed these tools to combine the most potent transformation practices so that you have the best possible support in creating the changes that you desire. The most important thing is that you continue to have positive forward movement along your path and if you feel like you are getting stuck I encourage you to work with these potent tools. You can find these products on my website www.thehabitofhappiness.org.

Bookios

Twenty years ago when I embarked on this journey of fulfilling my mission and sharing my tools with the world, I was driven by the desire to create a transformative tool. I have done everything possible with this book to fulfill that mission, and I am excited about how much transformation is possible for you within these pages. In my ever-increasing desire to go further and do more, I am happy to share my bookios, (all audio and video transformative tools) which are the perfect compliment to the book and the next level of fulfillment of this mission. The bookios guide you through the **experience** of transformation from your lower unhappy self to your higher happy self. You get the whole book on audio then at the correct moment; you have links that invite you to participate in the guided meditation transformative tools and the yoga videos that bring all the skills to life in the form of practices. Please go to the bookio page on my website (Address is at the end) to further explore these potent transformative tools.

The perspective of Purposefulness meditation:

This meditation helps you to find the pot of gold that exists within your life's challenges.

Guiding Principles meditation:

Offers a return to the deep inner values that restore our sense of peace, strength, and clarity.

Healthy habits meditation:

Reinforces your will power to align the subconscious mind with the conscious choices.

Mental Healing Meditations:

Our thoughts affect our emotional states, and this section supports you in changing mental patterns. The three steps to transforming fear-based consciousness to love based consciousness have three separate meditations.

1.) Mental Awareness: The awareness meditation (presence 1st then chakra clearing)

2.) Transformation: The transformation meditation (chakra empowerment) Practice:

3.) The nourishment practice is created with Chakra Healing meditation.

Emotional healing Meditations:

This section supports you in changing emotional states that in turn supports healthy thinking patterns. These three meditations help the three steps that support you in transmuting negative emotional states into positive, happy emotional states.

1.) Emotional Awareness Practice....... (Presence Practice meditation)

2.) Breath Awareness Practice .... (Chakra Balancing,........ All Yoga practices)

3.) Compassion meditation practice, (Chakra Healing. ... Yoga workshops)

Toolkits: (Or E-bookio's)

Contain the e-book with all the audio and video tools the meditations: Guiding principles, The Perspective of Purposefulness, Healthy Habits. All mental healing meditations (Written exercises) All emotional healing meditations (Written meditations)

Then targeted .....happiness archetypes, meditations, and yoga practices. 1-7

Targeted yoga daily practices and workshops. 1-7

THE TOOLS AND THE TOOLKITS:

PRESENCE PRACTICE

CHAKRA CLEARING PROCESS

CHAKRA REBALANCING PROCESS

CHAKRA HEALING MEDITATION

1ST - 7 TH CHAKRA YOGA IN PRINT

1ST - 7th CHAKRA MEDITATION

1ST - 7th CHAKRA YOGA DAILY PRACTICE VIDEO

1ST - 7th CHAKRA YOGA WORKSHOP VIDEO

1ST - 7th CHAKRA TOOLKIT (contains all of the above)

THE FOUR PILLARS TOOLKITS:

AWAKENING THE INNER LITE

AWAKENING INTUITION

MANIFESTING

DETOX

www.thehabitofhappiness.org

Printed in the United States
by Bookmasters

Printed in the United States
By Bookmasters